Environmental

Inequalities

ENVIRONMENTAL INEQUALITIES

Class, Race,

and Industrial

Pollution in

Gary, Indiana,

1945–1980

The

University

of North

Carolina

Press

Chapel Hill

and London

A n d r e w   H u r l e y

Manufactured in the
United States of America

The paper in this book meets
the guidelines for permanence
and durability of the Committee
on Production Guidelines for
Book Longevity of the Council on
Library Resources.

Portions of this book have
previously appeared in the
following articles: "The Social
Biases of Environmental Change
in Gary, Indiana, 1945–1980,"
Environmental Review 12 (Winter
1988): 1–19, and "Challenging
Corporate Polluters: Race, Class,
and Environmental Politics
in Gary, Indiana, since 1945,"
Indiana Magazine of History 88
(December 1992): 273–302.

Andrew F. Hurley is assistant
professor of history at the
University of Missouri–St. Louis.

Library of Congress
Cataloging-in-Publication Data

Hurley, Andrew, 1961–
    Environmental inequalities: class, race,
and industrial pollution in Gary, Indiana,
1945–1980/Andrew Hurley.
        p.   cm.
    Originally presented as the author's thesis
(Ph.D.).
    Includes bibliographical references and index.
    ISBN 978-0-8078-2174-9 (cloth: alk. paper)
    ISBN 978-0-8078-4518-9 (pbk.: alk. paper)
    1. Environmental policy—Social aspects—
Indiana—Gary.   2. NIMBY syndrome—Indiana—
Gary.   3. Pollution—Social aspects—Indiana—
Gary.   4. Gary (Ind.)—Environmental
conditions.   5. Social classes—Indiana—Gary.
6. Gary (Ind.)—Race relations.   7. Gary (Ind.)—
Social conditions.   I. Title.
HC108.G3H87   1995
363.7'009772'99—dc20   94-17932
                                                                CIP

cloth   06 05 04 03 02   6 5 4 3 2
paper   11 10 09 08 07   10 9 8 7 6

For my parents,

John and Frieda Hurley,

and in memory of

my grandmother,

Clara Hurley

Contents

Figure and Maps

Figure

Maps

Tables

Preface

It was no coincidence that the age of ecology was also an age of environmental inequality. Between 1945 and 1980, the United States witnessed the rise and maturation of a popular movement that promised to curb the environmental excesses of industrial and economic growth. Yet everyone did not benefit equally from the achievements of environmental reform. Despite the strength of organized labor, the rise of a civil rights movement, and a liberal political order that pledged itself to uplifting the nation's underprivileged, the political process and the dynamics of the marketplace gave industrial capitalists and wealthy property holders a decisive advantage in molding the contours of environmental change. Those groups who failed to set the terms—African Americans and poor whites—found themselves at a severe disadvantage, consistently bearing the brunt of industrial pollution in virtually all of its forms: dirty air, foul water, and toxic solid wastes.

Exploring this historical process requires a marriage of two scholarly fields: environmental history and social history. Still a relatively young discipline, environmental history explores the interrelationship between humans and the natural world: how environmental conditions have shaped human activity and how, in turn, humans have transformed the physical world around them. Although this approach to history has yielded many first-rate works, environmental historians have tended to neglect the importance of social divisions. More commonly, the field's practitioners have framed their analyses in terms of holistic economic and cultural systems. Many of the best works on the United States, for instance, have described the ecological transformations associated with the transition from the Native American subsistence economy to European capitalism. But social historians have taught us that capitalism, particularly industrial capitalism, involved social differentiation along the lines of class, race, gender, and ethnicity. Surely these divisions produced a variety of environmental experiences, objectives, and behavioral patterns. My aim, then, is to approach the process of environmental change as the product of competing environmental agendas forwarded by specific social groups.[1] Considering the intensity of environmental disputes since World War II, such an approach seems warranted.

Thinking about environmental history in terms of social divisions also invites us to reconsider the way we assess environmental change. Environmental historians are well aware of the pitfalls encountered in evaluating ecological change. Recently, ecologists have thrown the concept of equilibrium into question, thereby making it difficult for historians to measure environmental change against any objective standard.[2] The concept of social equity provides historians with an alternative. Thus, we can attempt to determine who benefited and who suffered when a particular society altered its relationship with the surrounding natural and built environment. Utilizing this approach to study one of the nation's most polluted cities, Gary, Indiana, I will demonstrate how divisions of race and class were instrumental in creating patterns of environmental inequality in recent urban America.

This argument is developed through a chapter organization that balances chronology and theme. Following a brief introduction that sets the study in a broader historical context, we turn to Gary in the years just after World War II, exploring the interrelationship between social organization and industry's use of natural resources. The next three chapters focus on specific social groups—the white middle class, the white working class, and the African American community—examining how each defined and responded to its environmental predicament. The final two chapters, which concentrate on the 1970s, illuminate the interaction among these groups in the context of the environmental movement and a corporate-engineered environmental backlash. Chapter 6 charts the rise and fall of a multiclass and multiracial environmental reform coalition, while chapter 7 offers an assessment of postwar environmental change in terms of social equity. A brief epilogue carries Gary's story into the 1980s and traces its broader implications.

Acknowledgments

It is a great pleasure to acknowledge those who have assisted me in this project through its many alterations to its present form. Bob Wiebe shared his wisdom at different stages of the work, demonstrating throughout an uncanny knack for giving the right advice at the right time, especially with regard to the overall structure and organization of the book. Arthur McEvoy stimulated my interest in environmental history, and this book surely would not have been written without his inspiration. I thank him for his unfailing support and encouragement. No one has seen more drafts of this work than Patty Cleary, and as a result of her efforts, it is much more readable than it would have otherwise been. I am fortunate to have such a generous friend and colleague, always willing to take just one more look at a paragraph.

Over the years, many people have taken the time to read and critique individual chapters or the entire manuscript. Henry Binford, Michael Sherry, Lane Fenrich, and Catherine Sardo Weidner offered useful suggestions at the early stages, while Jan Reiff helped me muddle through the statistical data. More recently, Ken Goings and Eric Sandweiss offered critical advice on certain chapters. Marty Melosi and Ted Steinberg kindly read the entire manuscript and provided incisive criticism.

I have benefited from the assistance of many archivists in the course of conducting my research, one of whom deserves special mention. Steve McShane at the Calumet Regional Archives in Gary consistently exceeded the call of duty to help me track down valuable source materials. It has also been a pleasure working with Paul Betz, Kate Torrey, and Lewis Bateman at the University of North Carolina Press. I thank them for their support.

My task was made easier by research grants provided by Northwestern University, the Indiana Historical Society, and Rhodes College. Furthermore, because this book took shape during many late nights in corner booths with countless cups of coffee, I would like to thank the folks at the K&K Diner in New York City, the Gold Coin Coffee Shop in Chicago, the Arcade Restaurant in Memphis, and Bar Italia in St. Louis for allowing me to monopolize prime table space into the wee hours of the morning.

Perhaps the most fulfilling aspect of this project has been the opportunity to interview some of the people who played a role in this story. To all of those who took the time to share part of their lives with me, I owe a debt of gratitude.

This book is dedicated to my parents and my grandmother, who have always been more than generous with their love and support.

Environmental

Inequalities

Class, Race, and

the Shaping of the

Urban Landscape

Georgia Jones awoke to the sounds of sirens on the morning of April 14, 1987. Several hours earlier, two storage tanks containing more than 27,000 gallons of hydrochloric acid had leaked their contents onto the premises of the Gary Products factory, engulfing the surrounding area in a cloud of toxic fumes. In response, civil defense officials organized a mass evacuation of the predominantly African American neighborhood, announcing the emergency with bullhorns and sending buses to remove residents. Upon hearing the news, Jones climbed out of bed, collected about a dozen neighbors, and drove off in a packed car to the Genesis Convention Center in downtown Gary. There she joined nearly 2,000 refugees who were biding their time reading, conversing, playing cards, and consuming the hamburgers and coffee that had been donated by McDonalds, Wendys, and Burger King.

Medical personnel were on hand to administer oxygen to several children who had either passed out or begun to hyperventilate because of the toxic fumes. For some adults, the effects of the spill were even more serious. Dennis Simpson had been painting the exterior of his house early that morning, shortly after the spill occurred. Exposed to a large dose of the acid fumes, Simpson became ill and was taken to nearby Methodist Hospital, where he received treatment for burning eyes and severe nausea. A total of 110 other residents required hospital care for breathing difficulties, skin irritation, and other minor ailments. Among the many disruptions caused by the industrial accident were the cancellation of classes at local schools, the closing of neighborhood stores, and the interruption of most operations at the northwest Indiana mail distribution facility, located only a few blocks from the Gary Products factory. Although Gary's postal workers had proven their commitment to delivering the mail in sleet and snow, they were not prepared to brave toxic fumes.[1]

How are we to decipher the meaning of this incident? Varying perspectives suggest alternative translations. For Gary Products, a manufacturer of cleaning solvents and antifreeze, the spill was a minor inconvenience, an expected cost of handling hazardous materials. For the afflicted population, the acid leak was one of many environmental mishaps that caused tremendous social dislocation and disruption, occasionally of tragic proportions. More striking, however, was the way in which the events of that April morning highlighted the hierarchy of environmental power in this manufacturing city. Here was a situation that occurred because the needs of industrial capital clearly took precedence over concerns for the quality of residential life. This skewed scheme of priorities may appear surprising given the fact that the previous half century had witnessed a labor movement, a civil rights movement, and an environmental movement, all of which in some fashion strove to cushion Americans from the harshest environmental consequences of industrial capitalism. Although all of these movements contributed to a reshuffling of environmental arrangements in Gary, this incident suggests that the city's African American and largely impoverished residents were powerless to prevent this sort of disaster from occurring. In this context, the accident at Gary Products makes an even more profound statement about the structure of power relations in recent U.S.

history. For, despite shifts in public debates and political agendas, what remained consistent was the influential position of private capital in ordering the urban landscape for its own ends.

Especially since the rise of industrial capitalism in the mid-nineteenth century, the urban environment, in both its natural and human-altered forms, has been contested terrain. While some have sought to control urban space for the purpose of accumulating profits, others have displayed more variegated motives, including habitation, recreation, and the assertion of social status. Of course, the competition over who would dictate the rules governing the urban environment did not take place on an even playing field. Historically, the ability to control others, through the political process and through the dynamics of the capitalist marketplace, gave certain groups a decisive advantage in the struggle to organize and manipulate the urban landscape. In other words, one's place in the social and economic hierarchy proved a reliable predictor of one's ability to advance and secure a set of environmental objectives.[2] For much of the history of the United States, this hierarchy was organized around divisions of class and race.

During the late nineteenth century, industrial capitalism molded urban society into two distinct groups: those who owned capital and those who sold their labor to the capitalists. Into the early twentieth century, this bifurcation corresponded closely to divisions of wealth and power. Although commercial capitalism had driven a sizable wedge between haves and have-nots much earlier in the nation's history, the limited skill requirements of mechanized manufacturing rapidly expanded and defined the laboring class by creating a virtual army of interchangeable workers with little bargaining power. The massive flow of European migration to U.S. cities between 1840 and 1917 contributed significantly to this split by creating a surplus of unskilled labor. With relatively meager incomes and foreign customs, the European immigrants who rolled cigars, stitched garments, stoked boilers, and tended machines lived a world apart from those who owned factories, shops, and banks. Indeed, when Robert Lynd and Helen Lynd visited Muncie, Indiana, to write *Middletown*, the classic sociological portrait of an American community in the 1920s, they emphasized the division of society into a working class and a business class as the fundamental cleavage governing virtually all aspects of cultural life outside the work place. According to the Lynds, "the mere fact of being born upon one or the other side of the watershed" largely determined where one lived, what products one purchased, with whom one socialized, where one worshipped, and even what time one awoke in the morning.[3] Also, despite the emergence of ethnic political machines that distributed essential services and jobs to working-class citizens in many industrial cities, it was the business class that most commonly held the reins of power in municipal governing structures.[4]

With the slowing of European immigration after the outbreak of World War I, manufacturers increasingly turned to African Americans to fill the lowest ranks of the industrial hierarchy, thereby adding a racial dimension to urban social arrangements. Eager to escape the oppressive sharecropping system in the American South, nearly 5 million African Americans migrated to northern cities between World War I and 1960 to work in packinghouses, auto plants, and steel mills. As a general rule, however, northern manufacturers hired African Americans only as a last resort. Thus, most black migrants who entered the industrial labor force ended up working in the least desirable and most dangerous positions. An even larger number of urban blacks were forced to settle for lower-paying jobs in the service sector, performing menial tasks such as washing dishes, waiting tables, carrying luggage, and operating elevators.

The influx of African Americans had the effect of splitting urban society along racial lines. Industrial corporations deliberately pitted white workers against black workers—for example, by hiring African Americans as strikebreakers—in order to quash any incipient working-class solidarity. Although industrialization did not create racism, industrialists' hiring practices sustained and deepened it. The resulting racial animosities spilled over into community life, in which white residents systematically excluded African Americans from important civic institutions, social venues, and political structures.[5]

Further complicating the urban social structure was the emergence of a distinct white-collar middle class in the early twentieth century. Writing in 1951, sociologist C. Wright Mills observed that during the first half of the twentieth century, white-collar workers became the driving force behind the American middle class, shaping its mores, expectations, and cultural values. Whereas petty proprietors had once set the standards for appropriate social behavior and aspirations among those of middling rank, salaried employees working for large corporations and government institutions now defined middle-class values and life-styles according to their distinct needs. In contrast to the business class, which championed the ethic of hard work and thrift, members of the white-collar middle class satisfied their social aspirations through participation in the expanding culture of consumption. This "new" middle class, by virtue of its size, introduced an important and influential dynamic to the social and political scene of the post–World War II United States.[6] Ultimately, the drive for consumer amenities would emerge as a major organizing principle for all of urban society.

For all of these groups—middle-class whites, working-class whites, and African Americans—the negotiation of social status involved attempts to organize and control the urban landscape. Through the accumulation of private property and the manipulation of governmental authority, privileged Americans used their wealth and power to construct a hierarchy of place around divisions of race and class. At the upper end of the social order, the wealthy were able to price their neighborhoods beyond the reach of the poor. By the twentieth century, large-lot zoning and the liberal use of restrictive covenants in many cities ensured that elite neighborhoods would retain their homogeneity. Working-class whites, on the other hand, relied on discriminatory real estate practices to separate themselves from racial minorities of comparable economic standing. African Americans seeking housing found little available to them outside the crowded inner-city ghettos that had become fixtures in most cities by World War II. To further assure the racial homogeneity of neighborhoods, schools, and recreational facilities, whites often resorted to harassment and outright violence toward nonwhites.[7] This characterization is not to suggest that the social mapping of urban space remained fixed. Population pressures, social mobility, and advances in transportation provided for a constant reshuffling of land-use patterns in industrial cities. Furthermore, shifting environmental values altered the matrix of demands placed upon particular urban places. These dynamics, however, did not change the essential fact that, at least until the middle of the twentieth century, those with wealth and white skin enjoyed a superior ability to manipulate the urban environment for their own ends.

Of all the actors on the urban-industrial scene prior to World War II, however, none enjoyed more power to control physical resources than industrial capitalists. Manufacturers displayed a voracious appetite for air, water, and land in the process of converting raw materials into finished products, and for the most part, they managed to secure whatever resources they needed. Indeed, industrialization in the United States flourished within a legal system that encouraged the manipulation of both public and private property for productive use. Courts routinely upheld the rights of corporations to expropriate natural resources and pollute the nation's air and waterways for the sake of economic growth, nuisance laws notwithstanding. In an era when private capital maintained a tight grip on local political structures, city governments were reluctant to impose any meaningful restrictions on industrial exploitation of the environment.[8] Within this context, urban populations maneuvered among themselves to acquire the remaining environmental amenities and to escape the worst effects of industrial pollution.

Scattered evidence suggests that by the early twentieth century, those at the bottom of the industrial capitalist hierarchy found themselves subjected to the worst effects of industry's offensive environmental practices, not only inside factories but also in their residential neighborhoods. For example, the Eastern European immigrants who came to Chicago to work in the stockyards around the turn of the century were assaulted by the ever present stench of slaughterhouses, fertilizer plants, and rendering vats. Members of the largely working-class population of East St. Louis, Illinois, which by World War I included large numbers of African Americans, carried on their daily activities amid aluminum and iron factory dust and noxious packing plant fumes.[9] And in the mill towns of Pennsylvania, workers and their families suffered for much of the twentieth century as temperature inversions trapped factory discharges between mountain folds, drenching their communities in industrial soot.[10] Affluent whites, on the other hand, usually managed to monopolize those areas with the least congestion, cleanest air, and most pleasing vistas. Yet despite these tendencies, the constricted spatial arrangement of U.S. industrial cities guaranteed that few citizens—rich or poor, black or white—could fully insulate themselves from the environmental consequences of industrial production during the early part of the twentieth century.

Industry's demand for urban air, water, and land continued unabated into the post–World War II era. Indeed, higher production levels, the application of new manufacturing technologies, and the trend toward capital intensification significantly amplified the environmental strains imposed by industrial production. Manufacturing output soared in the decades after 1945 as U.S. factories churned out automobiles, refrigerators, and other household appliances to meet the rising demand for consumer commodities. One consequence of this impressive spurt of economic growth was the burning of more oil and coal. Petroleum, used primarily for transportation, heating, and powering industrial machines, emerged as the nation's chief energy source after World War II and hence ranked as a major source of pollution. Offshore drilling installations discharged crude oil into waterways, refineries released dangerous hydrocarbons into the atmosphere, and gasoline combustion in motor vehicles enveloped urban areas in blankets of photochemical smog. The burning of coal, primarily for the purposes of railroad transportation, home heating, steel production, and electric power, also contributed to rising pollution levels by spewing a variety of toxic wastes into the atmosphere, including sulfur dioxide, nitrogen oxides, and small particles of soot, known as particulate matter.[11]

Many technologies that were developed during World War II and later applied to industrial production introduced even more long-lasting and far-reaching hazards. The postwar boom in plastics, chemicals, drugs, food additives, fabrics, and pesticides, for example, introduced a host of synthetic compounds into the environment. Many of these new chemical compounds, such as polychlorinated biphenyls (PCBs), polybrominated biphenyls (PBBs), dichloro-diphenyl-trichloro-ethane (DDT), and Kepone, were later linked to serious medical disorders such as cancer, brain damage, and liver failure. Unlike the wastes emitted by older, heavier industries, these synthetic materials tended to decompose more slowly and therefore remained in a hazardous state much longer.[12]

Despite industry's intensified assault on the urban landscape, a drive for social equality among industrial laborers and African Americans, widespread affluence, and a more pluralistic political structure all created the potential for a more democratic environmental order in the years between 1945 and 1980. With the support of powerful labor unions, industrial workers chipped away at managerial prerogatives inside the factory by demanding safer working conditions. Meanwhile, African Americans used the civil rights crusade as a vehicle for gaining access to scarce environmental amenities in industrial cities, such as parks, beaches, and clean neighborhoods. In less organized fashion, a democratization of affluence also worked to remove some of the impediments that had previously prevented many Americans from fulfilling their environmental aspirations. Especially for those in the expanding middle class, economic prosperity afforded the opportunity to create new residential communities in remote suburbs, far removed from the soot and smells of inner-city industrial districts.

The crystallization of a liberal capitalist political order in the two decades following World War II provided a means of propelling divergent environmental perspectives and agendas into the realm of public discourse and policy. In contrast to unfettered industrial capitalism, the liberal variety promised to soften and equalize the burdens imposed by the self-regulating market by investing the state with limited powers of intervention on behalf of social welfare. In this effort to cushion the harshest social blows of industrial capitalism, liberal politicians vaunted themselves as powerful allies of those who wished to reformulate environmental arrangements. By establishing the legal underpinnings for collective bargaining, outlawing the most overt forms of racial discrimination, and underwriting the costs of suburbanization through home mortgage insurance programs and highway construction, liberal regimes—particularly those associated with the Democratic party—directly assisted the efforts of black, working-class, and middle-class Americans to redefine their relationship to the environment.

Of course, the most explicit challenge to industry's environmental supremacy, and the one that made the most direct use of expanded governmental authority, was the popular and powerful environmental movement that arose in the years after World War II. With roots in the preservationist crusade of the early twentieth century, postwar environmentalism nonetheless marked an unprecedented attempt to reclaim the nation's natural resources for public use and enjoyment. In particular, environmentalists targeted the practices of manufacturers, thereby clashing with corporations over issues of resource extraction, waste disposal, and the location of industrial facilities. Hoping to harness the power of federal, state, and local governments, reformers pressed legislators to redirect environmental priorities through law. By the late

1960s, as widespread concern catapulted environmental protection near the top of the liberal agenda, the U.S. Congress responded with a flurry of legislation that placed responsibility for controlling the problem firmly with the federal government. Of particular importance were the National Environmental Policy Act of 1969, amendments to the Clean Air Act in 1970, and amendments to the Federal Water Pollution Control Act in 1972. By authorizing federal officials to set specific emission standards and monitor the discharges of individual polluters, these laws placed industrial corporations on notice that they would be held accountable to the U.S. government for their environmental misdeeds.[13]

Given the importance of the environmental movement in contesting entrenched environmental privileges, it is essential that we ground it firmly in its appropriate social context. Although mainstream environmental activists claimed to represent the general public interest, we should probe carefully for any social biases in either the movement's popular base or its stated objectives. What were the specific social circumstances that gave rise to postwar environmental values? Who were the most active and influential advocates of environmental protection? And most importantly, whose interests were served by the movement's triumphs? Fortunately, these questions have been addressed by both scholars and contemporary observers, many of whom have suggested that the mainstream environmental movement spoke most directly to the needs and aspirations of white, affluent Americans.

In the most sophisticated analysis of environmentalism's social roots, historian Samuel P. Hays linked postwar environmental values with the rise of an affluent consumer-oriented society. According to Hays, widespread affluence and an abundance of free time in the years following World War II enabled many Americans to reorder their priorities and channel their energies toward the pursuit of consumer amenities, leisure, and physical fitness. In the process, they developed a new appreciation for clean and healthful surroundings, an appreciation that ultimately found expression in organizations and political initiatives aimed at protecting valued environments.[14] Lending support to Hays's formulation, the membership rolls of prominent environmental groups and data from public opinion polls conducted in the 1960s showed a strong link between class and levels of environmental concern. For the most part, upper-income, suburban citizens—those most fully engaged in a culture of leisure, health, and consumer amenities—displayed the strongest commitment to environmental reform.[15]

Lower-income groups and racial minorities, on the other hand, demonstrated less consistent support for the mainstream environmental protection agenda. On occasion, labor unions and civil rights organizations openly criticized environmental reform measures, especially those aimed at industrial polluters, on the grounds that their constituents would ultimately bear the costs of regulation through higher consumer prices or job loss. Some of the harshest critiques of the environmental movement came from African Americans and labor leaders who chastised middle-class activists for their insensitivity to matters of social justice. For example, when a group of white students at San Jose State University buried a new automobile as part of the nationwide Earth Day celebration in 1970, a group of African American students decided to picket the event. To the counterdemonstrators, the interred car represented wasted resources; the money spent on the car should have been used to alleviate poverty in the ghetto. Thus, the African American protesters advanced a powerful message: the environmental movement, insensitive to the problems of the poor, smacked of arrogance.[16] Whitney Young, director of the National Urban League, put the matter more bluntly in 1970 when he stated, "The war on pollution is one that should be waged after the war on poverty is won."[17]

To many critics of the movement, this tension between African Americans and industrial workers on the one hand and much wealthier environmental advocates on the other confirmed that the ecology crusade was elitist at the core. In a conference paper delivered in 1972, Peter Marcuse characterized environmentalists as "escapists" because of their tendency to "protect the privileged lifestyles they now have, and isolate themselves personally from the effects of pollution."[18] Perhaps the most scathing indictment of environmentalism along these lines came from William Tucker, a contributing editor for *Harper's* magazine. Tucker, in his 1982 book *Progress and Privilege*, observed that environmentalists were drawn from the wealthiest sectors of society and directed their efforts at protecting their environmental amenities from the incursions of the poor and minorities. By limiting economic growth in the name of environmental protection, they denied the underprivileged the affluence necessary to enjoy access to national parks, shoreline preserves, and clean suburban neighborhoods. Hence, Tucker concluded, environmentalism was nothing less than elitism.[19]

Yet for all the indications pointing toward an upper-class bias in the environmental movement, contradictory evidence also existed. The simple formulation that the wealthy supported environmental protection whereas minorities and the poor opposed it does not accurately describe the dynamics of postwar environmental struggles. In many instances, efforts to abate pollution and preserve existing landscapes coincided with the interests of workers and minorities, and at times, African Americans and blue-collar workers collaborated with environmentalists. Labor unions that worked to defeat certain environmental measures on other occasions applied political pressure on behalf of environmental legislation. The Safe Drinking Water Act of 1974, the Toxic Control Substances Act of 1976, and the important amendments to the Clean Air Act and the Federal Water Pollution Control Act earlier in the decade all enjoyed strong union backing. The United Automobile Workers, in particular, stood out as a staunch advocate of environmental reform during the 1960s and early 1970s, opposing the construction of nuclear power plants, urging greater investment in mass transportation, and sponsoring several environmental conferences.[20] Just before his death, Walter Reuther, the union's president, made the unheard-of suggestion of incorporating environmental issues in the collective bargaining process. His successor, Leonard Woodcock, demonstrated a similar commitment to the environment. Woodcock rejected the notion that a clean environment came at the expense of jobs. In testimony delivered to Congress in 1971, he lashed out at job blackmail tactics and called for legislation that would enable workers to sue companies for damages suffered as a result of layoffs associated with pollution control efforts.[21]

Although collaborative ventures between environmentalists and African American groups occurred infrequently, they did take place. In some instances, the two groups found themselves confronting a common enemy, even when they did not share the same objectives. When the Sierra Club and the National Association for the Advancement of Colored People (NAACP) joined forces to stop new highway construction in Oakland, California, in 1972, each group had its own reasons: the Sierra Club wanted to prevent pollution while the NAACP wanted to protect low-income housing slated for demolition.[22] For all the condemnation heaped upon insensitive middle-class environmentalists, many African American leaders recognized that industrial pollution was a serious health hazard for blacks who lived in congested inner-city neighborhoods. Thus, when prominent African American leaders from across the nation convened in Gary in 1972 to chart a course for independent black politics, they included several planks about industrial pollution in their manifesto for change.[23]

Clearly, the ecology crusade did not rest on a monolithic social base. As the previous discussion suggests, the social dynamics that underpinned environmental controversies were quite fluid during the postwar years, changing over time and generating unpredictable alliances. Although middle-class whites provided the most consistent support for environmental protection, the outcome of environmental conflicts often hinged upon the positions taken by racial minorities and working-class citizens. To fully comprehend the involvement of lower-income and minority groups, we must examine environmentalism issue by issue to determine who supported what issue and how the nature of that support changed over time in accordance with broader historical trends.

Moreover, we need to broaden the concept of environmentalism beyond the narrow formulation advanced most forcefully by middle-class activists. Divergent historical experiences and social objectives generated competing environmental agendas, not all of which fit neatly into the programmatic package set forth by the Sierra Club, the National Wildlife Federation, and other organizations dominated by affluent whites. Efforts to improve occupational health and to equalize access to urban resources, although not considered part of the mainstream environmental agenda, nonetheless reflected the deep-seated concerns of workers and minorities about the quality of physical surroundings. Simply measuring commitment to environmental reform against a middle-class standard is inadequate. Such a perspective illuminates a narrow slice of environmental conflict, whereas we ought to identify the full range of social responses to pollution.

Once we account for all social perspectives, we are in a much better position to explain the contours of environmental change and to interpret its larger meaning in the context of postwar power relations. Because the drive to curb industrial pollution and to defend endangered landscapes had the potential to unite individuals otherwise divided by race and class, participation in environmental struggles could be empowering. Yet despite the social changes induced by the labor, civil rights, and environmental movements, the postwar years did not witness any sort of environmental democracy. Challenges to prevailing environmental arrangements met stiff resistance, especially on the part of industrial corporations. The liberal political arrangements that granted shares of power to industrial laborers, African Americans, and middle-class environmentalists left plenty of room for industrial corporations to wield their clout in public and private spheres. Because liberal doctrine held that economic growth was the most effective, and no doubt most convenient, route to social justice, policy makers at all levels of government tended to defer to private capital on important matters. Liberalism might broaden political representation and deploy public resources on behalf of social welfare, but it would neither disturb fundamental property rights nor intrude on the managerial prerogatives of industrial capitalists. So although the social and political developments of the postwar years promised to reconfigure environmental arrangements, the outcome was by no means predictable.

This study attempts to identify the winners and the losers in the environmental struggles of the postwar era. In the process of pressing industry to alter its environmental practices, which groups secured their objectives and which groups fell short? How did the social distribution of industrial wastes change between 1945 and 1980? In answering these questions, we may come closer to uncovering the structure of power relations in recent U.S. history. Moreover, measuring environmental change by its differential impact on society's members enables us to test liberal capitalism's ability to reconcile competing environmental objectives and, indeed, its ability to balance the imperatives of industrial growth and social welfare.

An intensive study of one community, Gary, Indiana, between 1945 and 1980, promises to illuminate these themes. As a major center of steel production, Gary embodied the workings of mature industrial capitalism with its powerful corporations and its highly stratified social structure. The magnitude of demands on the local environment generated a competition for resources that had few parallels elsewhere in the nation. And although Gary industrialists enjoyed virtual autonomy in manipulating the landscape as they saw fit until World War II, the postwar years witnessed a variety of challenges to corporate control of the environment. After 1950, the city saw the birth and maturation of a self-conscious environmental movement, which, as it did in other areas of the country, drew primarily on middle-class whites. Inside the factories, industrial workers, both black and white, pressed for better working conditions. Equally in line with developments elsewhere, African Americans and white working-class citizens thrust themselves into local environmental politics after 1960.

Gary's experience, however, was by no means typical. The presence of powerful labor unions and the successful drive for black political power gave industrial workers and African Americans unprecedented opportunities to advance their distinct environmental agendas. Moreover, much of the thrust of environmental reform was directed at one particular company, the U.S. Steel Corporation. As a result of these unique factors, environmental conflicts were played out with unusual clarity and intensity, thereby making Gary an ideal setting for exploring the influence of race and class on the process of environmental change and for demonstrating the enduring influence of race and class in organizing patterns of both human and environmental control.

The Perils of Pollution in the Steel City, 1945–1950

Steel production permeated the environment of Gary, Indiana, during the late 1940s. Every evening the mills presented viewers with a display of giant torches, erupting sparks, and massive factories engraved against a glowing red sky. Day and night, black and red smoke wafted through the atmosphere while oils, greases, and chemicals streaked across rivers and lakes. For those who lived and worked in Gary, pollution was inescapable. And although affiliations of class, race, and ethnicity conditioned individuals' precise relationship to the environment, the social costs of industrial pollution impinged upon the entire urban population. African Americans, European immigrants, native-born whites, factory workers, white-collar professionals, affluent families, and poverty-stricken individuals all endured certain hazards and inconveniences associated with industry's manipulation of the nat-

15

ural environment. Yet despite the pervasiveness of industrial pollution, manufacturers encountered little popular resistance during the 1940s. A political order grounded in the pursuit of industrial growth effectively reconciled social objectives with patterns of natural resource exploitation, thereby allowing manufacturers to maintain their environmental hegemony.

Prior to U.S. Steel's arrival in 1906, neither industry nor any other kind of human activity exerted much influence on the site of Gary, Indiana. The Native American Potawatomis who had roamed the Lake Michigan shores until the 1830s moved westward when white pioneers pushed through the area, leaving behind a landscape bereft of humans. The white settlers concentrated in Chicago, which by 1900 boasted a population of over 1 million. Only thirty miles eastward, across the Indiana border, swamps and dunes still dominated the landscape. Majestic sand mounds hugged the lakeshore, giving way to a series of shorter sand ridges further inland. Marshes, lagoons, and swamps filled the intervening depressions. This habitat supported a diverse animal population that included wolves, ducks, and bald eagles. Two rivers, the Grand Calumet and the Little Calumet, meandered through the region, sustaining a varied fish population. Railway tracks cutting through the sand dunes and marsh grass, along with a few scattered farming villages, marked the only human imprint on this section of northwest Indiana.[1]

Although industrialists displayed little enthusiasm for the area's rich ecology, they were impressed by the location's suitability for steel production. In 1905 the U.S. Steel Corporation, headquartered in Pittsburgh and the nation's largest steel producer, decided to expand operations in the Midwest. The Gary site proved attractive, not only because the Chicago market was nearby but also because it was ideal for plant construction and the transportation of both raw materials and finished products. Abundant land allowed sufficient room for steel mills and subsidiary manufacturing plants. If the company required additional space, it could extend the shoreline by filling the lake. Steelmaking demanded vast amounts of water for cooling; Lake Michigan furnished an endless supply. Moreover, the lake provided a water route to the rich Mesabi ore fields in Minnesota, while existing railway lines connected the site with eastern coalfields and midwestern steel markets.[2]

These geographic assets prompted U.S. Steel executives to transform the rural duneland into an industrial city. As the founders of Gary, corporate executives enjoyed free rein to mold the environment as they wished. And because U.S. Steel built Gary as a company town, it possessed unrestricted power to structure the relationship between social activity and the physical landscape, at least in the city's formative years. After purchasing 9,000 acres of lakefront property in northwest Indiana in 1905, the company began building the world's largest integrated steel mill, Gary Works, the following year. Construction entailed massive environmental manipulation. The corporation altered the Lake Michigan shoreline by building a boat harbor, cutting a ship canal, and extending the coastline 700 feet further into the lake. Because the Grand Calumet River traversed the middle of the proposed plant site and often flooded to a width of 1,000 feet, corporate engineers moved the river one-quarter of a mile to the south and confined it to a straight channel. Construction crews leveled the terrain by removing 12 million cubic yards of sand and draining swamps on proposed factory sites. In building 56 open-hearth ovens, 8 blast furnaces, a coke plant, and various mills for making billets, rails, plates, and bars, U.S. Steel had replaced thousands of acres of dunes and marshes with concrete foundations, steel buildings, heavy machinery, and fiery furnaces.[3]

Construction of Gary Works merely marked the beginning of steel manufacturing's intrusion on the landscape. In 1906 the corporation supervised the building of a city to house its workers.[4] Paved streets, houses, shops, churches, and saloons sprang up just across the recently diverted Grand Calumet River from the steel mills. Two main thoroughfares—one running east-west alongside the river, the other traveling due south from the main factory gate—guided the growth of Gary in a T-shaped pattern, with the densest development just beyond the main entrance to the mills.[5] But as Gary's population swelled from 10,000 in 1908 to over 110,000 by the outbreak of World War II, urban development shifted toward Gary's outskirts, filling in areas that had once been woodlands, swamps, and dunes.

North of the Grand Calumet River, industrial expansion accounted for intensified environmental manipulation in the decades following 1908. For example, U.S. Steel continued to modify the natural shoreline of Lake Michigan by extending it over 500 acres.[6] Filling the lake enabled the corporation to dispose of slag, a rock by-product of steel production, with the added benefit of providing additional space. Still, huge quantities of slag had to be disposed of elsewhere, as did other more hazardous wastes such as tar sludge, acids, and steel scales. So the company took advantage of the plentiful swampland along the lakefront by using it as a repository for much of this refuse. Slag, tar, and other wastes were discarded in vacant pits and lagoons scattered throughout the property. New plant construction also consumed additional portions of land. The expansion of Gary Works included an axle mill, a slabbing mill, two blooming mills, three new open-hearth shops, and a sintering plant. Stretching from Gary Works in both directions along the lakefront, the company built factory complexes for the Gary Sheet and Tin Mill, the National Tube Company, and the American Bridge Plant, subsidiary firms that relied on steel produced at Gary Works. In addition, U.S. Steel operated a cement plant at the extreme western end of its property that utilized blast furnace slag from Gary Works.[7] By the start of World War II, the integrated network of industrial facilities sprawled along seven miles of lakefront property, with factories, waste disposal pits, railroad tracks, and storage yards. Only the 400-acre tract of land at the east end of the company's property, adjacent to the town of Miller, eluded industrial development.

U.S. Steel's presence encouraged several smaller firms to establish manufacturing plants in Gary, further embellishing the city's industrial landscape. Businesses that needed steel for their operations preferred to locate near their supply source. Hence, producers of screws and bolts; steel wires, bars, and rods; and steel springs dotted the periphery of steel company property. Manufacturers of windshield wipers, hosiery, and trousers added to the matrix of industrial establishments.[8] Although the cumulative environmental impact of Gary's smaller enterprises was not insignificant, these secondary manufacturers did not occupy much space, and they placed relatively little strain on the city's air and water resources.

Steel manufacturing, on the other hand, discharged several hundred tons of waste annually into Gary's atmosphere and waterways. Of the industrial refuse produced, only a small portion went into landfills on company property. Smokestacks and pipes carried most of the wastes beyond the company's borders into the community's air and water. In each of the discrete steps involved in the production process, steelmaking placed unique demands on Gary's air and water resources. Only by following this process from the preparation of raw materials to the perfection of the finished product can we fully comprehend the vast array of waste materials and the complex genesis of each.

U.S. Steel engineers organized the production process so that materials flowed in an orderly fashion from east to west. At the east end of the property, workers prepared and combined raw materials to produce basic steel. Here, laborers transformed coke into coal, iron ore into pig iron, and pig iron into steel. The rolling and shaping of finished steel into precise forms occurred in the western mills. Figure 1 depicts the flow of operations at Gary Works. As the processes moved from east to west, they generally yielded smaller and smaller quantities of refuse and less harmful wastes.

The coke plant, located at the eastern end of U.S. Steel's property, was the dirtiest section of Gary Works. Each step in the transformation of coal to coke generated pollutants. The frequent moving and handling of coal along the way dispersed large amounts of dust. As coal baked at temperatures of nearly 2,000 degrees, suspended carbon particles, tars, hydrocarbons, carbon monoxide, methane, and sulfur dioxide escaped from the ovens. And when workers doused the cooked product with cooling water, the resulting steam lifted tiny coke particles into the air. The used quenching water also contained coke residue, along with the by-products ammonia and phenol.[9]

When the corporation found it profitable, wastes were recycled. Corporate managers, who maintained exclusive authority over production, made decisions according to cost accounting principles and the concept of long-term corporate stability. They engineered waste disposal systems that maximized profit, and at times, pollution control made good economic sense. For example, coking produced many gases used in the production of perfumes, aspirin, sulfa drugs, DDT, fertilizers, and paints. By drawing fumes directly from the coke ovens with exhaust fans, U.S. Steel recovered these by-products for sale to chemical companies. Meanwhile, the unmarketable portion of the hot gas was recycled back to the ovens and used as heating fuel.

When waste recovery promised no monetary gain, U.S. Steel allowed the particles and gases to follow their natural course, upward and outward. Gas and dust that escaped from leaky oven doors floated into the

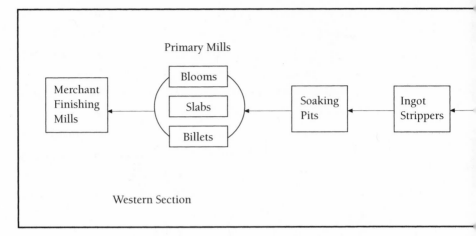

Figure 1. Production Flow at Gary Works

atmosphere along with the particulate-laden steam discharged from the water-quenching towers. Clouds of tar, hydrocarbons, sulfur, methane, carbon monoxide, and carbon hovered in and around the coke plant, then dissipated across the city or Lake Michigan, depending on the wind direction. At least 1 percent of the original coal ended up in the atmosphere by the conclusion of the coke-manufacturing process. Unwanted liquid wastes were piped into the Grand Calumet River along the company's southern border.[10]

Just west of the coke plant, the furnaces converting iron into steel emitted their own distinct wastes. Sintering plants combined iron ore fines with metallurgical dust to form an agglomerated chunk strong enough to bake in the blast furnaces. Here, workers shot hot air into huge cylindrical stoves containing ore, coke, and limestone. The molten iron that spewed from the furnaces every four or five hours was then carried on a giant ladle to the open-hearth furnaces, where it was baked once again, this time in combination with metals such as manganese, chromium, and nickel, to produce finished steel. Each of these processes released small particles of iron into the atmosphere as well as smaller amounts of carbon, limestone dust, hydrogen sulfide, and sulfur dioxide. In addition, the blast furnaces and open-hearth furnaces yielded slag, unwanted solid impurities that collected above the molten metal. According to one estimate, the blast furnaces alone generated 1 million tons of slag annually.[11]

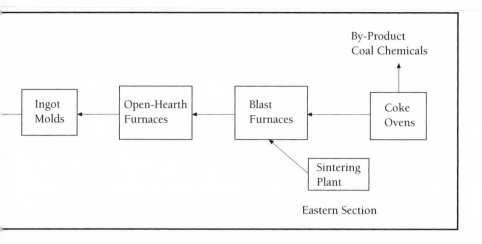

By-Product
Coal Chemicals

| Ingot Molds | Open-Hearth Furnaces | Blast Furnaces | Coke Ovens |

Sintering Plant

Eastern Section

The western portion of the plant, where workers shaped finished steel into various forms, produced much smaller volumes of waste. After emerging from the open-hearth furnaces, molten steel went to one of several rolling mills, where it was shaped into billets, blooms, or slabs. Further refinements occurred either at the merchant mills of Gary Works or at the U.S. Steel subsidiaries, the Gary Sheet and Tin Mill or the National Tube Company.[12] These finishing mills generated relatively little air pollution but presented some solid and liquid waste disposal problems. Rolling operations produced unwanted scales that accumulated on the surface of the finished steel. Workers blasted the scales away with high-power water jets and sluiced them into lagoons located on company property. Lubricating oils and greases flowed along with the wastewater. Eventually the scales settled to the bottom of the lagoons, where they were recovered and recycled back into the steelmaking furnaces. The corporation pumped the remaining water into the Grand Calumet River. Another cleansing procedure known as pickling used large amounts of sulfuric acid to remove impurities from the finished steel. The acidic fumes rising from the pickling tanks constituted one of the few air pollution hazards in the western mills. When the acid lost its strength, it became of little use to U.S. Steel, and the spent pickle liquors were deposited in company pits or flushed into the river following a neutralization procedure.[13]

The cement plant that U.S. Steel operated several miles away from the mills, in the far northwest corner of Gary, also contributed to the city's pollution load. The preparation of cement involved grinding down limestone, sand, and slag collected from the blast furnaces. This crushing process released dust as mechanized hammers pulverized the ingredients into a fine powder. More particles escaped into the atmosphere when the mixture baked in rotary kilns at temperatures of 2,700 degrees. Finally, water used to cool the finished product also accumulated cement fragments.[14]

U.S. Steel's environmental practices impinged upon all who toiled in its factories and lived in the surrounding neighborhoods. Pollution impaired health, damaged property, and forced adjustments in daily behavior. Moreover, the company's thirst for water and appetite for property limited public access to Lake Michigan, the Grand Calumet River, and much of the land in between. Although few escaped the deleterious effects of industry's environmental tampering, individuals' experiences with the industrial environment varied considerably. Exposure to dirty air or tainted water depended on where one worked, lived, and spent leisure time. These activities—employment, residence, and recreation— were shaped by one's position in a social hierarchy organized around class, race, and ethnicity. Yet social background did not always accurately predict exposure levels to pollution. Uncovering the precise relationship between social organization and industrial pollution patterns requires that we follow, step by step, the path of manufacturing wastes as they intruded on human activity both in the factories and in the neighborhoods.

Steelworkers encountered intense concentrations of pollution on the job. Each day steel production rotated 30,000 people, about half of Gary's labor force, from the residential neighborhoods into the mills.[15] Although U.S. Steel had hired a substantial number of women during World War II to compensate for the drain of male workers into the armed forces, men reclaimed their jobs once hostilities ended, making the shop floor an exclusively male domain once again. These male laborers encountered a wide range of work environments inside the mills during the late 1940s. Employees who toiled in the coke plant, sintering plant, blast furnaces, and open-hearth ovens suffered the most hardships. Coke battery workers, for example, faced blasts of thick smoke when they opened oven doors to insert or remove materials. Visibility sometimes became such a problem that workers rang bells and clanged shovels to communicate.[16] Duke Lee, who worked in the coke plant until 1946, remembered that conditions were so dusty that three years after leaving U.S. Steel he was still spitting up particles of coke.[17] Lance burners, who injected oxygen into the open-hearth furnaces, fastened themselves to one another with rope to navigate their way through the particulate fog.[18] Curtis Strong, who began working in the mills in 1943, recalled that in the sintering plant, "The dust was so bad, you couldn't see. You couldn't tell blacks from whites; everyone was completely red."[19]

Although in contrast to the eastern sections of the plant the rolling and shaping mills generated fewer environmental hazards, many who worked there during the 1940s recalled that conditions were less than desirable. Chris Malis landed a job in the rolling mills during World War II on the recommendation of his brother. In addition to the considerable amount of dust floating around inside the 160-inch plate mill, Malis remembered the tiny scales that constantly flew in all directions from the 160-inch steel slabs passing through the rollers.[20] Beginning in 1935, John Howard chipped steel with a large pneumatic drill in another section of the rolling mills. Looking back on his work experiences many years later, Howard remarked that he inhaled so much dust in the daytime that he would frequently spend entire nights coughing.[21] Despite these harsh conditions, both Malis and Howard conceded that they were probably better off than their counterparts in the coke plant and the basic steelmaking departments.

Steelworkers received meager financial compensation for the environmental hardships their work inflicted; in fact, exposure to hazardous wastes usually coincided with low pay. Company management and the United Steelworkers of America classified all production jobs in a numerical ranking that determined wages. Positions involving exposure to excessive noise, dirt, smoke, and heat merited a higher ranking on the scale. However, so many other variables entered the calculation that, in the end, work environment counted for little. In a 43-point rating system, on-the-job exposure to acids, fumes, and dirt was worth less than one point. Skill and training, on the other hand, counted for much more and largely determined an individual's wage. But because the most environmentally hazardous tasks usually required little skill, workers were hardly remunerated for the environmental burdens they endured. Most production jobs in the coke plant, sintering plant, blast furnaces, and open-hearth ovens ranked in the lower half of the wage hierarchy. Even in the relatively clean shaping and finishing mills, the few hazardous jobs paid poorly. For example, pickle loaders who worked amid sulfuric acid fumes were near the bottom of the pay ladder.[22]

U.S. Steel did not hire workers randomly; forty years of labor recruitment produced an occupational hierarchy built around racial and ethnic divisions. A series of labor shortages during the early twentieth century brought successive waves of unskilled labor into the steel mills, permitting some occupational mobility for existing workers. At first, European immigrants filled those jobs requiring light training and heavy toil. Poles, Slovaks, Serbians, and Croatians chipped steel, poured molten metals, and charged furnaces, while native-born whites supervised them and performed the more skilled tasks. Beginning with World War I, mill managers sought new labor sources as European immigration to the United States slowed. They turned first to southern blacks. When steelworkers in Gary struck for the right to organize in 1919, management recruited additional blacks to replace the strikers. Through the mid-1920s, African Americans comprised about 15 percent of Gary Works' labor force, while Mexicans, transported to Gary by railroad early in the decade, accounted for another 9 percent. Management placed both minority groups in the most menial positions; as of 1928, 80 percent held unskilled jobs. The steel production boom that coincided with World War II provided a third occasion for adding African American workers to the lower rungs of the job ladder. By 1945, blacks comprised 27 percent of the workforce at Gary Works, laboring almost exclusively in the coke plant and blast furnaces. The European-born employees, on the other hand, enjoyed opportunities to move into better positions. Discriminatory hiring practices translated into wage discrepancies; on the eve of World War II, black workers received 85 cents for every dollar earned by their white counterparts.[23]

Because unskilled, low-paying production jobs usually involved exposure to the most pollution, Mexicans and African Americans bore a disproportionate burden of environmental hazards within the mills. Mexicans toiled in the high temperatures of the open-hearth ovens because U.S. Steel executives believed them to be well-suited to the heat.[24]

Blacks worked mainly in the coke plant, the dirtiest section of the mills. One steel executive attempted to justify such hiring practices by claiming, "The Negroes shine in coke oven work where is there is much dust, heat, etc."[25] Black workers who secured employment in the cleaner west mills did not fare much better because they usually received jobs involving the greatest exposure to oil and grease.[26]

Within the mills, therefore, a distinct pattern emerged by World War II linking environmental exploitation with income, ethnicity, and race. Whites with northern European backgrounds working in management and skilled craft positions attained the greatest insulation from hazardous wastes and also received the highest wages. More recent European immigrants occupied a middling position; benefiting from upward mobility, they concentrated in semiskilled production jobs that paid moderately and involved some exposure to noxious waste emissions. Blacks and Mexicans fared the worst, earning the least and laboring under the harshest conditions.

Outside the mills, a more ambiguous relationship between pollution exposure and social standing prevailed. Smokestacks and pipes eventually carried steel manufacturing wastes beyond the company borders into the community. The population that encountered these wastes was considerably more diverse than the laboring class and the corporate executives who worked inside the mills. Professionals and operators of small businesses—shopkeepers, saloon owners, hotel managers, doctors, lawyers, and teachers—established themselves in Gary to serve the community's needs. This sector of the population comprised a full range of ethnic and racial groups, some rarely found in the steel mills, such as Jews. Except for Jews and African Americans, rigid barriers did not segregate the social lives of Gary's various ethnic groups and classes. Yet income and cultural preferences did, in effect, separate the population into discrete cells of social activity. The way these groups negotiated the use of physical space largely determined how the factory wastes interfered with the lives of Gary residents.

Airborne industrial emissions traveled according to wind patterns. Forty percent of the time, air currents blew from the south, directing dust and fumes away from the city, across Lake Michigan. When winds originated in the north, however, steel mill smoke enveloped Gary in a blanket of soot. Suspended particles of iron, cement, and coke hovered over the city and then rained down upon its citizens. Invisible sulfur dioxide from the sintering plant, blast furnaces, and coke ovens, along with hydrocarbons from the coke plant, accompanied the particulates.[27] Certain weather patterns exacerbated the situation. Cool, swift breezes blowing off the lake from the north trapped warmer air close to the ground, preventing the upward dispersal of pollutants. The sealed-in mill smoke formed a low-rolling plume that swept through Gary's neighborhoods. Stagnant air posed its own problems by keeping pollutants trapped at low elevations, close to streets and homes.[28]

Although the variability of wind patterns ensured that pollutants traveled to all sections of Gary, areas closest to the factories received a disproportionate share. Air quality was worst in downtown Gary, situated just across from the open-hearth furnaces (see map 1). Further east, residents were more likely to encounter emissions from the coke and sintering plants. On the more sparsely populated west side, citizens bore the brunt of cement plant discharges as well as emissions from East Chicago's steel mills.[29] In contrast to neighborhoods along Gary's northern tier, the southern and eastern fringes of the city escaped heavy doses of air pollution. The eastern lakeshore suburb of Miller, buffered from the mills by woodlands and insulated by prevailing wind patterns, received only half the dustfall of downtown. Industry sprayed equally small amounts of soot on Glen Park, the neighborhood located on Gary's southern periphery, six miles inland from Lake Michigan.[30]

The disparity in air pollution concentration among Gary's neighborhoods meant that those who lived in the shadows of the steel mills endured the greatest hardships. When winds blew in from the mills, the thick stench of steel and coke permeated the air of north side neighborhoods. Dust settled on streets, lawns, and houses, and during the summer, open windows drew dirty air inside homes. For those who lived in north Gary, air pollution entailed extra expense and work. Accumulations of industrial soot forced homeowners to clean windows and dust furniture regularly. In addition, these residents found themselves applying coat after coat of fresh paint to combat the smoke residue and coke fumes that tarnished exterior house finishes. Even drying laundry became a tricky matter as families had to take note of the wind direction before hanging clean garments on outdoor clotheslines.[31]

Furthermore, breathing polluted air damaged the health of many

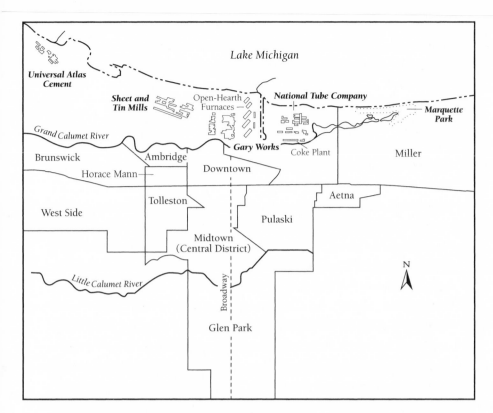

Map 1. Gary Neighborhoods, 1950

north side residents. During episodes of intense pollution, hospitals admitted patients suffering from various respiratory illnesses. Inhaling
sulfur dioxide and suspended particulates exacerbated heart and lung
ailments such as tuberculosis, asthma, and emphysema. Such short-
term health hazards threatened infants, the elderly, and the infirm, in
particular. Statistical data suggests that air pollution accounted for
abnormally high infant mortality rates in the neighborhoods bordering
the steel mills (see tables A.1 and A.2). Airborne wastes caused long-
term health problems as well. Coke ovens released carcinogenic gases,
while lead, cadmium, manganese, nickel, beryllium, and chromium
discharges caused ailments ranging from hypertension to lung cancer.
Thus, north side residents, particularly those clustered around the
downtown area, encountered the greatest health risks associated with
air pollution, often facing more danger than steelworkers inside the
mills, who tended to be younger and healthier.[32]

Who were these north side residents who suffered the greatest hardships from air pollution? For that matter, how did residential arrangements throughout the city bias exposure to dirty air? Gary's housing patterns failed to fit any simple model.[33] Certainly, distinct neighborhoods developed on the basis of race, class, and ethnic affiliations. African Americans clustered together, the wealthy and the poor lived apart, and working-class whites settled with others of similar economic and ethnic background. But these cells of social activity were small and, for the most part, were densely intermingled around the downtown area. Unlike air pollution levels, which varied directly according to distance from the steel mills, the socioeconomic characteristics of the residential population followed no consistent geographical pattern. Historical forces produced a jumbled patchwork of neighborhoods, such that no social grouping entirely escaped the hazards associated with dirty air.

U.S. Steel's initial plans for developing the city influenced the subsequent arrangement of Gary's neighborhoods. When the corporation founded the city in 1906, it constructed high-quality housing for its executives and skilled workers along strips bordering the mills to the east and west of downtown. Hence, the homes on either side of downtown were superior in quality to the tenements that filled many other industrial inner cities. The worst housing conditions existed in the section of Gary known as the "Patch," which was located 1.5 to 3 miles south of the steel mills. Here, immigrants and other impoverished workers, mostly single men, crowded into cheaply constructed boardinghouses and shacks.[34]

Over the next forty years, a complex set of forces modified the stark boundaries originally separating Gary's elite north side neighborhoods from the squalid south side. Social groups often pursued their own distinctive residential objectives; the motives that guided the foreign-born working class, for instance, did not necessarily explain the housing decisions of more affluent, native-born whites. Furthermore, discriminatory real estate practices prevented certain groups from exercising free choice in the housing market. Thus, by the 1940s, neither the original town layout nor simple market dynamics accounted for Gary's settlement patterns.

Among the affluent, the desire for more space, proximity to work, and access to good schools influenced residential choice, scattering elite neighborhoods throughout the city from the downtown area to the city's outermost fringes. Many white, native-born elites continued to inhabit the high-quality, company-built housing in Gary's north side neighborhoods. The Horace Mann section, situated along this northern tier two miles west of the open-hearth furnaces, remained Gary's most prestigious community, boasting the city's highest median income through the 1940s. Stately homes, a fine high school, and proximity to both downtown and the mills attracted the families of business executives and white-collar professionals. Beginning in the 1930s, this social class discovered similar amenities in Glen Park, located on the city's southern periphery. While this neighborhood's popularity in the 1940s reflected some disenchantment with inner-city living, its appeal was enhanced by frequent bus service to downtown and the steel mills. Toward the end of the 1940s, yet another remote suburb, Miller, emerged as an exclusive neighborhood. Previously strewn with ramshackle cottages and a few plush homes along the Lake Michigan shore, Miller suddenly experienced a steady influx of wealthy families. Its growth was hampered, however, by inconvenient access to downtown. For many of those who chose to settle there despite the lengthy commute, the scenic beauty of the lakefront community provided sufficient compensation. At the beginning of the 1950s, then, Gary's wealthiest whites still preferred to live near downtown, although the growth of Glen Park and Miller indicated a trend toward suburbanization.[35]

Ties of ethnicity kept most white working-class residents close to downtown, although outlying regions also supported a few blue-collar enclaves. Immigrants and their children constituted the bulk of Gary's blue-collar labor force. Indeed, as late as 1957, two out of five Gary residents were either foreign-born or first-generation Americans.[36] As in other industrial cities, Gary's foreign-born inhabitants relied on compatriots to procure employment, find housing, and perpetuate their cultural heritage.[37] The infusion of new immigrants from Eastern Europe immediately after World War II sustained the vitality of these ethnic networks through the 1940s. The central institution binding the ethnic community was the church. In addition to providing worship service, most ethnic churches offered parochial education for schoolchildren and supported a variety of musical, theatrical, and social clubs. Mutual aid societies also sprang from churches, providing members with insurance against economic hardship resulting from catastrophic illness or family death.[38]

From the city's beginnings in the early twentieth century, blue-collar neighborhoods coalesced around ethnic churches, most of which were situated just south of downtown, a short streetcar or bus ride from the mills (see map 2). The importance of these churches to blue-collar social life anchored many working-class families to downtown neighborhoods even as automobiles and expanded public transportation systems made suburban areas more accessible. When enough members of a particular ethnic group relocated to remote areas of the city, they established their own churches. Gary's Polish community, for example, was sufficiently large to support three parishes, two close to downtown and one further out in Glen Park. But for most blue-collar families who wished to remain within walking distance of their churches, residence coincided with the inner-city ethnic parish.[39]

In contrast to most white citizens, Gary's African Americans encountered more limited residential options as discriminatory housing practices kept them confined to the Midtown district, located in the center of the city. Ghetto formation came much later to Gary than it did to most northern cities.[40] When black migrants first came to Gary in sizable numbers after World War I, they settled amid the immigrant population on Gary's south side. Persistent housing shortages kept this area racially integrated for several decades, but as housing gradually became available in other parts of the city, the foreign-born whites moved out, leaving black residents behind. With the development of Glen Park further south, the south side became known as the Central district or Midtown. African Americans could not take advantage of the city's spatial growth because realtors refused to sell them homes in the new areas; newspaper advertisements noted whether homes were appropriate "for coloreds." Hence, Midtown became racially homogeneous.[41] As late as 1940, whites still constituted over 25 percent of Midtown's population, but by 1950, they comprised only 4 percent.[42]

Despite the stirrings of suburbanization among whites, the heavily polluted inner city continued to hold residents from the full spectrum of social groups. As of 1950, Gary's population remained concentrated around downtown, with over 70 percent of all residents living within 2.5 miles of Broadway and 5th Avenue.[43] Thus, although class, race, and

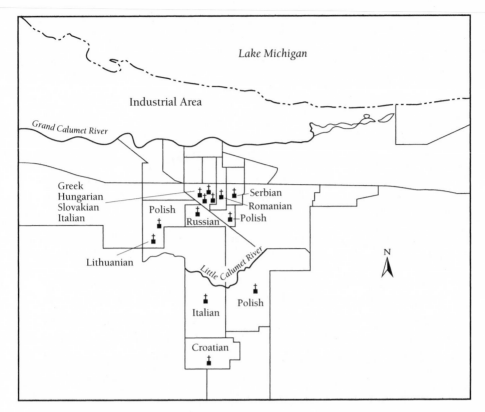

Map 2. Ethnic Parishes in Gary, 1950

ethnicity carved residential space into discrete neighborhoods, population density minimized social disparities in the distribution of air pollution. Those residents who lived along Gary's northern tier, directly
across from the mills, occupied the middle rungs of the social ladder. A
combination of immigrants and native-born whites, these citizens tended to work in semiskilled manufacturing jobs and earned incomes that
approximated the city's average.[44] Those above and below them in the
social hierarchy experienced comparable levels of pollution. African
Americans in Midtown and steel executives in the elite Horace Mann
neighborhood encountered similar doses of dirty air. The growth of
Glen Park and Miller on the suburban fringe meant that those who
breathed the cleanest air were somewhat wealthier than the average citizen. Even so, through the 1940s, neither class, race, nor ethnicity
served as a very reliable predictor of residential exposure to dirty air (see
table A.3).

Residence, however, was not the only social activity that brought individuals into contact with air pollution. Most people spent a great deal of time away from their homes. Where Garyites worked, shopped, worshiped, went to school, and played also determined exposure to airborne wastes. The primacy of downtown Gary to social life tended to offset any environmental inequalities resulting from more dispersed residential patterns.

Gary's central business district, the hub of commerce and civic activity, drew thousands of people downtown daily. Broadway, the city's main thoroughfare, cut a straight path from the steel mill gates south to the city limits in Glen Park. The hustle and bustle of urban life concentrated in the northernmost seven blocks of Broadway, the heart of downtown. Major civic, private, and recreational institutions lined Broadway or were located within a few blocks in either direction, and automobiles and buses plied the jammed roadway. City hall and the courthouse, standing across from each other at the intersection of Broadway and Fourth Avenue, marked the gateway to Gary's downtown, just beyond the border of factory property. The Gary National Bank, the major financial institution, and the Hotel Gary, where local businessmen met daily for lunch, stood further south along the main thoroughfare.[45] Lawyers, doctors, dentists, insurance salespersons, and realtors worked in nearby office buildings that offered striking views of cranes, factories, and belching smokestacks. The surrounding blocks contained many of the city's most important institutions, including the Steelworkers Union meeting hall along Fifth Avenue, the main branch of the Gary Public Library, and a regional campus of Indiana University. Gilroy Stadium, where all local high school teams played their football games, and the YMCA likewise stood within several blocks of Gary's main artery.

From Monday through Friday during the daylight hours, the main downtown attraction was the retail district. Beginning at Fifth Avenue and stretching south to Eleventh Avenue, department stores and more specialized retail shops lined Broadway, attracting shoppers from Gary and outlying communities. Gary residents routinely ventured downtown by car or bus to purchase clothing, furniture, and household appliances. Here, they could patronize the large department stores, Goldblatt's and Gordon's, or the smaller outlets such as Florsheim Shoes, Dreyfus Appliance and Furniture, and Seifer Lamar. Whatever store they ultimately chose, they more than likely did their shopping along Broadway; downtown shops absorbed about 75 percent of the city's total retail sales.[46]

The concentration of social activity in downtown Gary meant that dirty air touched the lives of even those who did not reside nearby. When winds blew from the north, which they did 60 percent of the time, smoke from the steel mills decreased visibility in the central business district, making driving treacherous. When U.S. Steel charged a coke oven or tapped a furnace, gusts of smoke swept across Gilroy Stadium, forcing officials to halt football games temporarily.[47] Downtown traffic congestion, which resulted in high levels of motor vehicle exhaust fumes, only added to the poor air quality. No ecological phenomenon better dramatized the pervasive nature of pollution than the convergence of social activity and dirty air in downtown Gary.

The only significant portion of the population that rarely ventured downtown was Gary's black community. A racially segregated consumer culture confined African Americans to the Midtown neighborhood for virtually all social functions. Whereas whites lived in neighborhoods throughout the city and congregated downtown, blacks lived in Midtown, shopped in Midtown, and pursued leisure activities in Midtown. For many African Americans, the daily journey to and from the mills represented the only occasion for leaving the ghetto community. This confinement was seldom a matter of choice. Downtown merchants and recreational institutions openly discriminated against African Americans. Black customers knew they were not welcome in most restaurants outside of Midtown, and at the YMCA and YWCA, discrimination was so blatant that one local minister suggested the institution change its name to the "Young Men's and Young Women's Organization of the Ku Klux Klan."[48] Furthermore, African Americans wandering beyond their neighborhood borders risked intimidation and violence from hostile whites. Hence, African Americans lived in a world separate from the white community. For black families, cultural and social life revolved around neighborhood churches, which offered entertainment, lectures, and meals. Single black men congregated in Midtown's pool halls and taverns. And those who wished to spend a few hours watching a movie were restricted to one of the local theaters that showed films designed solely for nonwhite audiences.[49] Ironically, the social isolation imposed on blacks kept them from breathing the city's very worst air. Located further from the mills than downtown, Midtown residents enjoyed slightly better air quality.

Water pollution, although less noticeable to Gary residents than air pollution, had an equally pernicious effect. Whereas the burden of water pollution fell unequally across the population, like dirty air, its effects were widely felt during the 1940s. Each day, U.S. Steel pumped over 300 million gallons of waste water into the Grand Calumet River and Lake Michigan, including about 37,000 pounds of oil, 10,000 pounds of ammonia-nitrogen, 1,100 pounds of phenol, and 1,200 pounds of cyanide. In addition, mill waste water carried small particles of iron, manganese, and chromium.[50] The introduction of these wastes into Gary's waterways imposed financial costs, interfered with recreation, and threatened human health.

Industry dumped most of its chemical and suspended solid wastes into the Grand Calumet River. Although many sediments settled on the river bottom, much of the waste flow eventually entered Lake Michigan after passing through the Indiana Harbor Canal just west of Gary. The gradual dispersal of wastes meant that water quality was worst in the river; the vast size of Lake Michigan diluted wastes there. Nevertheless, the southern part of the lake remained the most polluted. As early as 1933, one engineer cited southern Lake Michigan as having one of the nation's most serious water pollution problems.[51] Slow drainage out of Lake Michigan exacerbated the accumulation of industrial wastes. Therefore, although environmental degradation proceeded more rapidly in the Grand Calumet River than in Lake Michigan, industrial waste emissions altered the chemical and biological composition of both bodies of water.

For those who fished the lake for recreation or profit, the effects of water pollution were devastating. Two Miller families, the Carrs and the Sabinskes, watched their fishing businesses deteriorate as rising pollution levels transformed the ecology of Gary's waterways. Dick Sabinske remembered a time before the arrival of the steel mills when the Grand Calumet was "a wonderful river, clear and full of fish."[52] By the end of World War II, however, the waterway had become an industrial sewer, incapable of supporting any life except for blue-green algae and sludgeworms.[53] The effects of industrial dumping on Lake Michigan were less severe but equally noticeable. Fred Carr remembered observing multi-colored streaks in the water during the 1930s, each hue marking a different type of industrial discharge. Nevertheless, he claimed that the herring were so plentiful "you could scoop them out of the water with a hat."[54] Although Carr may have exaggerated the abundance of fish in the 1930s, the lake harvest certainly showed a sharp decline during the 1940s, especially with regard to sturgeon, trout, and yellow perch. Industrial pollution contributed significantly to species depletion by lowering oxygen levels and feeding algal blooms, which, in turn, displaced zooplankton and diatoms, the basic nutrition source for Lake Michigan fish. Of course, U.S. Steel was not solely responsible for changes in the lake ecology; industries ringing the lake from Chicago to Milwaukee contributed pollutants as well. Steel mill wastes, however, proved especially damaging to the aquatic habitats around Gary.[55]

Fish harvests improved in the late 1940s, but not to the liking of the Carrs, the Sabinskes, or other Gary anglers. After the war, species better adapted to the industrial lake habitat—carp, smelt, chubs, and alewives—invaded Lake Michigan from foreign waters. These new species were considered less desirable by most fishermen. The alewife, in particular, was seen as a pest because its aggressive hunting for dwindling food sources hastened the decline of the native fish. Hence, by 1950, lake trout disappeared from the lake and suckers, whitefish, and lake herring began a decline that would lead to virtual extinction by the 1960s.[56] Nevertheless, the Carrs and Sabinskes kept their businesses afloat until the early 1960s, eking out a meager living selling their catches to local retailers and renting boats to recreational fishermen.[57]

In contrast to the limited impact of fish extinction on humans, tainted drinking water affected almost all Gary residents. The chemicals and particles that flowed into Lake Michigan ultimately poured from household faucets. The Northwest Indiana Public Service Company (NIPSCO), the water utility that serviced most of the city, drew its water from Lake Michigan. Although the company positioned its water intake valve far enough into the lake to avoid the heavy flow of refuse passing through the Indiana Harbor Canal, iron particles and industrial chemicals entered the receiving pipe when currents circulated water to the east. In the absence of filtration mechanisms, these wastes then settled in the city's drinking water supply.[58] As a result, Gary residents complained that their water was murky and unpalatable. According to one individual, Gary water was so cloudy during the 1940s that it was impossible to see the bottom of a bathtub once it was filled.[59]

Perhaps the greatest victims of water pollution were the residents of western Gary. Unlike most city dwellers, many inhabitants of western Gary obtained their water from wells rather than from the utility company. This neighborhood, populated by a combination of fairly prosperous industrial workers and more impoverished Mexican immigrants, was the only place in Gary where the Grand Calumet River passed through a residential area. Highly permeable sandy soil increased the chance that polluted river water would contaminate household wells. Moreover, unsupervised children from the surrounding homes played on the riverbank and swam in the dirty water. If they absorbed toxic chemicals through their skin, they were vulnerable to a variety of health disorders. Chemicals from the coke plant, for instance, may have damaged skin tissue and contributed to liver and kidney ailments.[60]

Like air pollution, therefore, water pollution was distributed broadly across the population, with the worst effects felt by residents who, for the most part, occupied the middle ranks of Gary's social hierarchy.

In contrast to air and water consumption, industrial land use in postwar Gary rarely infringed upon the activities of Gary residents. Unlike water and air, land was privately owned and stationary. Once industry purchased a site, others rarely made competing claims on the property. Zoning regulations carved the city into distinct districts for industry, commerce, and residence, thus discouraging disputes over the type of use for a particular piece of property. As in most U.S. cities, Gary planners concentrated heavy industry in areas removed from residential neighborhoods, using commercial and light manufacturing districts as buffers. Although few residential properties bordered directly on steel mills or the cement plant, there was some intermingling of light manufacturing and living quarters. Both the Anderson Company, a windshield wiper manufacturer, and Bear Brand Hosiery were located in residential areas. Small manufacturers occupied little space, however, and sufficient vacant land existed throughout the city to satisfy the growing demand for residential property. Moreover, heavy industry had good reason to be satisfied with Gary's zoning plan because it set aside virtually all land north of the Grand Calumet River and several parcels along the city's western border for producers of metals, cement, chemicals, electricity, rubber, coal, petroleum, and asphalt.[61] This district contained over 40 percent of Gary's total acreage, far in excess of industry's immediate needs during the 1940s.[62] In addition to enjoying a vast reserve of land, heavy industry laid claim to those properties with the greatest access to railway lines, the Grand Calumet River, and Lake Michigan.

The Lake Michigan shoreline provided the only source of controversy concerning industrial land use through the 1940s. U.S. Steel originally purchased seven of the ten miles of city shoreline property. Almost immediately, the remaining three miles, located in Miller, became a matter of contention. The steel corporation sought the property for future industrial expansion. Drusilla Carr, who owned the coveted land, refused to sell and eventually waged a series of legal battles with U.S. Steel to prevent her beach from being "desecrated by huge industrial smokestacks."[63] She had the weight of popular opinion behind her because, as the city's only beachfront property, the area had become Gary's most prominent leisure resort and tourist attraction. By the 1920s, it featured a miniature railroad, a pleasure boat, a shooting gallery, a dance hall, a roller rink, and several nightclubs. Residents from Gary and Chicago owned summer bungalows along the beachfront. Only Gary's black population, denied access to white recreational venues, did not enjoy the use of Miller's beach. Despite the area's popularity, U.S. Steel continued to pursue the property, and in 1940 the company seized control of eighty-nine acres. Having no immediate plans for expansion, however, U.S. Steel turned the land over to the Gary Parks Department, temporarily quelling the lakeshore conflict.[64] At the end of World War II, city planners looked forward to renovating the park by expanding the beach and by building a bath pavilion, concession stand, fishing pier, and boat harbor.[65]

Thus, in contrast to the situation at the work place, where race and class largely determined exposure to pollutants, the burdens of industrial resource use generally fell evenly across Gary's residential communities. Industry's demands on the environment impinged most acutely on those who lived near the steel mills—the north side citizens who breathed the dirtiest air, the west side inhabitants who bordered the Grand Calumet River, and the Miller families who feared the loss of their beach. But these residents were a heterogeneous lot. Indeed, they comprised the bulk of Gary's population. Moreover, the polluted areas—Miller beach, the lake, and downtown—were utilized by a much larger population than those living nearby. Hence, industrial resource exploitation was very much a community problem in the years immediately following World War II.

Despite such pervasive environmental manipulation on the part of industry, manufacturers encountered little public pressure to amend their practices. Although citizens complained about factory odors and "murky and unpalatable" drinking water, a political structure grounded in the promotion of industrial growth left little opening for any serious environmental reform initiative. Historically, city governments in the United States have tended to make economic growth their first priority, whereas the specific strategies employed to attain growth have varied considerably according to time and place.[66] In Gary, the overwhelming economic importance of U.S. Steel encouraged public officials to identify industrial production as the key to local prosperity. Moreover, by the 1940s, city leaders had concluded that the best way to sustain healthy industries was to leave economic decision making in private hands. Fearing that pollution control would constrain industrial production and infringe on management's prerogatives, local officials allowed manufacturers full freedom to manipulate the environment as they saw fit.

By World War II, local government had established a precedent of noninterference with U.S. Steel's operations. Earlier in the century, civic officials and U.S. Steel had struggled to define the parameters of corporate involvement in community affairs. Fearing that Gary might remain a company town indefinitely, voters elected Tom Knotts, a Democrat and an outspoken opponent of the corporation, as the city's first mayor in 1909. Knotts incurred the company's wrath by awarding the electric trolley franchise to a firm that promised to build its lines far from U.S. Steel's residential properties. Gradually, animosities abated as the steel company and a series of Republican administrations in power between 1914 and 1935 worked to smooth relations. Having learned its lesson, U.S. Steel withdrew from active meddling in community affairs, content to leave governance in the hands of a small business elite. By the late 1930s, the steel company had divested its residential property holdings.[67] In return for U.S. Steel's retrenchment, city officials relinquished the right to police company property. For all practical purposes, city government stopped at the steel mill gates. With its own security force, fire department, and power plant, the corporation had little need for local government services and, indeed, barred city and county officials from the plant, even for the purposes of tax assessment. Within its property boundaries, U.S. Steel's actions went unchecked, including its manipulation of the environment. Although the city kept a 1910 smoke control ordinance on its books, the law did not apply to the area north of the Grand Calumet River, that is, property owned by U.S. Steel. Likewise, zoning regulations that outlawed excessive noise and smoke were not enforced on corporate property.[68]

The ascendancy of the Democratic party in the late 1940s posed no threat to this compact between local government and U.S. Steel. Just as Franklin Roosevelt had joined corporate capital, industrial workers, and middle-class citizens in an enduring coalition, local party leaders fashioned a new political regime that balanced the interests of a newly empowered working class with the imperatives of industrial growth. Gary's business elite continued to espouse a laissez-faire doctrine. According to Chamber of Commerce wisdom, government served the community best by confining its role to holding down corporate tax rates and funding only those public improvements that facilitated commerce, such as better street lighting and larger parking facilities.[69] Democratic party leaders, eager to promote local prosperity, were not averse to such a limited, economic role for government. But they also needed some mechanism to secure the allegiance of working-class citizens who formed the core of the New Deal coalition. Ironically, the resulting arrangements closely resembled the machine structures that were already beginning to crumble in many other U.S. cities.[70]

Patronage, distributed through ethnic networks, emerged as the basis for working-class support for the new political regime. Municipal government employed over 600 workers, most of whom received their jobs through a network of political loyalties. Employment applications required the signature of a precinct committee member, who was usually affiliated with one of the city's many ethnic political clubs. For groups such as the Slovak Political Club, the Polish American Democratic Club, and the Roumanian Democratic Political Club, these patronage jobs were the rewards for marshaling voters to the polls on election day.[71] In African American neighborhoods, precinct committeemen performed a similar function, mobilizing voters in exchange for patronage positions, while operators of gambling and prostitution houses received tacit permission to conduct illegal activity in return for their electoral support.[72] Content with a share in the spoils of patronage politics, ethnic groups demanded little else from government.

The presence of organized labor also undergirded working-class allegiance to a conservative political regime. After a long history of unsuccessful attempts, U.S. Steel workers organized in 1937. Suddenly, nearly 50 percent of Gary's workforce found itself backed by a powerful national union in its struggle to find a comfortable status in industrial capitalist society. From this point on, the union became the principal institution through which Gary's working class pursued social mobility. Hence, during the prosperous postwar years, workers expected the Steelworkers Union to ensure a fair distribution of the dividends of growth. Confident of its ability to win pay increases through private negotiation with corporate management, organized labor asked little else from government than a neutral police force during strikes.[73] Thus, despite the empowerment of Gary's working class, local political arrangements did not initially produce the sort of activist, welfare-state orientation that characterized political developments on the federal level.

Of course, the durability of the postwar political coalition depended on business's ability to deliver on its promise of economic growth. Hence, immediately following World War II, business leaders embarked on an aggressive program to diversify the city's economic base and entice new manufacturers to Gary. Less than a month after the United States dropped the second atomic bomb on Japan, the Chamber of Commerce met at the Hotel Gary to launch the Gary Industrial Foundation. In his keynote speech, Dean Mitchell, president of NIPSCO, reminded his audience that it had been the United States' industrial might that had won the war and that economic diversification was a necessary cushion against another depression. Moreover, he cautioned government against meddling in the affairs of business.[74] Armed with these principles, the Gary Industrial Foundation set out to attract new manufacturers to Gary by selling industrial real estate, offering business loans, and providing some direct grants. Although U.S. Steel was not formally represented in the new organization, the steel company volunteered several of its executives as technical advisers.[75]

The foundation's achievements, along with the impressive growth of steel production, guaranteed the health of Gary's economy through the end of the decade. At first, the foundation scored minor victories, luring several dozen small manufacturers to Gary, among them a toy aircraft propeller firm, a company that converted bacon rinds into cracklings, and an enterprise that de-inked old newspapers. Then in 1950 civic leaders, with the assistance of Gary's mayor and U.S. Steel, reeled in their first major catch, the Budd Company, a manufacturer of automobile body parts. Pledging to provide 1,000 jobs, the Budd Company would become the city's second largest employer.[76] Nevertheless, the steel company continued to drive the local economy. Buoyed by a rising demand for automobiles and consumer appliances, U.S. Steel maintained its wartime production levels, adding more than 3,000 workers to its payroll.[77]

Ultimately, politicians refused to challenge industry's environmental practices because they believed that doing so might jeopardize this economic growth and undermine the strength of the postwar political coalition. On the rare occasion when a gadfly city council representative raised the issue, other council members and the mayor's office quickly quelled discussion by arguing that pollution control was too costly, not only for the industries, which would be forced to purchase expensive equipment, but also for local government, which would be held responsible for enforcing any regulations. In 1950, for instance, Hobart Wiggerly, a representative from Glen Park, wondered aloud why the city had not enacted a meaningful smoke ordinance. Samuel Dubin, the city attorney, explained that any comprehensive abatement program would unduly squeeze the city's coffers. Eugene Swartz, Gary's mayor, added that the issue was very complex and warned the council against any hasty action. With strong opposition from the mayor's office, the council laid the matter to rest.[78]

Given this political context, the only acceptable environmental reform measures were those that imposed no burden on private enterprise. For example, public officials did not hesitate to address problems related to domestic sewage, an issue that was somewhat removed from the immediate concerns of private capital. Moreover, here was an issue in which the link between health and pollution was well established. By the turn of the century, public health professionals throughout the United States had identified bacteria as the primary cause of contagious disease.[79] When a typhoid epidemic ravaged Gary in the 1920s, citizens pressed for public health reforms including chlorinated drinking water and a modern sewage treatment facility. To ensure healthful drinking water, the Gary Public Health Department began inspecting Lake Michigan for the presence of harmful bacteria in the 1940s.[80] In instances where industrial wastes could be controlled without involving the manufacturers, civic leaders and legislators were also ready to take action. In 1947 and again in 1949 the city council tried unsuccessfully to prod NIPSCO, the local water company, into building a modern filtration plant. Filtration, it was hoped, would sift out iron particles and eliminate the metallic taste of Lake Michigan water. When the Gary-Hobart Company requested permission to take over operation of the water system several years later, the city council approved the transfer only on the condition that the new company filter Gary's drinking water.[81]

A laissez-faire approach to curbing industrial polluters also characterized state and federal environmental policy during the 1940s. Thus, both the U.S. Army Corps of Engineers and the Indiana Department of Conservation routinely approved permits that allowed U.S. Steel to extend the shoreline further into Lake Michigan.[82] Even after Indiana established the Stream Pollution Control Board in 1943 for the specific purpose of preventing industrial and domestic wastes from contaminating the state's water resources, U.S. Steel felt little pressure to amend its practices. Assessing conditions throughout the state, the board determined that the Gary area represented the most acute problem in Indiana. But even though the agency held the authority to set water quality standards and to mandate compliance by industries, it was reluctant to interfere with U.S. Steel's operations. Instead, it acted as a rubber stamp for virtually all of the steel company's requests for waste disposal modifications.[83]

State and local officials clearly demonstrated their cautious approach to industrial pollution control in a conflict with Chicago over steel mill wastes during World War II. Heightened wartime production took a noticeable toll on Lake Michigan water quality, especially in Chicago, where northwesterly currents carried wastes emitted from Gary factories. Citing complaints about the "great amount of undisinfected filth, sewage and poisonous and unhealthful and noxious matter" discharged by Indiana industries, Illinois sued Gary and three neighboring communities for excessive pollution in 1943.[84] The immediate response from Gary officials was denial; the problem had originated elsewhere, argued the superintendent of the city's sewer system. When the frailty of this argument became apparent, local and state officials devised a plan that they hoped would placate Chicago without unduly harming U.S. Steel. Under the supervision of the Indiana Stream Pollution Control Board, U.S. Steel would separate its domestic sewage from its industrial waste and send the sewage portion to the city's treatment plant. Chicago consented to the proposal, and when the war ended, U.S. Steel made the necessary modifications. Even though the Illinois attorney general had specifically identified industrial waste as a component of the excessive pollution in the lawsuit, the final agreement ignored the subject altogether.[85]

✻ In refusing to challenge industrial environmental practices, politicians and civic leaders merely reflected broader popular views. Most residents believed that despite the inconvenience, dirty air and water was the price one paid for industrial prosperity. Indeed, many viewed billowing smokestacks as evidence that industry was keeping up its end of the bargain. When factories shut down during strikes, newspapers printed photographs of the city under clear skies, an ominous sign in Gary.[86] When a columnist for a steel industry journal wrote in 1947 that "nature intended rivers to be useful, primarily, rather than beautiful," he expressed an opinion that prevailed throughout Gary.[87] With limited knowledge about state-of-the-art technology, most people assumed that pollution control was expensive and impractical. The notion that serious environmental reform came at the expense of industrial growth was firmly ingrained in the popular mind.

The connection between human health and industrial waste, on the other hand, remained obscure. Experience suggested that respiratory troubles coincided with smog attacks. Although many Gary citizens suspected a direct link, they lacked the scientific evidence to substantiate their beliefs and public officials remained unconvinced. Policymakers trusted chemists, biologists, and engineers to assess the health risks of industrial pollution. Although experts agreed that domestic wastes caused disease, they denied a link between health and manufacturing refuse. At most, industrial smoke might aggravate asthma and hay fever or irritate the respiratory tract. Medical opinion ruled out links between smog and either cancer or pneumonia.[88] In the case of water pollution, some local experts contended that industrial wastes actually improved public health. According to the superintendent of Gary's sewage treatment plant, wastewater discharges from Gary Works benefited the city by flushing domestic wastes from the Grand Calumet River.[89]

The reaction of residents to the arrival of the Budd Company neatly captured prevailing attitudes about industrial development and the urban environment. In a sharp break with the practice of locating large factories in the area north of the Grand Calumet River, the Budd Company decided to build its new plant in the Brunswick section of western Gary. Even though the factory would impart an industrial flavor to the residential neighborhood, families in the area welcomed the new addition. Company representatives assured Brunswick homeowners that the plant would produce little noise and smoke. Moreover, they promised to surround the factory with attractive landscaping. At a meeting of the Brunswick Community Club, a few residents expressed their fears that industrialization would diminish property values. Verne Washburn, representing the Gary Real Estate Board, countered that greater demand for housing would actually boost property values in the area. Most of those in attendance agreed with Washburn. Displaying their faith in industrial expansion, the club urged the city to rezone the proposed site from residential to light industrial use so that the manufacturer could move in promptly.[90]

As Gary entered the 1950s, then, the city was apparently content with its established pattern of resource allocation. Pollution did not seem to exert much impact on the organization of social life; most people, regardless of class, race, or ethnic background, continued to live and conduct important social functions close to downtown, the dirtiest part of the city. Likewise, political discourse did not reveal any significant popular opposition to industry's environmental practices. Following the informal accord that bound ethnic clubs, organized labor, and the business community in alliance, politics operated under the premise that Gary was more a place to work, buy, and sell than a place to live.[91] With the community united around the goal of promoting economic growth, civic leaders were content to allow manufacturers free rein in environmental matters for the sake of maintaining cordial relations with industry. As a result, industrial pollution remained an annoyance widely shared among the population.

Despite the system's stability, certain changes threatened to upset the social and political arrangements that supported postwar ecological patterns. Over the next twenty years, both industrial laborers and African Americans grew disenchanted with the social and political contract that wedded them to existing environmental practices. For these groups, the process of redefining social objectives unleashed latent frustrations about their environmental predicaments and alerted them to previously unknown dangers. But it was among Gary's middle-class citizens that the contradiction between social objectives and environmental practices first inspired a coherently articulated environmental program. The middle-class environmental reform movement of the 1950s and 1960s, then, represented the first significant challenge to industrial exploitation of Gary's environment.

Opposition to

Blind Progress

CHAPTER 3

Middle-Class

Environmentalism

Helen Hoock and Naomi Stern were unlikely candidates to become Gary's most prominent environmental activists. By 1968, the two women had developed a close friendship based on common experiences and interests. Both were raised in the New York City area, both moved to the suburban community of Miller with their families in the early 1960s, and both joined the League of Women Voters to meet friends with whom they could "talk about something other than children." Hoock and Stern often invited each other over for tea and chatted about a wide range of contemporary issues, including the civil rights movement and the Vietnam War. But environmental protection rarely came up in their conversations. Even though some of their acquaintances in the league had developed an interest in pollution abatement in the 1950s, the matter was of little concern to them. As they sat in Hoock's living room shortly before Thanksgiving in 1968, however, they could talk of nothing else. The Northwest Indiana Public Service Company (NIPSCO), the local utility company, had just announced its plans to build a 500-megawatt generating station along the Lake Michigan shore, less than two miles from their homes. Horrified by the prospect, the two women decided to organize a citizen opposition movement. Within two years, Hoock and Stern had roused over fifty families to action and were referring to themselves as "hard-core environmentalists."[1]

What made the notion of a power plant on Lake Michigan so offensive to Hoock, Stern, and their neighbors was that it threatened to undermine that which was most precious to Gary's white-collar middle class—the quality of residential life. Beginning in the 1940s, middle-class families channeled their social ambitions toward fashioning new suburban communities in the city's outlying districts. Environmental activism emerged out of the effort to protect those physical features of residential life—fresh air, pastoral landscapes, open space—that had become central components of middle-class identity. Through the 1970s, the preservation of suburban amenities would remain the driving force behind middle-class opposition to industrial pollution.

Whereas the basic motivation behind middle-class environmentalism remained constant, its rhetorical thrust and strategic formula changed considerably as reformers learned from their mistakes and developed more sophisticated political skills. Taking on industry required that middle-class citizens, for the first time, stake out a political presence. Middle-class homemakers, who embraced environmental protection as an extension of their responsibility to safeguard community health and welfare, were particularly effective in prodding local government to broaden its scope beyond promoting economic growth to include the enhancement of residential amenities. Convinced that these two goals were perfectly compatible, the reformers cooperated with business leaders to produce pollution control programs that infringed only minimally on the prerogatives of manufacturers. Only when the limitations of this approach became apparent in the late 1960s did middle-class environmentalists retreat to a more narrow and more stubborn defense of their suburban havens, calling for a moratorium on industrial growth. If they could not fully prevent the steel mills from spraying smoke across the city, they might at least keep landfills, noxious factories, and power plants out of their neighborhoods. With considerable support from those who viewed slow growth as a means of retarding the pace of racial integration, white-collar, well-educated suburban residents ultimately found themselves with the necessary financial resources and political skills to attain most of their environmental goals.

The emergence of a middle-class environmental protection ethic flowed from the growth of a consumer-oriented white-collar contingent. Prior to World War II, Gary's white-collar sector, wedged between manual laborers and entrepreneurs, remained small and lacked significant political clout. Although business proprietors and the heads of major manufacturing firms also represented a minority of the population, they exerted a far more identifiable presence, especially in politics, where they stood out as the most vociferous advocates of local business prosperity, low tax rates, and economic growth. Moreover, it was this business class that most effectively championed the ideology of limited governmental involvement in private capital's environmental affairs. However, as large firms displaced small retailers as the vendors of many consumer goods and services, and as many of the wealthiest business elites moved away from the city to neighboring lakefront communities that offered more space and prestige, the entrepreneurial class shrunk considerably.[2] By 1970, less than 1 percent of Gary's population counted themselves among self-employed proprietors, a drop from 3.5 percent twenty years earlier.[3] Moreover, top executives within the steel industry joined this exodus, thereby removing a powerful conservative element from Gary's civic life.[4] Although the business class remained a major force to be reckoned with, its numerical decline loosened its ideological grip and opened the door for other components of the middle class to reconstruct the city's political agenda. In particular, it enabled the growing number of white-collar families, that element of society that C. Wright Mills termed the "new middle class," to redefine the prevailing environmental wisdom.

The postwar economic boom underwrote expansion in the ranks of salaried, white-collar employees, those people who formed the backbone of the new middle class. From 1945 through 1970, Gary enjoyed almost uninterrupted prosperity, largely due to the accomplishments of U.S. Steel, which broke one production record after another.[5] The continued success of industrial diversification schemes during the 1950s, when the city welcomed a petroleum refinery, a paper towel manufacturer, and an electricity generating utility, further augmented Gary's economic bounty.[6] Although these manufacturers still depended primarily on manual labor, they also supported a growing number of white-collar employees. Automation, capital intensification, and the increasing complexity of coordinating production reduced industry's demand for blue-collar workers while stimulating a need for engineers, technicians, managers, and clerical staff. Gary Works alone kept over 1,000 clerical workers on its payroll through the 1950s and 1960s.[7] Nevertheless, the largest gains in white-collar employment came outside the manufacturing sector. Gary's professional class, dominated by accountants, doctors, lawyers, and teachers, doubled in number between 1940 and 1970, by which time it accounted for 10.2 percent of the local labor force. Clerical positions also multiplied as private firms, banks, government agencies, and retailers hired more bookkeepers, secretaries, clerks, tellers, and cashiers. By 1970, almost 16 percent of all employed adults fell into the clerical category. Thus, economic growth during the 1950s and 1960s transformed Gary's occupational profile, swelling the ranks of white-collar employees.

Relatively high incomes set this white-collar group apart from the rest of Gary's population. Certainly, earnings within the middle class varied considerably, with corporate executives, doctors, and lawyers at the high end and clerical workers at the bottom. Indeed, most clerical jobs paid roughly the same as semiskilled industrial labor positions. According to data from 1959, electricians, carpenters, machinists, and pipefitters—blue-collar workers with specialized skills—earned considerably more than bookkeepers, cashiers, and file clerks. A simple examination of wages, however, understates middle-class wealth because many clerical workers were women who worked to supplement family income. During the 1950s, women held about two out of every three clerical positions in Gary, with even higher concentrations among secretaries, stenographers, typists, bookkeepers, and cashiers. Census data reveals that the majority of female clerical employees lived in Gary's most affluent neighborhoods, suggesting that they were working wives or young single women affiliated with upper-income households.[8]

Double incomes, even if women worked only part time, enabled many middle-class families to raise their standard of living, perhaps enough to purchase more household items, a new car, or even a larger home in the suburbs. The case of Peggy and Glen is illustrative. While Glen held a supervisory position at U.S. Steel in the years just after World War II, his wife Peggy worked as a clerk in a research laboratory. Combined incomes enabled the couple to purchase a suburban home in Ross Township, just south of Gary, in 1947. When the family needed new furniture five years later, Peggy returned to work, this time as a clerk for the Elgin, Joliet, and Eastern Railroad Company. Thus, for this particular married couple, female clerical work was clearly a means of participating more fully in the middle-class world of consumption.[9] Teenaged clerical workers performed a similar function for middle-class families by helping relieve parents of expenses associated with raising children. Anne Suglove, for example, recalled that her after-school job at a local department store during the 1940s covered the cost of movies at the Roosevelt Theater and late-night social engagements at the Copper Kettle restaurant.[10] In analyzing the household, then, it becomes even more apparent that white-collar work bestowed significant material rewards upon those in the new middle class.

Because white-collar employees, in contrast to independent proprietors, did not fully control their work situations, they channeled surplus income toward purchases and activities that improved the quality of life away from work, in new suburban communities. Increasingly, middle-class families, in Gary and elsewhere, measured their social achievements according to specific standards of domesticity, consumption, and residence. The unqualified marks of success were a private home, a nuclear family, abundant leisure time, and a healthy stock of consumer goods that made life more comfortable and satisfying. Certainly, Americans valued homes, families, recreation, and consumer gadgets prior to World War II, but never before were these elements so clearly recognized as badges of membership in the middle class. Moreover, it was only in the postwar years that mass suburbanization enabled so many middle-class families to build from scratch the sort of setting that would promote these social and cultural objectives.[11]

If the postwar years were kind to the new middle class, it was in no small measure due to the largesse of federal programs that subsidized suburban development. Whereas New Deal rhetoric of the 1930s celebrated the "forgotten man" and highlighted the suffering of the nation's most underprivileged, post–World War II liberalism reflected a much greater sensitivity to middle-class quality-of-life concerns. Of particular significance were housing and transportation policies, many of which received bipartisan support. Despite the fact that Dwight Eisenhower touted the Federal Highway Act of 1956 as a national defense measure, the most significant consequence of this massive road-building program was the easing of automobile traffic in and out of major metropolitan areas. With the completion of interstate highway networks, suburban residents could escape all traces of the industrial inner city and still find themselves within easy commuting distance of downtown. Even more influential were the federal mortgage insurance programs sponsored by the Federal Housing Authority and the Veterans Administration. By lowering initial down payments and extending repayment schedules, these programs made private housing accessible even to families that had accumulated only moderate savings. Significantly, however, not all prospective homeowners could take advantage of these deals. The federal government avoided granting such mortgages in low-income, inner-city neighborhoods where investments were considered risky, and hence, middle-class families emerged as the prime beneficiaries.[12]

The combination of rising incomes, improved transportation, and liberal mortgages proved irresistible to Gary's middle-class families. By the mid-1960s, three interstate freeways crossed Gary, providing rapid access to new suburban communities in every direction. Anticipating the effects of government programs, developers established subdivisions in areas where federal housing agencies were more than willing to guarantee loans. The consequences were unprecedented. Between 1940 and 1960, new construction added 18,000 privately owned dwellings to the city's housing stock, marking nearly a threefold increase. With most of the new building in suburban areas, Gary's population decentralized. During the 1950s alone, the number of residents in western Gary, Glen Park, Aetna, and Miller jumped by 70 percent, more than twice the average growth rate for the city as a whole (see map 3).[13]

The well-to-do migrants who filled Gary's suburbs in the 1950s and 1960s selected and constructed their new communities according to specific environmental preferences. Environmental considerations had always been an important component of the middle-class desire for suburban living. Since the early nineteenth century, Americans prized sub-

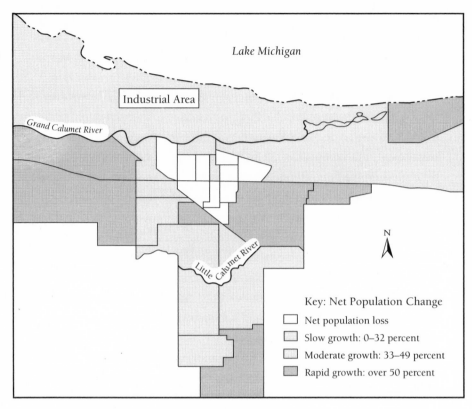

Map 3. Residential Movement in Gary, 1950–1960

urbs for their rustic settings, far removed from any visual reminders of industrial work.[14] Gary's affluent suburbs reflected the persistence of these values. Sales promotions for new suburban subdivisions during the 1950s frequently stressed the environmental amenities associated with particular pieces of property. Realtors, well attuned to consumer preferences, embellished their advertisements with descriptions and photographs of pastoral scenery and natural vistas. Promoters of the new Meadowdale subdivision in Glen Park assured potential home buyers that it was the "safest and healthiest environment" for raising a family, while an advertisement for a lakefront home in Miller described the scenery as "breathtaking." Just across the city line in Merrillville, a realtor promised "country living—close in."[15] By the late 1960s, many families were moving to the suburbs specifically to escape the physical effects of heavy industry. Authors of a 1968 planning report concluded that air pollution was a major factor driving prosperous families from the inner city.[16] When a high school teacher informed the Gary Air Pollution Control Division in 1971 that she was leaving the city due to the stench and haze of industrial emissions, she undoubtedly spoke for others.[17]

Within suburban communities, residents arranged their homes in a fashion that mimicked bucolic settings. The Morningside district of Glen Park, home to many of Gary's wealthiest corporate executives, temporarily interrupted the city's rectangular grid layout with its meandering lanes that conveyed the impression of a naturally contoured landscape. Homes in this area, like those in other middle-class sections of Gary, were detached and featured two or three bedrooms, a basement, and small yards in the front and back.[18] Homeowners typically adorned their yards with grass, trees, and perhaps a flower garden. Although lawns and small flower plots were no substitute for untamed wilderness, they nonetheless provided a pastoral contrast with the dense housing, littered alleyways, and industrial scenery of downtown districts.

Nowhere in Gary was the connection between environmental amenities and suburban development more overt than in Miller, which emerged as Gary's most desirable residential neighborhood during the 1950s. Nestled amid woods and sand dunes, bordered by Lake Michigan, and far removed from U.S. Steel's smokestacks, Miller was a nature lover's paradise. Earlier in the century, noted botanist Henry Cowles had conducted his pioneering ecological studies in Miller, taking advantage of the area's rich flora and fauna. Into the 1940s, Miller remained untouched by industrial development and sparsely populated—but not for long. Thousands of families armed with government loans and wartime savings invaded the area, purchasing dream homes in the woods, alongside lagoons, or on the lakefront. During the 1950s, Miller replaced Horace Mann as Gary's most prestigious neighborhood, ranking highest in median income and property values.[19] The new settlers fit the stereotypical social profile of the U.S. middle class. As of 1960, almost 60 percent of Miller residents in the paid labor force were employed in white-collar occupations as professionals, managers, technicians, and clerical workers. Blue-collar laborers comprised a mere 29 percent of the working population, and most of them were skilled workers with relatively high incomes. Only 22 percent of all employed residents worked in the steel industry, the lowest percentage in the city. Higher education levels among residents also distinguished Miller from the rest of the city. A city planning report published in 1966 noted that of all Gary communities, Miller "came closest to middle class Americana, the essence of family stability with its white collar occupations, high school educations, home ownership and children."[20] More than anywhere else in Gary, environment acted as the magnet that drew the affluent to suburbia.

The pursuit of pastoral landscapes converged with other middle-class objectives in shaping the physical character of Gary's burgeoning suburban enclaves. Low-density development, in addition to permitting open spaces and parks, allowed for house plots large enough for the purpose of raising big families and showcasing consumer purchases. Front lawns and backyards not only provided greenery but also insulated families from neighbors, an important amenity for a middle class preoccupied with domestic relations. Of course, this liberal use of space also kept the price of admission to suburbia high enough to ensure racial and class homogeneity. Gary's suburbs were exclusively white. Although systematic residential segregation insulated upper-income whites wherever they lived during the 1940s and 1950s, racism would eventually become one of the most important impulses behind suburbanization. Indeed, it would become clear by the late 1960s that in the minds of middle-class residents, whiteness enhanced both the psychological and economic value of suburban property. Thus, the appeal of suburbia lay in the fact that it brought together all those qualities that middle-class families found lacking in the inner city.

Having arrived in the suburbs, however, many discovered that, despite the promises of real estate agents, they could not completely escape the perils of industrial pollution. Indeed, suburban living introduced middle-class families to environmental menaces they had not encountered in the inner city. Moreover, they grew increasingly worried that rising pollution levels would re-create in the suburbs the very sort of physical settings they had fled. Ironically, then, suburbanization sparked a heightened sensitivity to industry's environmental practices.

As middle-class families spent more time outdoors and developed a preoccupation with health and fitness, air pollution became a more pressing concern. Especially during the summer months, Gary citizens visited city parks and athletic fields with increasing frequency.[21] Sales jumped at local sporting goods stores, reflecting this obsession with outdoor recreation and exercise.[22] Although the levels of particulate dustfall were far lower in the remote suburbs than in the downtown districts, those people who spent more time outdoors increased their exposure to the pollution. Also, largely as a consequence of physical fitness concerns, many began to wonder about the connections between air pollution and human health. When unpleasant odors invaded Glen Park one January day in 1950, residents barraged the Gary Health Department with telephone calls. Above all, they demanded to know what effect the smells would have on their health. Apparently they were appeased by assurances that the odors were harmless because nothing further came of the matter.[23] As the local and national media informed citizens about scientific studies attributing lung cancer, emphysema, and bronchitis to industrial smoke, however, suspicions became convictions and the popular resolve for clean air stiffened.[24]

Suburban living also brought recreational demands into conflict with industry's use of local waterways. In the years after World War II, Lake Michigan became a playground for Gary's affluent. On hot summer days, swarms of bathers and sunseekers descended on Marquette Park beach in Miller, requiring the city to extend the beachfront an additional mile in 1953.[25] Waterskiing, sailing, and offshore fishing became so popular that beginning in the 1940s public officials considered the possibility of building a small boat marina in the lake.[26] However, just as more Gary citizens found their way onto the water, escalating steel mill emissions tarnished the lake, reducing the availability of desirable fish and covering the surface with unsightly streaks of oil and grease.[27] Swimmers encountered their own particular hazards from waterborne industrial wastes. Factory discharges nourished the growth of cladophora, a type of floating green algae. First sighted in small tufts during the 1950s, cladophora mats swelled to several feet in length by the 1960s, large enough to drape unsuspecting bathers in a coat of green slime. If it was no longer safe to go in the water, the beach offered little improvement. Cladophora masses drifted ashore in long tangled rows, and oil slicks dispersed tarry material along the sandy beach.[28] According to one irate Miller resident, conditions had deteriorated so much by 1963 that it was impossible to use the beach without getting one's shoes and clothes covered in oil.[29] Beach lovers undeterred by algae and oil also had to contend with piles of rotting fish. Possibly as a result of high water temperatures in the 1960s, millions of alewives died and washed ashore on Gary's beaches, where they created a stench that bathers claimed was "unbearable." Frustrated city workers complained that the incoming tides discarded dead fish faster than they could remove them.[30]

In response to these disagreeable developments, some middle-class citizens searched for a political solution, prodding local government to take greater responsibility for community welfare. Sociological studies of the 1950s tended to depict the U.S. middle class as politically aloof. As long as their social objectives were focused on moving to the suburbs, and as long as the federal government aided this process with its generous housing programs, Gary's middle-class families fit this stereotype by placing few demands on local government. But when it came to keeping their residential communities free from pollution, they clearly belied the conventional wisdom. Upon discovering that moving further from the inner city did not guarantee environmental bliss, some residents demanded more aggressive action from local authorities. Since liberalism promised to soften the blows of industrial capitalism, Gary's middle class pinned their political hopes on some sort of pollution control law. Hence, the first challenge to laissez-faire environmental arrangements came from a middle class intent on preserving the quality of residential life.

Many of those involved in the early push for governmental action on the environmental front were women, who, as the recognized guardians of domestic welfare, accepted primary responsibility for the maintenance of suburban communities. Cultural norms of the 1950s dictated that women find fulfillment in the home, as housekeepers and as family caretakers. Even though an increasing number of middle-class women were participating in the paid workforce, their jobs were usually temporary excursions for the purpose of supplementing the family income. Few women in Gary, or elsewhere, pursued careers, which were disparaged.[31] As Betty Friedan would later expose in her 1963 best-seller, *The Feminine Mystique*, these rigid social expectations stirred resentment and discontent among educated women who yearned for more challenging responsibilities. For many, environmental reform provided a viable alternative to domestic confinement. Keeping the neighborhood clean could be justified, and was sanctioned, as a natural extension of women's familial obligations. Women activists were simply fostering the proper environment for a healthy and comfortable suburban family life. Thus, smoke abatement initiatives and pure water campaigns provided women with an opportunity for meaningful public service within the context of prevailing gender norms. For this reason, Gary's middle-class environmental movement was very much a women's movement.[32]

Removed from local party structures, these middle-class women advanced their cause through civic groups and community organizations, thereby introducing a new dynamic to Gary politics. Patronage politics was irrelevant to the middle class; white-collar citizens neither needed nor wanted low-paying government jobs. They considered preserving the quality of residential communities far more important, and hence they expected government to underwrite the trappings of suburban living. These demands found expression in organizations that drew people together on the basis of community membership, either as citizens of the entire city in the case of civic groups or as residents of smaller areas in the case of neighborhood associations. Relying on media support, the force of popular opinion, and the strength of the middle-class voting block, these new groups encouraged politicians to negotiate in the currency of issues rather than favors. It was largely due to their efforts that local officials eventually responded to middle-class demands for environmental protection.

Perhaps the most influential of these civic groups during the 1950s and 1960s was the Gary chapter of the League of Women Voters. Drawing heavily from the middle-class neighborhoods of Glen Park, Miller, and Horace Mann, the league tapped into the growing discontent among women trapped in a revolving door of shopping, cooking, cleaning, and chauffeuring children.[33] When the chapter presented a skit for prospective members in the 1960s, it opened the performance with an exasperated homemaker's exclamation: "I've had it! This housewife routine is getting me down. Every day the same damn chores." The play concluded with the protagonist's zest for life being restored after she discovers the Gary League of Women Voters.[34] Thus, the league consciously promoted itself as an antidote to the suburban housewife's malaise identified by Friedan. Through its study groups, the organization offered women an opportunity to analyze issues, make policy recommendations, and influence political officials. Elaine Kaplan, who joined the group in the 1950s after moving with her husband to a suburban home in Miller, recalled, "It was a way of feeling productive."[35]

The league edged its way into the male world of local politics carefully, choosing the least controversial approach. Through the 1940s, the organization built its agenda around issues that emerged from women's domestic role, such as monitoring the local school board and ensuring the purity of milk. Even though league members were concentrated in a few neighborhoods, they framed their goals in terms of the betterment of the entire city. This was not altogether a product of crass political calculation. Middle-class neighborhoods were scattered throughout the city; a citywide approach to problem solving made sense for them. Moreover, even those from the remote suburbs of Miller and Glen Park continued to identify with Gary as a unified entity. Suburbanization in the 1940s and 1950s represented the goal of separating home life from inner-city aggravations, not the complete abandonment of the city. In essence, the league hoped to protect and enhance the quality of middle-class life by applying its social and cultural standards to the entire city.

In addressing the slightly more contentious problem of water quality, the league simply expanded this approach. In 1953 the league became embroiled in the national controversy over water fluoridation. Designed to stem tooth decay, especially among children, fluoridation excited paranoid fears about a communist plot to poison the nation's drinking water supplies. The league attempted to foster a more rational discussion by disseminating scientific information. From there, it was merely a series of short steps to the issue of water filtration and, finally, industrial pollution in Lake Michigan. In part, the chapter's sudden interest in water was due to a directive from the national office to investigate local water quality. However, especially when it came to the matter of industrial pollution, Gary members had very specific reasons for concern.[36]

For Lotte Meyerson, water quality was an important component of the quality of residential life. She and her husband had moved with their two daughters to Gary from Chicago in 1952. Having been raised in inner-city apartments, they were overwhelmed when a real estate agent showed them a wooded tract in Miller only half a mile from Lake Michigan. They purchased the property on the spot. Meyerson recalled, "We [had] . . . beautiful beaches," but "some of that was threatened by pollution. Sometimes we couldn't go swimming." Hence, upon joining the

League of Women Voters a few months later, she became one of several women to investigate ways in which the city might reconcile industry's appetite for water with residents' environmental demands.[37]

While some members of the league devoted their energies to fighting water pollution problems, others were bringing air quality to public attention. In 1955 Milton Roth, a young attorney and husband of a league member, made clean air the cornerstone of his campaign for city council representative. When he gained election, the league recognized an opportunity for testing its political strength and thus shifted its focus from water to air pollution.

For his part, Roth saw smoke abatement as a means of rousing a dormant political establishment. Upon returning from law school in 1950, Roth moved to Miller, where he fell in with a group of people he described as "young, intellectually curious liberals" interested in "remaking the world." At the very least they would try to remake Gary. Attending a city council meeting, the young idealists were alarmed by what they considered to be "a grade school level of intelligence and expression." They decided that one of them should run for office, and Roth was selected. As a candidate for an "at-large" position on the council, Roth desperately wanted to introduce new issues into the discourse of local politics. After some deliberation, he settled on environmental amenities. In campaign advertisements and public addresses, the candidate called for more parks, a boat marina, a fishing pier, and a local smoke abatement law. Traveling around the city, he discovered that his plea for clean air struck a chord among voters, especially suburban homemakers. Much to the surprise and horror of the local machine, he won the election.[38]

Intent on pursuing smoke abatement as a city council representative, Roth elicited the animosity of his colleagues. Earlier attempts to raise the air pollution issue in the council had been quickly shot down, and Roth had little reason to expect more favorable treatment. Peter Mandich, Gary's mayor, urged Roth to abandon the cause, calling it "insane." Local legislators were equally cool, but hoping to avoid a showdown, they simply tabled Roth's proposal for an air pollution law and placed the matter under study indefinitely. Privately, they expected the proposal to languish.[39]

Had it not been for the League of Women Voters, the matter might well have been put to rest. The women activists came to Roth's aid, keeping the issue in the spotlight and maintaining the pressure on recalcitrant politicians. Inviting speakers to their meetings and scouring medical reports, they learned about the health hazards associated with dirty air and became fluent in the intricacies of pollution control. Armed with this knowledge, they visited legislators and appeared at city council meetings in support of a local smoke abatement ordinance. By the early 1960s, the league was able to count on the assistance of several other middle-class civic organizations, most notably the Gary Junior Chamber of Commerce, a group loosely affiliated with the Chamber of Commerce but far less closely aligned with business interests. More importantly, they won the endorsement of the *Gary Post-Tribune*, which ran a series of articles and editorials lamenting the poor quality of local air.[40]

In trying to sell the concept of pollution control, Roth and his allies worked diligently to shatter the prevailing attitude toward smoky skies. The association between pollution and prosperity remained well ingrained in the public mind. Into the early 1960s, Chamber of Commerce literature extolled the beauty of Gary's "mighty blast and open hearth furnaces in her horizon-long sweep of mills with their up-thrust stacks and her flame-lit nights pulsing with the reflected fires of hot coke and molten steel," all of which heralded the city as a "lusty symbol of American enterprise."[41] Of course, the corollary view that smoke abatement would impair economic growth posed the fundamental challenge to the advocates of pollution control.

Rather than minimize the importance of economic growth, the reformers emphasized its compatibility with a sensible pollution control program. They argued implicitly that cleaner skies would help the economy by improving the city's national reputation. As a positive example, they cited Pittsburgh, where smoke abatement formed a vital component of downtown revitalization. In contrast, Gary remained a national embarrassment.

Still, legislative triumph would await the explicit approval of Gary's business leaders. From the beginning, Roth believed that industry would be amenable to some sort of antismoke law. Indeed, early on in his campaign he received encouragement from Granville Howell, vice president for operations at U.S. Steel. In 1955 Howell sent his sister, a close friend of the Roth family, to give the candidate the message that the steel company was prepared to do something about air pollution; if the city passed legislation, the corporation would comply. Later on, Howell personally informed Roth that although he should not expect any active help from steel executives, the company would not reject any reasonable set of regulations.[42]

Once they received such assurances, reformers proved perfectly willing to dilute regulatory policy for the sake of business support. Roth may have been an idealist, but he was no anti-industrialist. As he later recalled, he never had any intention of harming U.S. Steel. He was convinced that clean air required only minor technological adjustments on the part of manufacturers. Still, architects of the law took pains to construct an ordinance that would minimize any hardships on industry. And as business leaders recognized that the middle-class proponents of clean air had no desire to reduce their profits, they warmed to the idea. Furthermore, Gary's manufacturers had their own reasons for supporting such a law. As they looked to the future, they recognized the possibility of state and federal antipollution regulations. In public and private statements, business leaders expressed a preference for cooperating in the formulation of local regulations rather than facing outside control further down the road. Howell voiced such sentiments as early as 1955. Seven years later one Chamber of Commerce member announced that he favored local regulation because "that's where we can get at it."[43] But it was not until business leaders publicly endorsed smoke abatement that the city council summoned the courage to pass legislation. Faced with the immediate possibility of a tougher state law, U.S. Steel went on record supporting a municipal air pollution control program in the fall of 1962. Although Roth no longer sat on the city council, having lost his seat three years earlier, the legislature passed Gary's first smoke control ordinance in December.[44]

A political strategy based on accommodation combined with optimistic expectations about the efficacy of pollution control promoted a regulatory policy that made minimal demands on Gary's industries, particularly U.S. Steel. Crafted by city officials in consultation with steel company executives, the law set limitations on the density of smoke emissions and established fines for violations. However, it also exempted several steelmaking facilities from the regulations, including open-hearth furnaces, Bessemer converters, sintering plants, and coke ovens. A key clause enabled industry to avoid compliance if it promised to take steps toward the gradual reduction of air pollution. U.S. Steel applied for an exemption, submitting a plan to bring the company into compliance with the 1962 law by 1973. According to the proposal, the corporation would replace worn-out equipment with more modern machinery fitted with smoke abatement devices. In essence, U.S. Steel submitted a schedule of equipment retirement. Anxious to secure the company's cooperation, city officials approved U.S. Steel's air pollution control program.[45]

Now that an air pollution ordinance was on the books, the League of Women Voters turned its attention back to water, cooperating with federal and state officials to produce a similar set of guidelines for industrial waste emissions in Lake Michigan. By this time, the federal government had developed an interest in water quality, especially in Lake Michigan, where cladophora proliferation and alewife die-offs signaled serious ecological trouble. Beginning in 1965, the Federal Water Pollution Control Administration organized a series of conferences at which government bureaucrats and corporate executives hammered out long-term agreements on pollution control strategies. To encourage public participation in the process, federal regulators invited citizen groups to testify at conference proceedings. The League of Women Voters accepted the invitation, intent on counterbalancing the cautious approach of the conferees. Like their local counterparts, federal and state officials were reluctant to push too aggressively for pollution control for fear of impinging on economic growth. Perry Miller, who represented the state of Indiana at many of the meetings, put the matter bluntly. "It is not reasonable," he told the *Chicago Sun-Times*, "to expect water draining highly industrialized areas to have the same appearance as water draining non-industrial areas. We are anxious to promote industry in the area."[46] Not surprisingly, industrialists in attendance sought to minimize their obligations. Granville Howell suggested that U.S. Steel be given twenty years to complete its pollution abatement program. Spokespersons from the Gary league, along with representatives from other chapters in Indiana, Illinois, Michigan, and Wisconsin, presented the case for more urgent action. At the very least, they argued, the conferences ought to set rigid timetables for compliance and uniform standards for polluting industries ringing Lake Michigan.[47]

Given the political constraints inherent in a political process that favored business interests, Gary's environmental reformers had reason to be proud of their accomplishments; by the late 1960s, they had altered the rules of environmental manipulation, subjecting industrial decisions about resource use to the scrutiny of public officials and citizen groups. As a result of new regulations, local industries embarked upon expensive pollution control programs, something they surely would not have done without the compulsion of legally binding agreements. U.S. Steel spent over $60 million on new equipment during the 1960s alone. Baghouses, electrostatic precipitators, and scrubbers sucked unwanted particles from smokestacks, while separators, clarifiers, and scale pits filtered impurities from wastewater. In 1962 the company began dismantling its open-hearth furnaces and replacing them with cleaner basic-oxygen furnaces.[48] In an effort to improve its image, U.S. Steel built a deep well for the storage of caustic acids in 1966 even though it was not compelled to do so by law.[49] Georgia-Pacific, a tissue paper manufacturer, stopped dumping its wastes directly into the Grand Calumet River in 1969 and initiated a $17 million pollution abatement program.[50] Although NIPSCO had installed dust collectors when it built its power plants in 1956 to prevent escaping particulate matter from corroding giant fans located in the smokestacks, the utility company invested over $4 million on additional electrostatic precipitators in 1967.[51] As for Gary's smaller manufacturers, they too made adjustments, attaching pollution control equipment to their smokestacks, switching their fuel from oil or coal to natural gas, and building treatment facilities for liquid wastes.[52] Most remarkably, reformers secured these achievements with the cooperation of the business community. Although industries may not have relished new pollution controls, they acquiesced, trusting that their involvement in the policy-making and regulatory processes would keep their obligations to a minimum.

Middle-class activists found little cause for celebration, however. For all the expenditures on pollution control, air and water quality showed little noticeable improvement during the 1960s. For all the regulations and enforcement mechanisms, polluters managed to circumvent the law when they so desired. For all their political accomplishments, middle-class reformers still found themselves on the losing side of a battle against encroaching industrial development. Hence, by the early 1970s, the dynamic sector of the middle-class environmental movement abandoned the regulatory approach to pollution control and embraced a theory of slow growth, ultimately calling for a virtual moratorium on new industrial activity in Miller.

Even after smoke abatement and wastewater regulations had been in effect for several years, progress was difficult to detect. A 1966 investigation conducted under the auspices of the Federal Water Pollution Control Administration revealed rising amounts of phenols, iron, and cyanide in the Grand Calumet River.[53] Three years later, tests indicated that although phenol levels had decreased, other measures of industrial pollution were unchanged.[54] Although the data on airborne particulates looked somewhat more promising, skies still glowed red in the evening from open-hearth charges and black clouds from the coke ovens continued to obscure vision during the day. Newspaper reports informed citizens that Gary's air quality continued to rank among the worst in the nation. If anything, the multicolored streaks emblazoned across the horizon appeared even more menacing in the wake of well-publicized medical studies linking a host of respiratory disorders with industrial air emissions.[55]

Progress came haltingly not because the pollution control devices failed to work properly but because rapid industrial growth generated greater quantities of waste. At the same time that U.S. Steel was installing oil separators, filtration plants, and dust collectors, it was conducting a vigorous expansion program that added a cold reduction mill, a hot strip mill, a continuous caster, an annealing furnace, and several bar mills to its productive arsenal.[56] Moreover, a favorable business climate lured several metal fabricators, a lime kiln, and at least three chemical firms to the city during the 1960s, all of which contributed to the aggregate sum of pollutants.[57] Of course, because these new processes were subject to existing environmental regulations, their waste emissions were less than they might otherwise have been. Nonetheless, for much of the 1960s, industrial growth undermined pollution control efforts.

While the disappointing pace of environmental progress alone might have been enough to make local reformers question their approach to pollution control, it was primarily renewed attempts to industrialize the Lake Michigan shoreline in Miller that pushed middle-class activists toward a strategy that was at once more defiant and more parochial. During the 1960s, Miller emerged as the last refuge for prosperous whites, a haven for those enamored of environmental amenities and troubled by social dislocations. In other parts of the city, upwardly mobile African Americans, assisted by fair housing laws and emboldened by newly acquired political power, moved into previously forbidden neighborhoods, prompting a mass exodus of white homeowners. By 1970, whites had all but abandoned the Horace Mann district, once considered the most desirable neighborhood in the city. Housing integration came more slowly to Glen Park, but an influx of working-class whites diminished the neighborhood's appeal among the well-to-do. Most of the departing middle-class whites left Gary altogether, taking up residence in one of the remote suburbs to the south or east of the city. But a substantial number moved into Miller, drawn by the area's scenic beauty as well as its racial stability. Thus, for the first time, virtually all of Gary's middle-class environmentalists lived in the same neighborhood. When industry began making expansionary forays into Miller in the late 1960s, residents demonstrated a fierce resolve to defend their environmental paradise.

U.S. Steel fired the first salvo in the battle for Miller in 1967 by announcing its intention to fill a portion of Lake Michigan with solid refuse. Eleven years earlier, the Gary City Council had granted U.S. Steel permission to deposit furnace slag over 373 acres of the lake, adjacent to the eastern portion of its property, near Miller. The matter generated little opposition or debate at that time. When U.S. Steel received a construction permit from the Army Corps of Engineers the following year, all legal requirements were satisfied. For the moment, however, the steel company had enough space elsewhere on its grounds for the storage of slag waste, and the landfill project was held in abeyance until the next decade.

When news reached Miller that the steel company was ready to fill the lake in 1967, the League of Women Voters immediately questioned the environmental consequences. The issue was of particular concern to the league because by this time, almost all members lived in Miller and would be directly affected by the project. According to their investigation, the extension of land into the lake would create a pocket of stagnant water susceptible to garbage accumulation. Hence, Marquette

Park beach would become seriously polluted. Insisting that the project should be aborted, the league wrote letters of protest to U.S. Steel, the Army Corps of Engineers, and the secretary of the U.S. Department of the Interior.[58]

Even though the league found an ally in A. Martin Katz, Gary's mayor, U.S. Steel would not be deterred. Until the landfill episode, Katz could boast no better than an uneven record on environmental protection. Like most Gary politicians, he deferred to leading business elites before endorsing any pollution abatement measures. For example, when Katz arranged a plan to coordinate air pollution programs in three northwest Indiana counties, he appointed Harley Davenport, a prominent downtown businessman, as chairman.[59] Also, rather than follow up Gary's air pollution ordinance with similar water pollution legislation, the mayor announced his preference for cooperating with local industries to reduce pollution.[60] As an avowed liberal, Katz was not averse to using governmental authority to further social welfare. Yet until this time, strong electoral support from Gary's African American community caused Katz to make civil rights reform the cornerstone of his liberal agenda. By 1967, however, it was clear that African Americans would field their own candidate in the next mayoral election. Thus, Katz may well have seen in the Miller lakeshore controversy an issue that would win him the backing of a new constituency—the white middle class. Perhaps Katz merely wished to tap into the current of ecological enthusiasm that electrified the entire nation in the late 1960s. Whatever his motives, Katz urged U.S. Steel to reconsider its plans, noting that although Gary welcomed industry, the health and welfare of citizens and the continued use of beaches for recreational purposes deserved higher priority.[61] Katz had little firepower to back his rhetoric, however, and after a temporary delay, U.S. Steel proceeded with construction.

Just as the landfill controversy faded, NIPSCO reignited the fury of Miller residents with its plans for a generating station on the Lake Michigan shoreline. The local utility needed additional capacity to accommodate the spurt of population and economic growth that swept northwest Indiana during the 1960s. Lacking sufficient room for expansion at the Dean Mitchell site in western Gary, NIPSCO surveyed the region for another location and eventually selected a tract of woods and sandy beach along the Lake Michigan shoreline between Miller and U.S.

Steel property. The area provided several advantages: proximity to transmission lines, access to rail transportation, and a location at the geographical center of NIPSCO's customer network. Above all, Lake Michigan offered a plentiful water supply for NIPSCO's cooling operations.[62] However, NIPSCO was not alone in its desire to purchase the lakefront property. The Gary Parks Department also eyed this tract in hopes of constructing a small boat harbor to satisfy the mounting recreational demands of Gary's affluent citizens. Further complicating the matter, U.S. Steel owned the desired parcel and wished to retain it for future plant expansion.

In 1968 the three parties—NIPSCO, U.S. Steel, and the Gary Parks Board—resolved the conflict with an ingenious compromise. U.S. Steel agreed to sell 100 acres of its eastern lakefront property to NIPSCO for the site of a 500 megawatt generating station in exchange for receiving a discount on electricity rates. To provide additional space for the NIPSCO plant, U.S. Steel promised to dredge sand from lagoons on its eastern property and use it to extend the shoreline of Lake Michigan. According to the scheme, the small lake created by the sand dredging would then be turned over to the Gary Parks Department for use as a small boat harbor. To sweeten the deal, U.S. Steel threw in a donation of 145 acres of parkland to the city. In what became known as the "three-way deal," each party got what it wanted: NIPSCO obtained land for its new power plant, the Gary Parks Department procured a harbor for its marina, and U.S. Steel received cash and cheaper energy rates. At a city hall press conference in November 1968, George Jedenoff, superintendent of Gary Works, announced that the deal was set.[63]

Although there was considerable public support for the marina, Miller residents did not take kindly to the notion of a 500 megawatt power plant in their backyard. For Helen Hoock, the news was particularly disturbing because the lakefront had become a source of personal contentment and an integral part of her domestic routine. It was the beauty of the lake and surrounding dunes that had convinced Hoock and her husband to rent a waterfront apartment seven years earlier. In 1965 they purchased a home several blocks away. During the summer months, she regularly accompanied her children to the beach, where they swam and played with other neighborhood children. Often, her husband met them there in the evening before they returned home for dinner. Hoock's immediate concern about the three-way deal was that a pollution-spewing power plant would ruin the beach and mar the beauty of the lakefront. So when her friend, Naomi Stern, suggested that they organize citizens in opposition to the project, Hoock was willing to give it a try, although, as she later recalled, "I really didn't know what I was getting into."[64]

Even though both Hoock and Stern belonged to the League of Women Voters, they concluded that an independent organization would be more effective. They certainly intended to draw upon the experience of league members who had cut their teeth on environmental issues in the 1950s, but they also wanted the flexibility to act quickly and use more militant tactics. The league, after all, was primarily a study group. Moreover, a new single-issue organization would be better able to arouse disgruntled citizens, male and female, throughout Miller. After assembling about fifty concerned citizens, they selected a name for their organization, Community Action to Reverse Pollution, or CARP, a reference to the garbage-eating fish. Hoock became the group's first president.[65]

The depth of middle-class fears about the fate of Miller provided CARP with an army of committed citizens. Virtually all the group's members resided in Miller, many living near the lake. They tended to be white, college-educated, white-collar workers. CARP members, then, fit the profile of middle-class citizens who found in Miller's scenery and recreational opportunities the means of pursuing the good life.[66] Consistent with the group's perspective, its literature and public relations rhetoric stressed fears that the power plant would destroy all that was special about Miller. CARP complained that the plant would spew 105,000 tons of sulfur dioxide into the atmosphere annually in addition to fly ash, a form of particulate dust. Even worse, these emissions would combine with iron oxide discharges from the steel mills to form a sulfuric acid mist over Miller. CARP members worried that spent cooling water discharges would raise the temperature of Lake Michigan to produce an oxygen-starved stew of rotting organisms and green slime. The potential destruction of Miller Woods, an ecologically unique area of sand dunes and forest that stood in the way of U.S. Steel's harbor-dredging operations, was yet another matter of concern. Miller residents cringed at the idea of railroad spurs and power transmission towers dominating a landscape once occupied by rolling sand ridges, lagoons, and trees. In essence, CARP sought to protect what was distinctive about Miller, in other words, to prevent the neighborhood from becoming like the rest of Gary.[67]

To achieve this end, the Miller activists left few stones unturned, appealing to federal, state, and local officials. In contrast to the landfill controversy several years earlier, the environmental villain, in this case NIPSCO, needed approval from the Army Corps of Engineers and several state agencies, in addition to permits from the Gary Air Pollution Control Division and the Gary Plan Commission and the continued support of the Gary Parks Board. Hence, CARP barraged these offices with letters citing expert testimony from ecologists, biologists, and doctors. CARP also took advantage of recent environmental laws. In 1969 the U.S. Congress had passed the National Environmental Policy Act, which allowed citizens to request environmental impact statements for any projects that involved federal agencies. CARP demanded that the Army Corps of Engineers conduct such an investigation, hoping at least to gain some time and to throw an obstacle in NIPSCO's path.[68]

Within Gary, CARP aimed its campaign at the mayor, Richard Hatcher. At first, Hatcher spoke favorably about the three-way deal, calling it "a mutually advantageous arrangement between the public and private sectors."[69] Hatcher was not strongly committed to the project, however, and Hoock sensed that he could be swayed. Although Hatcher enjoyed little political support in Miller, he was not particularly friendly with Gary's large corporations. Thus, CARP worked at gaining the support of the mayor, sending delegates to confer with him, providing testimony at public hearings, and collecting endorsements from other groups in the city to demonstrate widespread citizen support. CARP climaxed its campaign with a picnic on the grounds of the proposed power plant on May 17, 1970. The organization invited the mayor to the event, hoping to demonstrate widespread public opposition to the power plant and to convince him that the area was too beautiful to be destroyed for the sake of industrial development.[70] The picnickers must have been pleased with Hatcher's address that afternoon. Although the mayor did not speak directly about the power plant issue, he nonetheless affirmed his commitment to oppose "the further rape of the lake, . . . the further befouling of our air, or . . . the further use of land for the needs of the few rather than the many."[71] If any doubts remained about the mayor's position, they vanished over the next several months as Hatcher became more outspoken in his opposition to the power plant. With the mayor's backing, city agencies fell into line and denied NIPSCO approval to build a new facility in Miller.

The battle to preserve the Miller shoreline did not end with the collapse of the three-way deal, however. NIPSCO continued to explore the possibilities of a lakeshore power plant after the original scheme fell through.[72] Even more disturbing were rumors that U.S. Steel intended to expand its facilities further east into Miller Woods. These potential threats induced CARP activists to broaden their mission beyond the specifics of the three-way deal to include any sort of industrial intrusion. Carol Wilmore, who succeeded Helen Hoock as the organization's president, stated the group's goal bluntly in 1972: "Our basic premise is that there is no place for further industrialization of our lakeshore."[73] It was this sentiment that prompted CARP to join several other citizen groups in a campaign to incorporate all remaining natural areas of Miller in a federally regulated national park preserve.

The idea of a national park in Gary drew legitimacy from the recent success of environmentalists several years earlier in gaining national park status for an area just east of the city known as the Indiana Dunes. In 1952, when several steel companies attempted to construct new mills along the lakefront in neighboring Porter County, twenty-one women responded by forming the Save the Dunes Council to prevent the industrialization of Lake Michigan. Their strategy was to convince Congress to declare the Indiana Dunes national parkland and therefore off-limits to industry. By the 1960s, membership in the Save the Dunes Council swelled to more than 2,000, some of whom lived in Gary. Consistent with the social profile of most environmental associations in the 1960s, affluent whites dominated the group; their primary concern was the preservation of the area's unique ecological formations for recreation, aesthetic appreciation, and scientific study. After years of hearings, investigations, meetings, and letter-writing campaigns, Congress devised a compromise between the demands of environmentalists and those of industrialists, allowing Bethlehem Steel to build a new plant along the shore but setting aside 8,600 acres for a park. With the establishment of the Indiana Dunes National Lakeshore in 1966, the Save the Dunes Council could at least claim partial victory.[74]

Five years later, the cry "Save the Dunes" came to Gary. After the passage of the bill creating the Indiana Dunes National Lakeshore in 1966, the Save the Dunes Council sought to place more natural areas under federal protection. An investigation by one of its committees revealed that the lakefront property under siege by NIPSCO and another tract in south Miller sheltered precious wildlife and flora. The area wedged between Marquette Park, Lake Michigan, and Gary Works, known as Miller Woods, encompassed a series of habitats in various stages of succession. Young dunes with grasses, orchids, and poplars stood alongside oak forests with thick grass carpets and sparkling lagoons ringed with lilies and cattails. The second area, the Long Lake section, formed a narrow strip that ran parallel to Lake Michigan, just south of Miller's lakefront residential district. Wetlands there provided a temporary stop-over point for migratory birds as well as nesting grounds for blue heron.[75] With the Save the Dunes Council's support, environmentalists persuaded Indiana representative Edward Roush to introduce legislation in 1971 that would add 5,328 acres to the Indiana Dunes National Lakeshore, including Miller Woods and Long Lake.

Besides advancing CARP's aims of keeping heavy industry away from the beach, the park expansion bill also tapped a much broader constituency that saw environmental protection as a means of preserving Miller's racial composition. When several African American families moved into Miller's lakefront district around 1970, panic engulfed the neighborhood. "For Sale" signs sprouted on front lawns like spring flowers. Afraid of inciting the wrath of neighbors, a few families packed their belongings and departed in the night. One individual distributed an anonymous circular explaining his reasons for leaving, citing his fears that the influx of African Americans would lead to unsafe schools, unsafe homes, and falling property values. Perhaps more to the point, he concluded by declaring, "My kids are not going to marry outside their race or get raped by a bunch of animals."[76] Not all Miller residents were prepared to abandon their community so readily, however. Hence, when Clarence Borns, Fred Eichorn, and Moses Dilts proposed the idea of a homeowners association as a stabilizing force in July 1971, more than 400 citizens signed up to join the Miller Citizens Corporation.[77] In its first newsletter, the organization reminded members, "An area cannot turn black if there are few homes for sale. . . . The pattern of other communities which have undergone rapid racial change need not be ours."[78]

Judy Smith saw the Miller Citizens Corporation as a final line of defense against Miller's disintegration. She had moved to Miller with her husband in 1956 and over the next fifteen years discovered the neighborhood to be ideal for raising a family and making friends. When her children began inquiring about the sudden profusion of "For Sale" placards, she grew worried. She had watched the west side of Gary "turn black, block by block," and she feared that Miller was undergoing the same transformation. It was not that Smith objected to blacks living among whites. Indeed, her reputation as an advocate of housing integration moved Eichorn, Dilts, and Borns to discourage her from joining the Miller Citizens Corporation, fearing that she might frighten away those who felt differently. As far as she was concerned, the crux of the matter was timing. She later explained: "The rapidity of change destroys neighborhoods. You wanted to slow things down."[79] Regardless of residents' precise racial beliefs, and undoubtedly there was much difference of opinion, Miller stalwarts agreed that the primary task of the new homeowners group was to slow down the process of change.

If past experience was any guide, however, the Miller Citizens Corporation had little chance of success. As early as 1961, forty families on Gary's far west side had organized a similar group, the Chase-Clark Community Council, to prevent panic selling among fearful white homeowners. Seven years later, residents of the affluent Horace Mann and Ambridge districts formed the Northwest Side Civic Association with much the same goals. Both groups sought to bolster community pride by sponsoring beautification projects and pressing municipal government for more efficient delivery of city services. Both groups failed to meet their objectives: by 1970, virtually all white families had abandoned these neighborhoods.[80]

However, the Miller Citizens Corporation had the advantage of Miller's unique environment, and the group's leaders readily used references to the pristine surroundings to dissuade whites from leaving. Literature distributed by the organization highlighted the lake, the beach, and the ubiquitous sloping sand formations covered with wild grasses and trees. One such brochure asked rhetorically, "Where else could you catch salmon or trout in the morning, be in easy access to your metropolitan office, attend a major league game in the afternoon, and still enjoy a dinner with the family in a home near the big water or nestled in the wooded dunes?"[81] Accordingly, one of the group's stated objectives was the preservation and enhancement of Miller's natural beauty.[82] In this way, environmental protection efforts were energized by the broader quest for neighborhood stabilization, which included a significant racial component.

The overriding concern with maintaining social equilibrium even conditioned the Miller Citizens Corporation's support for a national park in Miller. Although members hoped that a national park would prevent unwanted industrial development, they balked at the possibility that recreational facilities might lure unwanted outsiders to Miller. Hence, they opposed the widening of County Line Road on Miller's eastern boundary to allow increased traffic flow into a proposed high-density recreation area at West Beach. Not only would traffic congestion pollute the air, they objected, but the proposed complex of parking garages, snack shops, and swimming pools would ruin unique ecological and botanical formations. Only further along in their arguments did they state what was for many the heart of the matter: increased visitors would infringe upon Miller's tranquillity and "upset the stability of the community."[83] Park administrators eventually scaled down their plans for the recreation facilities, thereby enabling the Miller Citizens Corporation to throw the full weight of its constituency behind the citizen lobbying effort.[84]

Congress approved the national park expansion in 1976, over the objections of industry, particularly U.S. Steel. In congressional testimony, the steel corporation passionately opposed the inclusion of its eastern property into the national park. The corporation maintained that Miller Woods, littered with abandoned railway tracks, construction equipment, and solid wastes, was ecologically worthless.[85] In other words, U.S. Steel argued that since it had ruined the property already, it might as well be allowed to keep it. More importantly, however, the company needed the space for future plant expansion, according to L. Keith Smith, superintendent of Gary Works. Hence, the national park extension jeopardized industrial growth.[86]

In contending that environmental protection would damage the local economy, U.S. Steel brandished industry's most powerful weapon.

Whether the issue at hand was stricter air pollution laws, a landfill in Lake Michigan, a power plant in Miller, or a national park in Gary, industry consistently resorted to the argument that a cleaner environment would necessarily come at the expense of a healthy economy. The point might be conveyed positively—as when NIPSCO promised that a Miller generating station would attract new industries to Gary—or in the form of a threat—as when NIPSCO warned that stiffer regulations on sulfur dioxide emissions would force it to double electricity rates.[87] Gary's industrial leaders first linked environmental reform with economic damage in 1966 when steelmakers and oil producers from northwest Indiana convened to thwart tougher air pollution laws. The group issued a warning: excessively restrictive regulations would prohibit heavy industry from continuing operations in the Calumet region.[88] Over the next ten years, U.S. Steel employed this argument more than any other firm in Gary, maintaining that pollution controls were too costly and that further regulations might force the company to flee Gary. On one occasion, U.S. Steel executives speculated publicly about the possibility of relocating to Texas.[89]

Industry's formulation of the environmental dilemma in economic terms did little to diminish middle-class support for environmental reform; instead, it forced many middle-class citizens to reconsider their commitment to the concept of economic growth. Through the 1950s and early 1960s, when environmentalists collaborated with business leaders, reformers saw no conflict between pollution control and a vibrant economy. To Milton Roth, the League of Women Voters, the Junior Chamber of Commerce, and other proponents of Gary's first smoke abatement law, pollution control meant technological tinkering, not altering the pace of economic development. But it became difficult to ignore the economic implications of environmental reform when U.S. Steel threatened to move to Texas. Although some environmentalists accused industry of exaggerating the financial costs of pollution control, many also concluded that if a choice had to be made, it would be preferable to forego growth.

Battles over the Lake Michigan landfill, NIPSCO's power plant, and the national park brought home most powerfully to Miller residents the fact that continued economic growth had a price: specifically, the destruction of those environmental amenities that for the middle class constituted an important aspect of social success. Postwar affluence rewarded many Gary residents with abundant recreational opportunities and picturesque surroundings. Ironically, the economic advancements that enabled them to fulfill their social aspirations now threatened their cherished life-styles. They understood that a clean environment was not compatible with all forms of economic development; each proposal for new development in Miller exposed the conflict starkly. For their purposes, industrial expansion had gone far enough. Gregory Reising, Miller's representative in the state legislature, expressed his constituents' sentiments in congressional testimony on behalf of the lakeshore park expansion bill by declaring, "The corporation [U.S. Steel] has told me that they need the area to help Gary progress. My city is dying from this type of progress."[90] Similarly, CARP's motto, "Not blind opposition to progress, but opposition to blind 'Progress,'" neatly captured the tempered middle-class attitude toward economic growth.

In adopting the discourse of limited growth, Gary's middle-class activists exposed themselves to the charge, readily leveled at the time, that environmentalism had become little more than a pretense for social exclusion.[91] In the case of the Miller Citizens Corporation, such a critique may have been warranted. By the mid-1970s, the powerful homeowners group was opposing any sort of development that threatened to alter the neighborhood's character—trailer parks, apartment complexes, high-density recreation facilities, and so forth—often citing environmental disruption as a justification for their position.[92] If nothing else, the Miller Citizens Corporation demonstrated the ways in which racial concerns could energize the slow-growth movement. But to reduce the slow-growth philosophy to racism would be to misinterpret the underlying foundations of middle-class environmentalism.

From the 1950s onward, Gary's middle-class activists saw environmental protection as a means of sustaining the suburban ideal. They had built their suburban communities according to specific environmental preferences and were determined to safeguard those amenities. In this respect, Miller's environmentalists were remarkably successful. Starting out as political neophytes, they gradually became so skilled at fact-finding, public demonstration, and lobbying that by the 1970s they represented one of the city's most powerful interest groups. By raising the banner of limited growth, reformers broadened and strengthened their popular base, bringing into the environmental fold citizens who were alarmed by social dislocation in their neighborhood. Of course, high incomes and white-collar positions made it relatively easy for reformers to formulate an environmental critique that targeted excessive industrial growth as the fundamental problem. Few Miller activists, after all, depended on U.S. Steel or any other manufacturing firm for their livelihood. Although drastic swings in the regional economy certainly affected families who lived in Miller, their dependence on local industry was at least a step removed from those directly employed by the mills. Thus, middle-class activists were able to spurn industry without fear of immediate retribution.

Not all Gary residents enjoyed this luxury. As middle-class environmentalists and industrialists squared off in the battle between environmental quality and economic growth, those with less financial security found it difficult to choose sides. Even by the 1970s, Gary remained a predominantly working-class community with almost half of the city's labor force employed in manufacturing.[93] For white industrial laborers, their families, and most African Americans, economic vulnerability limited their commitment to certain environmental initiatives. Furthermore, different social experiences imbued with them with distinct sets of environmental priorities. Although their pivotal role was not always appreciated by middle-class environmentalists, their position in public environmental conflicts influenced the outcome of environmental reform and the contours of environmental change in postwar Gary.

Tired of Working

in Pollution and

Having It Follow

Us Home

Working-Class

Environmentalism

Frustrated with organized labor's apathetic stance toward environmental health issues, Ray Quillen and Don Paulk resigned from their union posts as assistant grievance committeemen in January 1973. After working for over sixteen years in U.S. Steel's rolling mills, they had seen little reduction in dust and noise levels and they were convinced that furnace emissions were to blame for the heart ailments that had recently disabled three men in their department. Although they held the steel company accountable for creating such hazardous conditions, they were even more disappointed in their union, which showed no inclination to confront plant management on the matter. To Quillen and Paulk, the union had failed to live up to its responsibilities, a failure that was especially unfortunate considering that industrial laborers were perhaps the most aggrieved victims of pollution in the city. After all, blue-collar workers were forced to endure smoke and dust not only on the job but in their residential communities as well. As an exasperated Quillen explained, "We are steelworkers who are sick and tired of working in pollution and having it follow us home."[1]

As Quillen's comment indicated, Gary's industrial workers perceived their environmental predicament in quite different terms than their middle-class counterparts. For those who toiled in the factories, work place relations remained central to the development of an environmental consciousness. Even as social objectives outside the work place swung between the pull of ethnic loyalties and the lure of a middle-class consumer culture, blue-collar families never lost sight of the fact that their fortunes rested on their ability to act collectively, especially in opposition to industrial capital. From the 1940s onward, workers retained a particularly keen sense of class on the job, interpreting exposure to deadly fumes and searing heat as forms of corporate exploitation. Indeed, it was inside the steel mills that workers first engineered an organized response to pollution, fighting for better working conditions through their union, the United Steelworkers of America. Ultimately, it was disenchantment with union leadership that prompted steelworkers such as Quillen and Paulk to seek alternative strategies for fighting pollution. Yet even as working-class activists moved toward a community-based approach in the 1960s, they preferred to operate through their own organizations rather than join established middle-class reform groups.

The U.S. working class had entered the postwar era more homogenized than at any other time during the twentieth century.[2] The triumph of organized labor and the rise of the New Deal political order during the previous decade eroded the insular ethnic culture that had fragmented working-class society in the 1920s and 1930s. Whereas blue-collar families had once relied on a variety of religious and nationality-based institutions to ease their transition into urban-industrial life, they now looked to unions and government for help in attaining the economic means and psychological security to engage in a mass consumer culture organized around middle-class standards. Yet blue-collar workers encountered financial and cultural constraints in their pursuit of middle-class life-styles. Less bound by ethnic affiliations yet not quite middle class in their behavior and outlook, Gary's blue-collar residents encountered a unique set of environmental experiences and, hence, developed a distinct brand of environmentalism. Indeed, in circumventing the union in pursuit of distinctive environmental objectives, workers gained the freedom to broaden their environmental agenda and to reinvigorate a critique of corporate capitalism that had been stifled by the cooperative spirit of collective bargaining.

The experiences of the 1930s and World War II imbued Gary's steelworkers with a defiant spirit as the postwar period began. Militant action among rank-and-file workers over the previous decade had produced significant gains, most notably union representation. Fed up with autocratic foremen, job insecurity, low pay, and poor working conditions, thirteen disgruntled steelworkers had secretly convened in a tavern basement in 1933 to plan a union drive at Gary Works. In 1936 they joined forces with the Steelworkers Organizing Committee, which was orchestrating a movement to unionize steel mill laborers throughout the country. Despite harassment by mill management, the insurgent labor activists gradually won over enough workers so that by the following year, U.S. Steel decided to recognize the union rather than face a protracted strike. Immediately, the Steelworkers Organizing Committee, later renamed the United Steelworkers of America, became the primary bargaining agent for thousands of U.S. Steel employees, whether they worked in Gary, Pittsburgh, Birmingham, or elsewhere. In their first contract, unionized steelworkers obtained a wage hike, reduced hours, a formal set of procedures for resolving grievances, and some seniority rights. As the nation gradually shifted toward a war economy over the next four years, and as the demand for steel products grew, unionists in Gary called strikes to secure more wage increases and a dues checkoff system.[3]

During World War II, the union consolidated its gains, but at the price of a constrained range of worker authority on the shop floor. Eager to keep the war economy running as smoothly and efficiently as possible, the federal government granted organized labor important concessions in return for a promise to refrain from work stoppages. In particular, the National War Labor Board endorsed the principle of the closed shop, which guaranteed union security by requiring workers to maintain their union memberships for the duration of their contracts. Abiding by this compact required that union leaders keep rank-and-file workers on a short leash in order to discourage independent strikes. Moreover, labor leaders tacitly agreed to leave all decisions about production in the hands of corporate management. Although Philip Murray, president of the Steelworkers Union, advocated the establishment of industrial councils that would bring union representatives and management officials together in the economic planning process, the idea was not received warmly by either business or government. Thus, labor relations during World War II set a precedent for limited worker involvement in any matter beyond wages, benefits, and minor shop floor disputes. Furthermore, wartime developments established a trend of limited rank-and-file participation in industrial relations.[4]

Despite pressure from above to refrain from militant behavior, Gary's steelworkers maintained their assertive spirit through the war and into the postwar period, challenging management directly on a variety of issues, including health and safety. So confident were workers of their newfound power, they frequently ignored formal procedures for resolving grievances and, without waiting for official union approval, walked off their jobs in protest. Not only in Gary but across the country, buoyant industrial workers engaged in wildcat strikes—spontaneous work stoppages not authorized by union leaders—to resolve shop floor conflicts.[5] Because wildcat strikes staged by only a handful of laborers could be extraordinarily effective at crippling production, striking workers often won concessions from management. For example, when forty-five cleaner line employees at the Gary Sheet and Tin Mill walked off their jobs for two days in 1953 to protest a speedup, they idled 450 workers in other departments and held 6,000 tons of tin hostage.[6]

Gary steelworkers used the wildcat strategy to protest, among other things, excessive smoke and fumes inside the mills. Early union contracts had little to say about dangerous working conditions, although the initial round of bargaining did produce a provision that allowed individual workers to walk away from any job they deemed unsafe. This clause, however, provided no means for rectifying the hazard in question. Hence, through the early 1950s, steelworkers in various departments fell back upon their own resources to compel ameliorative action on the part of mill management. Especially in the coke plant, where environmental hazards were most severe and workers were most militant, shop floor leaders staged frequent strikes to improve physical conditions. In 1953, for example, 450 coke plant workers walked off their jobs for two days after management ignored a list of grievances about working conditions. The strikers demanded that management repair warped furnace doors and provide more protective clothing for laborers who worked near the hot ovens.[7] Shortly thereafter, a group of workers in the Sheet and Tin Mill decided they could no longer tolerate the fumes from the nearby enameling process. When their complaints produced no results, the grievance committeemen ordered workers off the job. Management responded immediately by sending a team of engineers to the site, assuring workers after a few hours that an exhaust fan would be installed.[8]

At the same time that workers used the wildcat tactic, they took advantage of formal union procedures for resolving grievances, although this approach proved to have limited effectiveness. The grievance system established in the 1937 contract steered worker complaints through a hierarchy of committees staffed by both management and labor officials. In the event that no agreement could be reached, the dispute was settled by federal government arbitrators. Because the grievance mechanism operated on the principle of mutual consent, settlements invariably minimized any interference with the production technologies of steelmaking. Grievance committeemen knew that in making a case for safer working conditions, they were more likely to get results if they proposed solutions that required only the most superficial alterations to the work setting. Although the wildcatters did not necessarily demand radical changes in the manufacturing process, the grievance process essentially locked workers into a mode of conflict resolution that would, at best, insulate workers from existing hazards rather than treat the problems at their source.

Grievances involving excessive exposure to smoke and fumes, for instance, usually culminated in the installation of exhaust fans. Corporate managers were loath to spend money on any health and safety improvements, but they saw exhaust fans as a relatively cheap way to mollify discontented workers. Recognizing this fact, union representatives often requested fans in order to bring grievances to a quick resolution. Such was the case when crews at several coke loading stations lodged a formal protest about excessive dust in 1946. According to the complainants, dust constantly spewed from the coke shoots in their unventilated work area, thereby creating a serious health risk. But instead of urging management to reduce the level of dust emissions, they requested exhaust fans to draw the offensive coke particulates elsewhere.[9]

Another method used to reduce exposure to environmental hazards was to spread the burden more evenly among a greater number of workers. One of the first attempts to employ this strategy occurred in 1951 when seven workers who dumped coal into the coke ovens and replaced the lids on furnaces complained that high temperatures on top of the batteries posed risks to their health. Indeed, it was not uncommon for coke plant workers to suffer heat exhaustion. In this particular case, the aggrieved employees charged that their situation was especially injurious because the furnaces to which they were assigned were enclosed on both sides by gas mains and standpipes. Not only did this arrangement inhibit air circulation, but it left workers without any space to step aside for temporary relief from the heat. When the union submitted its grievance, however, it did not request that the company adjust the position of the coke ovens or reconstruct its piping system. Rather it asked that crew sizes be increased from four to five men so that workers could take turns resting.[10] Over the next two decades, the union adopted this approach regularly, prodding the company to hire additional personnel to spell workers in areas of intensive heat. As workers grew more concerned with the health implications of dust emissions, union representatives sought to apply the spelltime formula to smoky jobs in the coke plant as well, although it was not until the early 1980s that this complaint was settled to the union's satisfaction.[11]

While steelworkers in the early postwar years relied on a combination of independent action and formal union procedures to redress their environmental grievances, the cooperative spirit and bureaucratic style that increasingly defined industrial relations eroded workers' ability to secure health and safety reforms through militant action from the mid-1950s onward. Through a series of strikes and settlements between 1946 and 1959, labor and management incrementally constricted the range of worker authority in the plant. In return for better wages and fringe benefits, the Steelworkers Union relinquished control over many work place decisions, particularly those relating directly to the production process. Anxious to participate in the consumer cornucopia of the postwar United States, few workers objected to the terms of the trade-off. Indeed, few among the rank and file protested as union negotiations of all sorts became increasingly centralized. In the process, local issues —those problems peculiar to particular plants, including health and safety matters—received scant attention.[12]

Further impeding worker militancy on health and safety issues was the union's strategy of establishing cooperative relations with management from the mid-1950s onward. Union officials, convinced that uninterrupted steel production was in the best interest of workers, openly encouraged cooperation and peaceful negotiation between management and labor. In 1953 David McDonald, president of the International United Steelworkers of America, sent word down through the ranks that wildcat strikes must end.[13] The following year, McDonald advanced the concept of "mutual trusteeship," whereby labor and management, in an effort to maintain high productivity levels, would resolve differences peacefully through joint committees and negotiations conducted by labor bureaucrats. Mutual trusteeship for the sake of economic growth ultimately curtailed work stoppages of any kind. After a bitter five-month walkout in 1959, steelworkers abandoned the strike as a means of securing improvements in pay or working conditions.

Through the 1960s and 1970s, industry used the specter of rising steel imports to maintain the union's allegiance to labor-management cooperation. McDonald's successor, I. W. Abel, continued down the conciliatory path of accommodation, sometimes with even greater resolve. Committed to increasing production as a hedge against foreign competition, Abel set up productivity committees in each mill. These joint labor and management committees worked to ensure the smooth flow of steelmaking. Under Abel's leadership, the union and the steel industry joined forces in a propaganda campaign to convince workers that they would have to sacrifice certain rights for the sake of productivity. They produced a movie, "Where's Joe?," which delivered the message that the average American steelworker was likely to lose his job to a counterpart in Germany or Japan. Only by cooperating with management could Americans prevent this scenario. Union-management cooperation reached its climax in the 1973 Experimental Negotiating Agreement. Under this pact, the union voluntarily relinquished the right to strike during contract negotiations in exchange for hefty wage increases.[14]

In the spirit of mutual trusteeship and cooperative industrial relations, unions increasingly relied on joint labor-management committees to resolve health and safety conflicts after 1950. For the most part, these committees expended their energies on the problem of industrial accidents; the corporation, after all, wanted to reduce insurance claims and costs related to lost hours. Hence, discussions often centered around precarious walkways, poor lighting, and dangerous vehicular traffic around work areas. Yet workers also used the health and safety councils to tackle particularly thorny environmental problems. When they did, the resulting agreements usually mimicked those generated by the grievance mechanism. During the late 1950s and early 1960s, for example, the joint safety committees considered the problems of fumes at the gantry crane yard in the open-hearth department, smoke from scarfing machines at the rail mill, and furnace emissions from the coke ovens. In each case, the union pressed for exhaust fans, and usually management acquiesced.[15]

Workers also used the health and safety committees to prod management to supply them with personal protection devices such as uniforms, helmets, and shoes for better insulation from acids, oils, grease, and heat.[16] The precedent for this approach was set in the 1940s when coke plant workers demanded outfits that would better protect them from smoke and heat. At the time, these laborers received only the most rudimentary protective gear: goggles, safety shoes, gloves, and, for those who toiled atop the batteries, a crude plastic mask to reduce smoke inhalation. Grievance committeemen, therefore, conducted lengthy negotiations with company officials to secure clothing with better insulation and more efficient respirators.[17] Over the next two decades, workers from other sections of the mill brought similar demands to joint safety committee meetings. During the late 1960s, for instance, union officials convinced U.S. Steel to supply laborers in the smoky gantry crane yards of the open-hearth department with respirators. And by the 1970s, those who performed tasks near hot steel were provided with aluminized suits.[18]

In general, the occupational health remedies established through bureaucratic negotiation and consensus had limited effectiveness. Although personal protection devices helped somewhat, placing the responsibility for protection on the workers created other problems. Some workers refused to wear protective clothing on the grounds that it was uncomfortable. Furthermore, exhaust fans in the coke plant and rail mill often did little more than transfer smoke from one part of the mill to another.[19] Spelltime slightly reduced individual workers' exposure to hazardous conditions, but only at the expense of subjecting additional workers to the environmental hazards. Postwar health and safety modifications at Gary Works made no attempt to reduce the level of pollution inside the mills. Thus, despite several decades of efforts, the mills remained dirty and dangerous places through the 1970s.

Even the passage of the Occupational Safety and Health Act (OSHA) in 1970, which permitted the federal government to regulate factory environmental conditions, did not convince the union to take a more militant posture on the environmental health front. OSHA represented an effort to bring the federal government into the realm of worker health and safety, much as the Clean Air and Clean Water acts brought the government into the business of regulating the ambient environment. Toward the end of the 1960s, a coalition of consumer advocates, government bureaucrats, and other health and safety activists based in Washington, D.C., along with several unions, pressed the U.S. Congress for some sort of an occupational health law. The Steelworkers Union, which lobbied more vigorously for OSHA than any other union, adopted the cause only after it became evident the measure would pass. Moreover, with the exception of a group of activist steelworkers in Pittsburgh, the Steelworkers Union's involvement in the formulation of OSHA was restricted to top union officials.[20]

Once OSHA became a law, however, the Steelworkers Union leadership failed to use its provisions to secure substantive work place reforms. OSHA empowered the federal government to set standards for the concentration of hazardous substances in the work place, gave workers the right to participate in standard setting, and permitted employees to call for work place inspections. But these provisions meant little as long as the union lacked the will to act upon them. Although the Steelworkers Union included some mild health and safety clauses in its 1971 contract and lobbied for tough coke oven standards under OSHA, the international office did little to stimulate activity among its locals. Plant health and safety problems continued to be resolved through joint committees.[21] A Steelworkers Union in-house analysis of OSHA in 1979 concluded, "The lack of grass roots political support . . . indicates an area in which our approach must change."[22] In the absence of union pressure, the federal government was slow to develop standards. By 1980, the government had devised exposure standards for less than two dozen hazardous substances. Of those substances, the only ones that had a significant impact on the steel industry were coke oven emissions, chromium, and lead.[23] Thus, OSHA neither challenged industry's control over production nor charted a new course for organized labor.[24]

Local labor officials in Gary displayed no more enthusiasm for OSHA than did the top union leadership. Even as Steelworkers Union lobbyists in Washington, D.C., pressured the federal government to establish strict coke oven emission standards, local unionists remained aloof. In 1973 the international office sponsored a coke oven conference to consider strategies for including coke oven provisions in upcoming contracts. Although the Gary Works local 1014 received invitations to the conference, it declined to send representatives.[25] When OSHA turned its attention to coke oven conditions at Gary Works, local union officials stood on the sidelines while the federal agency and the company wrestled over the matter.[26]

The only health issue that prompted the union to employ OSHA provisions in Gary during the 1970s was one that had no connection to the steelmaking process—the quality of water in washroom showers. Although U.S. Steel provided city water for drinking, it drew its wash water directly from Lake Michigan. During the 1960s, as concern for environmental hazards increased, workers began to complain about wash water quality. In particular, they objected to the putrid smell, the oily sheen that covered their bodies after bathing, and the dead fish that sometimes passed through the showerheads. Some workers even claimed that the untreated lake water induced hair loss.[27] When Harry Piasecki challenged the entrenched All-American party for leadership of the local in 1970, he made the wash water problem a major campaign issue.[28] Once elected, Piasecki attempted to fulfill his campaign promise to solve the problem, and along with Bronko Stankovich, the Safety and Health Committee chairman, he applied pressure on both U.S. Steel and OSHA to improve water quality in the showers. During contract negotiations in 1972, Piasecki obtained a weak commitment from U.S. Steel to switch its water supply, but the company procrastinated. The following year, Piasecki and Stankovich traveled to Washington, D.C., to appeal to OSHA officials for a ruling that would compel the steel company to use potable water. This time their efforts succeeded. Prodded by an OSHA edict, U.S. Steel pledged to switch from lake to city water by 1978.[29]

If the union moved cautiously with regard to occupational health hazards inside the mills, it was even more reluctant to address environmental problems on the outside, where industry's environmental practices often frustrated the social aspirations of Gary's blue-collar families. As the material benefits secured by organized labor conferred a measure of prosperity upon industrial workers, and as the lure of a mass consumer culture oriented around middle-class standards gradually eroded the moorings of an insular ethnic culture, blue-collar families began to share some of the environmental concerns and objectives that preoccupied their white-collar counterparts. Thus, in the decades following World War II, steelworkers and their families displayed an unprecedented commitment to obtaining suburban housing, outdoor recreational facilities, and clean air and water in their neighborhoods. Yet Gary's working-class residents operated within cultural and economic constraints that limited their ability to attain these goals. The environmental programs put forth by middle-class reformers, therefore, did not fully resonate with the particular needs of blue-collar citizens. Ironically, the cultural pull of middle-class consumerism made blue-collar families more cohesive as a class, thereby facilitating a collective community response to environmental conditions that featured a distinctive agenda, ideology, and organizational framework.[30]

The package of tangible benefits secured by organized labor during the 1940s and 1950s was perhaps the most important factor in reorienting working-class social life around middle-class norms. As historians of the U.S. working class have noted, this cultural transition dated back to the 1920s when national movie distributors, commercial radio stations, and chain grocery stores first vied with local ethnic institutions for the loyalty of working-class consumers. But through the 1930s, economic insecurity and a distrust of national institutions to a large extent kept workers wedded to ethnic banks, social clubs, and entertainment venues.[31] After World War II, the shift toward mass culture accelerated as the gains secured through collective bargaining allowed workers to share more fully in the bounty of economic prosperity. Considering wages alone, average hourly earnings at U.S. Steel increased from 72 cents in 1936 to $3.78 in 1968.[32] In addition, unionized workers received retirement pensions, paid vacations, and reduced work schedules, all of which allowed blue-collar families to adopt at least some of the consumption habits and recreational activities of their white-collar neighbors.

Working-class receptivity to a national, middle-class consumer culture was reinforced by the growing number of second-generation Americans within the blue-collar contingent. Since many older immigrants had died, without a comparable influx of newcomers to compensate, Gary's foreign-born population fell from 15 percent in 1940 to 8 percent in 1960. Even in the older working-class districts near downtown, European immigrants accounted for less than a third of all residents by the latter year.[33] Unlike their parents, the swelling contingent of second-generation Americans spoke English as a native tongue; most were educated in public schools that deliberately inculcated youths with middle-class values and culture. Furthermore, as historian Lizabeth Cohen noted in her study of Chicago's working class just prior to World War II, "Young people's struggle for emotional autonomy from parents converged with efforts to assimilate into American society, making adolescence a time to escape the confining ethnic worlds of their families."[34] If anything, this tendency was even more pronounced among the children of immigrants in post–World War II Gary.

The shifting cultural orientation associated with a prosperous, second-generation working class was reflected in the decline of ethnic institutions that had once focused community solidarity and helped to maintain the security of vulnerable immigrant populations. Prior to World War II, for example, most Eastern Orthodox churches offered language and religious classes for schoolchildren late in the afternoon, after the public schools closed. After the war, however, these Serbian, Greek, Russian, Romanian, and Bulgarian churches abandoned their afternoon programs.[35] The same fate befell many social clubs that drew upon specific European ethnic constituencies, such as the Dom Polski Club, the American-Serbian Athletic Club, and the Albanian Beneficial Society. Finding it difficult to sustain their memberships, about half of them vanished from the Gary scene by the late 1960s.[36] Another indication of shifting cultural affiliations was the increase in chain store sales, suggesting that fewer consumers did their shopping in neighborhood "mom-and-pop" stores that dispensed specialty ethnic items. Among grocery stores, for example, chain stores such as A&P and Kroger's received 59 percent of city sales in 1963, up from only 30 percent in 1939.[37] Although independent proprietors with Eastern European surnames—such as Ampeloitis, Delgrado, Kuzmicki, Malopszy, Nestorovich, Svetcoff—continued to dominate the retail grocery trade in the older immigrant district, self-service supermarkets selling national name brand products secured the loyalty of shoppers in second-generation neighborhoods.[38] Thus, abundant evidence pointed to the decline of the insular ethnic culture that had once shaped working-class life.

The durability of working-class social networks and impediments to economic mobility, however, prevented industrial laborers from melding completely into a homogeneous middle class. In the first place, second-generation families did not wish to sever all connections with Old World traditions. Most steelworkers still attended their ethnic churches, even after they moved away from the old neighborhoods. Also, while many ethnic clubs disbanded, others persevered. Gary's Polish community alone supported an athletic club, a cultural club, a women's society, a new immigrants club, and a Polish army veterans organization through the mid-1960s. The Polish National Alliance, which sold insurance, sent financial aid to Poland, and served as a vehicle for social gatherings, boasted seven separate lodges and 1,600 members as late as 1966.[39] Likewise, the Croatian Catholic Union flourished well into the 1960s and made a special effort to secure the allegiance of second-generation Americans through social and athletic youth clubs.[40] Furthermore, distinct working-class spheres of social interaction were reinforced by political and labor organizations. Ethnic affiliations provided the basis for the political clubs that mediated between working-class voters and the Democratic party machine, even though ethnicity had little to do with the purpose of the clubs. Workers' involvement in unions provided another forum for social interaction that solidified class networks both in and out of the factory. The Steelworkers Union, for example, sponsored athletic tournaments for workers and a variety of family events, including picnics and an annual Christmas party.[41] Even if industrial laborers wished to rub shoulders with their white-collar counterparts, limited incomes often prevented them from doing so. Despite rising incomes, the average semiskilled worker simply could not afford the life-style enjoyed by most white-collar employees. While prosperity certainly affected the habits and activities of industrial laborers, their experience of affluence was different from that of the new middle class. Hence, when blue-collar families reacted to industrial wastes, they did so in the context of separate social networks, distinct environmental experiences, and a unique set of considerations and constraints.

Although young working-class families followed the middle-class practice of abandoning inner-city dwellings for private homes in outlying areas of the city, ethnic attachments and limited finances imposed geographic restrictions on the settlement process, thereby diminishing the environmental rewards of migration. Once married, the children of Gary's immigrant population tended to move away from the ethnic districts. Anxious to abandon cramped, inner-city rental quarters, they were receptive to realtors who promised more space, greater privacy, and cleaner surroundings in new private homes. Real estate brokers occasionally emphasized environmental features when selling homes in outlying working-class communities. For example, a 1948 advertisement for a development in Aetna described the homes as "convenient to downtown, . . . yet out of the smoke and dirt."[42] However, although well-paid steelworkers, especially those who qualified for veterans' loans, benefited from the same government housing programs that underwrote white-collar suburbanization, they could rarely afford the expensive homes that dotted the Miller lakeshore or lined the meandering lanes of Glen Park's Morningside district. Moreover, far-flung neighborhoods such as Miller were too remote for those who wished to maintain close contact with relatives and churches in the older immigrant district. For the working class, interurban migration usually involved modest geographical leaps. The most popular destinations for skilled craft and semiskilled workers were those neighborhoods just east and west of the older ethnic districts, although a fair number of well-paid skilled laborers also opted for modest homes in Glen Park on the city's southern fringe. Furthermore, although relocation generally brought some environmental improvement in the form of cleaner air and more open space, working-class families did not escape industrial pollution to the same extent as their middle-class counterparts.[43]

Especially when compared with the settlement of Miller, the peopling of Gary's western suburbs revealed the ways in which working-class families balanced environmental preferences with other residential objectives. As in Miller, Gary's undeveloped western reaches experienced a rapid influx of homeowners during the 1950s. Indeed, as of 1960, homeowners outnumbered renters by a ratio of more than four to one in both communities. But whereas Miller attracted many white-collar families, the modest one-story bungalows and ranch-style homes on the city's western fringe tended to draw large numbers of blue-collar families. Over 40 percent of the breadwinners in western Gary worked in the steel mills, mostly in well-paying positions.[44] Also distinguishing western Gary from Miller was the high proportion of second-generation Americans. The area's proximity to the older immigrant district appealed to families who wished to maintain ties with relatives and former neighbors. Above all, however, it was environmental conditions that set the two suburban neighborhoods apart. In stark contrast to Miller, western Gary was developed for both residential and industrial purposes. A broad swath of industrial property, which by 1960 included U.S. Steel's cement plant, a coal-fired power plant, a detinning factory, sewage treatment facilities, and an oil refinery, cordoned western Gary inhabitants from Lake Michigan. Moreover, within the residential section, zoning regulations allowed manufacturers to locate alongside private homes. At the same time that developers erected rows of frame houses for working-class families, they lured prospective firms by advertising the area's attributes making it suitable for industrial production: access to railways, proximity to sources of raw steel, and the availability of swampy land for waste disposal. Businesses responded enthusiastically, and soon chemical companies, salvage yards, and metalworks lined the city's western border.[45] So although working-class settlers of western Gary found affordable homes close to downtown, they did not fully escape the industrial environment.

Shifting recreational habits also informed the environmental perspective of Gary's working class. The triumph of organized labor in 1937 initiated the forty-hour work week, thereby ending the exhausting schedules that sometimes had laborers toiling on twelve-hour shifts with only one day of rest each week. Over the next thirty years, union negotiators chipped away further at workers' time obligations so that by 1970, steelworkers received eight paid holidays in addition to between one and four weeks of paid vacation annually, depending on seniority.[46] Shorter working hours and longer vacations not only translated into more leisure time but also encouraged the adoption of more elaborate recreation habits. Among male steelworkers, social activity had once centered around the saloon.[47] After a grueling day in the mills, steelworkers routinely stumbled into one of the many downtown taverns to swill beer and drink whiskey for a few hours before staggering home to bed. George Horvath recalled that after tending the open-hearth furnaces through the night, workers would assemble at the Ingot Tavern across from the steel mill gates to "drink shots and beer through the mid-morning." The following night, after several hours of sleep, "they would be ready to work the furnace like nothing happened."[48] After World War II, however, saloons lost much of their popularity. Whereas Gary boasted 1 saloon for every 88 persons in 1911, that ratio had dropped to 1 for every 1,000 persons by 1957.[49] If laborers were spending less of their time on bar stools, they more than compensated with family-oriented recreational pursuits that involved more time and expense. Few activities matched bowling in its appeal to Gary's postwar working class. No less than six bowling alleys competed within a few blocks of one another in the heart of downtown. Unions and ethnic clubs frequently sponsored bowling tournaments, touting the pastime as a wholesome activity for the entire family. The Croatian Catholic Union, perhaps somewhat more obsessed with the sport than other organizations, used bowling as a vehicle to forge friendships among Croatians throughout the Midwest. A typical activity was the five-hour bowling marathon held in January 1956 at the Hawaii Lounge just outside of Chicago, which was followed by dinner, kolo dancing, and an accordion performance by Dick Candiano of the Gary lodge.[50]

Most importantly, however, with respect to the development of an environmental consciousness, workers spent much of their newly freed time outdoors. For some, this took the form of relaxing in the backyard and chatting with neighbors. The more energetic took up fishing, hunting, and a variety of athletic activities. During the summer months, organized labor sponsored men's baseball leagues and softball tournaments for both men and women in various parks around northwest Indiana.[51] Although golf was not known to have many devotees within the working class, the Croatian Catholic Union organized its first golf tournament in 1955, making special arrangements for the novice golfer.[52] Fishing and hunting captured a far larger working-class constituency during the postwar years, prompting many Gary steelworkers to join organizations such as the Izaak Walton League and the Lake County Fish and Game Association. When a reporter asked a lathe operator how he planned to spend his free time in the event of a strike in 1955, the steelworker replied emphatically, "I'm just going to fish and fish and fish!"[53] Perhaps the greatest inducement for outdoor recreation was the paid vacation. With weeks off from factory duty, millhands traveled with their families to far-off places, taking cross-country drives, visiting the nation's capital, and vacationing on the beaches of Florida.[54]

Out of these new residential and recreational experiences came a set of environmental concerns that was unique in many respects. With greater time spent outdoors in their neighborhoods, where there was a heavy concentration of manufacturing, blue-collar families developed the sort of alarm about air pollution that gripped middle-class environmentalists. But because they lived in different parts of town, the two groups focused their wrath on different pollution sources. Also, although outdoor recreation inspired campaigns for better parks among both groups, they did not always support the same parks. Steelworkers were not prominent among the activists who attempted to "save the dunes" from industrial development in the lakefront tracts east of Gary during the 1950s, although the Steelworkers Union did announce its support for the cause. Yet a decade earlier, organized labor had championed the cause of a "working man's park" at Wolf Lake, several miles west of Gary. Situated across from a Standard Oil Company refinery, the park would lack the scenic beauty of the Indiana Dunes, but the site provided easy access by public transportation, an important consideration for the many steelworkers who still lacked automobile transportation.[55] Fishing inspired an awareness of water pollution among white-collar and blue-collar families alike, but different fishing practices somewhat divided the priorities of each class. Whereas upper-class anglers often lowered their hooks from privately owned boats, those of more modest means tended to cast their lines from jetties along the shore. By the late 1960s, a popular call for more fishing piers along Lake Michigan would emerge as an issue that resonated most powerfully among working-class citizens.[56]

Given the history of union involvement in community affairs, it was not unreasonable for workers to expect organized labor to address those problems of air and water pollution that affected blue-collar families most directly. The Steelworkers Union, although primarily concerned with representing workers inside the factories, was active in municipal politics and, at times, thrust itself into local controversies when it believed workers' interests were at stake. By endorsing candidates, financing campaigns, and mobilizing voters, organized labor accumulated political credits that it cashed in by influencing appointments on various government boards. At various periods during the postwar years, union representatives sat on Gary's school board, planning commission, housing authority, parks board, and police commission.[57] Through its participation in administrative agencies and by applying pressure on prominent political officials, the Steelworkers Union played an important role in fights for higher wages for schoolteachers, for local rent control, and for slum clearance during the 1950s.[58] Although organized labor moved slowly to address racial discrimination in the steel mills, the Gary Works local supported blacks' efforts to win civil rights legislation in the community, lobbying vigorously for a fair employment bill in 1950 and for open occupancy legislation in the early 1960s.[59] So when community environmental issues became politicized in the late 1950s and 1960s, many workers expected their union to take a strong stand.

For a brief time, union officials did just that, passionately endorsing the cause of environmental reform, particularly with regard to air pollution control. Although union leaders never initiated environmental reform campaigns, leaving that task to middle-class organizations and politicians, they nonetheless applied their political muscle once the campaigns were under way, recognizing that dirty air and water undermined their constituents' welfare. When the city formed its Air Pollution Advisory Board to help administer the 1962 smoke abatement ordinance, labor demanded a seat and the city promptly complied with the request. In March 1965 the Gary Works local made headlines by vowing to wage an all-out fight for an effective air pollution program. The union dispatched angry letters to the mayor and all Gary councilmen urging swift and aggressive action against polluters. Steve Bazin, president of the local, charged city officials with procrastinating in establishing an effective program.[60] When U.S. Steel proposed a pollution abatement plan for its facilities in Gary that same year, president of the Sheet and Tin Mill local, Carey Kranz, was one of the first community leaders to press Gary's mayor to reject the proposal on the grounds that it contained too many loopholes.[61]

Even at the peak of union enthusiasm for environmental reform in the mid-1960s, however, the Steelworkers Union endorsed environmental measures selectively. In particular, union support for lakeshore protection in Miller, an issue of great importance to middle-class residents, was at best lukewarm. Labor leaders understood that the Miller beaches offered workers an important recreational outlet. But because few working-class families lived in Miller, the beaches were frequented more often by white-collar residents. Furthermore, local labor leaders looked forward to the additional jobs that would be created by Miller's economic development. As an obstacle to further economic growth, shoreline protection ran counter to union objectives. Faced with conflicting pressures—the desire for recreational facilities on the one hand and the need for more jobs on the other—the Steelworkers Union adopted an ambiguous stance on issues pertaining to environmental protection in Miller. Despite prodding from Community Action to Reverse Pollution (CARP), the union showed little interest in the proposal of the Northwest Indiana Public Service Company (NIPSCO) for a lakefront power plant. Although the Steelworkers Union's subdistrict office supported the environmentalists on the issue of a national park in Gary, some of the city's less powerful unions lined up on the other side of the fence. Indeed, the Carpenters, Glazers, and Ironworkers unions, hungry for additional jobs, established a joint lobbying organization to stop the park expansion.[62]

If the mid-1960s witnessed growing union commitment to environmental protection in the surrounding community, at least on the part of the Steelworkers Union, then the late 1960s marked a retrenchment. Several factors accounted for the reversal. First, a tough stand against pollution conflicted with the union's efforts to establish more cordial relations with management, a goal that became more rigid through the late 1960s. Already tentative in its endorsement of environmental reform, the union retreated further in the 1970s as deteriorating race relations eroded its political clout and economic difficulties constricted its political vision.

With its constituency divided almost equally between blacks and whites, the Steelworkers Union walked a tightrope on the racial issues that had come to dominate local politics by the late 1960s. As African Americans began to make inroads against discrimination in housing and education, many working-class whites felt that civil rights reform had gone far enough. Thus, when George Wallace made a bid for the Democratic party's presidential nomination in 1964 on an anti–civil rights platform, many of Gary's white voters rallied behind him. Although the Steelworkers Union was officially committed to civil rights reform, white steelworkers were among those most opposed to further racial integration. Belatedly, the Steelworkers Union opposed Wallace, but most of Gary's white steelworkers ignored the union and voted for the segregationist. Although Lyndon Johnson's delegate carried the city by a slight margin due to solid African American support, the white working-class districts of western Gary, Aetna and Glen Park, backed Wallace by a more than two to one majority.[63] The 1967 mayoral election proved even more troublesome for organized labor. When the union threw its support to the incumbent, A. Martin Katz, in the Democratic primary, African Americans took their turn disregarding labor's mandate, voting en masse for Richard Hatcher. In the general election, local union leadership made only halfhearted efforts to assist Hatcher, then the Democratic nominee. Orval Kincaid, the Steelworkers Union's subdistrict director for Gary, organized a committee to help elect Hatcher but refused to allocate any funds.[64] Some union leaders, most notably the president of the Sheet and Tin Mill local, bolted to the Republican party rather than support Hatcher.[65] Most white steelworkers did the same and voted for the white Republican candidate. Nevertheless, Hatcher gained election, becoming Gary's first African American mayor.

The emergence of race at the forefront of local politics severely undercut the clout of the Steelworkers Union. The union's precinct organization fell apart, and rank-and-file participation in political campaigns ground to a halt. The union abandoned the practice of giving workers the day off to campaign for Democratic candidates.[66] Labor's traditional political agenda, based on securing higher standards of living for Gary's lower and middle classes, had little appeal for white voters concerned about whether blacks would be moving into their neighborhoods, going to the same schools as their children, or controlling the city's government.

Economic pressures also placed organized labor on the defensive. Fearful of competition from foreign steel producers, labor reconsidered its commitment to community welfare measures and returned its political objectives to the orbit of workers' immediate interests by the early 1970s. Corporate warnings about rising Japanese steel imports that had once elicited moderate concern now provoked alarm in the aftermath of the 1971 recession in Gary. Nervous about job security, workers grew susceptible to the threat of layoffs. In this climate, maintaining jobs became the overriding concern of the Steelworkers Union. Organized labor, acting more as a special interest group than a torchbearer of broad-based social change, viewed environmental reform with suspicion whenever it threatened to impede economic growth.[67]

By the 1970s, the union's 1965 pledge to conduct an all-out fight against polluters seemed a faint echo as labor leaders discontinued their active support for most environmental measures, including air pollution control. Labor's representative on the Air Pollution Advisory Board no longer attended meetings, and when the city eliminated the slot, the union raised no objection.[68] Similarly, representatives from the middle-class environmental groups CARP and the Miller Citizens Corporation received no encouragement when they sought union support for their initiatives in the early 1970s.[69] Especially as middle-class activists gave environmental protection priority over economic growth and jobs, they gained the reputation of "kooks" among union officials.[70] In April 1973 Harry Piasecki, president of local 1014, printed a front-page editorial in the union newspaper attacking local activists for insensitivity to job loss. In their pursuit of environmental protection, they expressed a "super-heated, fanatical desire," according to the union president.[71]

Not all workers shared these sentiments, however, and in the face of union intransigence, many sought to reorganize the union from within by ousting the entrenched leadership. Not only in Gary, but in labor unions across the country, the late 1960s marked a period of rank-and-file insurgency as industrial workers combined challenges to centralized authority with a call for a more confrontational posture toward corporate management. Usually the issue of health and safety was merely one among many anticorporate issues, but on some occasions it took center stage. The link between union democracy and occupational health first gained publicity when a group of insurgent miners, called Miners for Democracy, overthrew the corrupt chiefs of the United Mine Workers by exposing the union's refusal to press management on the problem of black lung disease. Around the same time, dissident teamsters clashed with their union bosses on the issue of truck safety.[72] Among Gary steelworkers, frustration with the union's handling of environmental matters found expression in Ed Sadlowski's rank-and-file campaign for district director in 1973. Among Sadlowski's platform planks was the inclusion of pollution issues into the collective bargaining process. Sadlowski also linked in-plant pollution with environmental conditions in the community. "If we as a union make [pollution] . . . a strong bargaining issue," he commented, "we can see that industrialists in a community keep that community in the same shape that they found it."[73] When he ran for president of the Steelworkers Union in 1977, Sadlowski continued to espouse a more militant position on industrial pollution. Rejecting industry's argument that pollution control meant job loss, Sadlowski claimed, "Unions must address themselves to the fact that you can make steel and you can have clean air at the same time."[74]

It did not take long for militant workers to recognize the limitations of the "reform from within" strategy. Most challengers lost their bids to unseat long-tenured union officials, while the few who won met stiff resistance when they attempted to institute reforms. Sadlowski, for example, constantly found his efforts blocked by higher ranking executives in the Steelworkers Union during his term as district director. Thus, workers committed to a more radical approach saw no other alternative than to take independent action. If the union refused to take advantage of OSHA or to confront U.S. Steel on health and safety matters, they would take matters into their own hands. Outside the mills, blue-collar families responded in similar fashion to the union's dwindling support for environmental protection. In the late 1960s, for the first time, working-class residents formed citizen organizations with explicit political aims, among them, the improvement of environmental conditions in blue-collar neighborhoods. The new environmental organizations, operating both in the mills and in the community, shared a common belief that working-class interests could best be served by adopting a more confrontational posture toward industry, a posture that the union had long abandoned.

Disgruntled steelworkers launched a more aggressive campaign to improve occupational health conditions inside the mills by circumventing the union and collaborating with a group of local scientists. Bill Walden, an industrial chemist, initiated the loose alliance when he offered the services of his pollution research organization to factory workers. A year earlier, Walden had set up a nonprofit pollution research laboratory along with another chemist, a veterinarian, and two biology students. The initial function of the laboratory was to provide ordinary citizens with the means for testing bacterial levels in water. Walden also began receiving many requests to examine the contents of factory discharges. While researching these industrial pollutants, he became convinced that workers inside the plants were suffering from high exposure to dangerous chemicals and fumes. Perhaps, he reasoned, his services could be put to better use in helping to improve the environmental plight of industrial workers. With this goal in mind, Walden formed the Calumet Environmental and Occupational Health Committee (CEOHC) in 1972. First, Walden and his associates contacted union officials throughout northwest Indiana, offering assistance in assessing health hazards and filing OSHA complaints. After top-ranking labor leaders responded coolly, CEOHC emissaries approached rank-and-file workers.[75]

In Gary, it was the latter group that responded most enthusiastically to Walden's offer. CEOHC selected Gary Works as one of its initial targets; as the largest steel mill in the region, it was an obvious choice. But the team of scientists made little headway with the union. Harry Piasecki, president of the Gary Works local, rebuffed the group. Walden sensed that Piasecki, along with other local union officials, resented a group of outsiders telling them how they ought to be handling health and safety matters. Thus, he took his proposal to informal caucuses that were overtly hostile to the entrenched union leadership. The steelworkers who participated in these dissident caucuses, younger and better educated than the average laborer, reflected the changing work requirements of steel manufacturing. As the steel firm relied more heavily on automated machinery in the 1960s, management sought workers with sharp minds rather than strong backs. Many of these newer recruits, eager for information about health hazards inside the mills and reluctant to defer to older union leaders, seized the opportunity to chart an independent course and welcomed CEOHC's assistance.[76]

Through education programs and direct prodding, CEOHC inspired a more aggressive response to occupational health hazards in Gary's steel mills. Walden recalled that to many steelworkers, smoke was merely smoke, not something worthy of apprehension. Through leaflet distributions at the factory gate and appearances before small gatherings of concerned workers, CEOHC alerted steelworkers to the dangers that threatened them. Once enlightened, workers began applying for CEOHC's technical assistance. In U.S. Steel's pickling plant, for instance, workers complained of exposure to toxic ammonium chloride fumes. The company contended, however, that workers faced no risks, supporting its claim with air quality measurements. Following CEOHC's instructions, workers conducted their own tests and found evidence to the contrary; ammonium chloride levels were dangerously high. Later that year, CEOHC encouraged workers to file OSHA complaints themselves if the union leadership refused to take the initiative. CEOHC understood that the mere passage of OSHA did not guarantee improved plant conditions. With limited funds and personnel, the federal agency rarely acted unless prodded by workers. CEOHC pressured federal inspectors to maintain close attention to problems in the Gary area.[77]

By the end of 1972, CEOHC had established enough contacts in the steel mills to assemble like-minded union dissidents in a worker-dominated organization, Workers for Democracy. Among the founding members were Ray Quillen and Don Paulk, the disgruntled unionists who quit their grievance positions to join the new group. Modeled after Miners for Democracy, the thirty-member steelworker group assumed responsibility for the aggressive pursuit of improved factory conditions, continuing to file OSHA reports independently of union leadership. In December Workers for Democracy requested OSHA inspections of the coke oven batteries, blast furnaces, sintering plant, and 210-inch plate mill at Gary Works. A federal investigator arrived in Gary in February and discovered a particularly dangerous situation in the coke plant, where workers inhaled levels of coal tar fumes far above legal limits. OSHA issued citations and mandated that U.S. Steel rectify the situation within one year. Pressing the matter further, Workers for Democracy sued U.S. Steel for excessive pollution, taking advantage of provisions in the Clean Air Act that permitted citizen lawsuits. At the same time, the insurgent steelworker group submitted a set of demands regarding coke oven controls to the steel companies and the U.S. Environmental Protection Agency (EPA). In the short term, it insisted on some of the same reforms that the union had urged, for instance, distributing hazardous work among more laborers so as to reduce the damage inflicted on each individual. But its list of demands also went on to include the replacement of faulty oven doors, the use of clean water for quenching hot metals and coal, continuous medical surveillance of workers, and procedural changes in the baking of coke.[78]

Workers for Democracy provided an outlet for steelworkers frustrated with the union's inertia. Its members made no secret of their opposition to the union hierarchy; many also joined Ed Sadlowski's rank-and-file rebellion against the entrenched leadership. Moreover, these angry steelworkers did not hesitate to use the new organization as a vehicle to attack high-ranking labor officials. When Mike Olzanski, an Inland Steel employee, spoke at a public meeting on air pollution compliance schedules in Gary in 1973, he chided the union chiefs by remarking, "We pay our union ten dollars a month in dues to protect our interests, but I don't see any local union representatives or district representatives down here today to speak to this issue that's of great importance to us." Olzanski then proceeded to criticize the Experimental Negotiating Agreement on the grounds that it prohibited workers from striking over local health and safety conditions. In this way, Olzanski effectively linked labor's indifference toward occupational health with its policy of accommodation toward corporate management.[79] In line with this reasoning, Workers for Democracy soon extended its critique to the hierarchical structure of the Steelworkers Union, consistently citing the no-strike pledge as evidence that the union had lost touch with rank-and-file workers.[80]

While Workers for Democracy compensated for union inertia on occupational health matters to some extent, a variety of sporting and outdoors clubs filled the vacuum created by organized labor's withdrawal from environmental politics in the community. Industrial infringements on fishing were particularly effective in igniting environmental activism among Gary's blue-collar citizens. Although the number of anglers enjoying area lakes, rivers, and streams had gradually increased throughout the postwar years, Indiana's lake-stocking program, which introduced coho salmon and steelhead trout into Lake Michigan in 1964, stimulated an unprecedented fishing frenzy. Suddenly, the lake teemed with game fish; for the first time in the century, the catch of prime game fish increased. But anxiety accompanied the euphoria as sportsmen worried that persistent industrial pollution from steel mills and power plants would eventually offset any gains brought about by the state's lake-stocking program. Apprehensive fishermen swelled the ranks of sportsmen's associations, transforming them from innocuous social clubs into political pressure groups. Winzell Stocker, president of the Lake County Fish and Game Association, recalled that the infusion of salmon into Lake Michigan was "like a stick of dynamite" as far as his organization was concerned. Whereas members had once gathered to reminisce about their fishing and hunting adventures, they now turned their attention to politics, protesting new construction along the waterfront, lobbying local, state, and federal legislators for stricter water pollution regulations, and conducting their own investigations of water quality in the region.[81] The Glen Park chapter of the Izaak Walton League, which boasted a high percentage of steelworkers, experienced a similar transformation. When the federal government convened its annual Lake Michigan conference in 1967, the Glen Park "Ikes" submitted testimony calling for regulations that would sustain aquatic life not only in the lake but in the Grand Calumet River as well.[82]

In the early 1970s, the working-class passion for fishing drew anglers into a direct confrontation with U.S. Steel over public access to fishing piers along Lake Michigan. For years, the blue-collar residents of western Gary had tolerated U.S. Steel's virtual monopoly on lakefront property. But as fishing fever peaked around 1970, sports enthusiasts there became frustrated at being unable to fish close to their homes. For some, this frustration led to despondency. In a letter to the *Gary Post-Tribune*, one Gary woman worried about her father, who "finds that there are no areas in Gary he can go fishing to. He has a limited income and he finds himself sitting around the TV or working in the yard."[83] Other fishermen took a more active approach. In 1970 a group of citizens, mostly from western Gary and the neighboring community of Hammond, set their sights on Buffington Pier, a one-mile jetty that protruded into Lake

Michigan from U.S. Steel's cement plant. Calling themselves the Buffing-ton Pier Community Coalition, the group demanded that the steel company either lease or donate the jetty and adjacent harbor to the public. The group contended that the company rarely used the property and that the facilities would be put to better use as a fishing pier, bathing beach, and boat basin.[84] U.S. Steel and its allies in the Chamber of Commerce opposed the plan. Corporate executives argued that despite the activists' claim, the company needed the pier for freight deliveries to its cement plant. Furthermore, they maintained that the area was unsafe.[85] Unsuccessful negotiations with the steel company prodded the coalition to turn to the Gary Parks Board for help. The group urged the city to purchase the property. Despite receiving petitions with over 3,000 signatures endorsing the plan, the board refused.[86]

Although the Buffington Pier Community Coalition disbanded following the Gary Parks Board's decision, Gary residents continued their fight to reclaim industrial property at Buffington Pier and other locations along the lakefront. In 1971, for instance, a loose coalition of fishermen from northwest Indiana revived the issue, this time demanding use of the pier at the industrial port of Indiana Harbor, several miles east of Gary. Over 300 fishermen, armed with rods and reels, threatened to seize the property and stage a massive "fish-in." Local boaters promised their assistance, vowing to prevent freighters from docking at the port by forming a blockade. "If we have to," warned one Gary resident, "we should string our boats across the harbor."[87] Hoping to avoid a confrontation, Indiana's governor declared the harbor open to the public.[88] Two years later, Buffington Pier was once again the center of attention as the city council representative from western Gary introduced a resolution encouraging the mayor to open the jetty to the public, even if it meant condemning the property. The measure passed, but U.S. Steel protested vehemently and nothing came of the matter.[89] In a more successful venture, however, the Lake County Fish and Game Association convinced NIPSCO, which owned land adjacent to U.S. Steel, to allow public fishing from its lakefront property in 1975.[90]

Of all the environmental groups and initiatives in and around Gary, the one that most explicitly addressed environmental issues from a working-class perspective was the Calumet Community Congress. Much like Workers for Democracy, the Calumet Community Congress vaunted itself as a militant alternative to organized labor. But where Workers for Democracy operated inside the steel mills, the congress worked outside, orchestrating community groups to forge a united blue-collar front against polluting industries. Rather than emphasizing workers' common occupational background, the congress brought citizens together on the basis of a shared historical experience outside the factories, specifically immigration from Europe, aspirations of upward mobility, abandonment by organized labor, and limited political clout. Nevertheless, the congress drew on the tradition of labor militancy by pinpointing corporate exploitation as the source of workers' troubles in the community. No issue better highlighted this connection than industrial pollution.

The Calumet Community Congress originated out of the frustrations of Jim Wright, a steelworker from Gary. Like his father, who had migrated from Mexico after World War I, Wright toiled at the Inland Steel factory in East Chicago. In 1968, however, disturbed by the pessimism and hostility that pervaded the working-class communities around Gary, Wright turned his full attention to community activism. As he surveyed the attitudes among his coworkers and neighbors, Wright detected a deep sense of alienation from political life and progressive social causes. Many working-class whites, he found, blamed their troubles on the civil rights movement. Squeezed by escalating taxes and inflation, they resented the federal and local poverty programs that assisted poor African Americans but ignored blue-collar whites who experienced only slightly better living standards. Moreover, these whites feared the consequences of the black power movement, believing that any gains achieved by African Americans came at their expense, a sentiment that accounted for the large blue-collar turnout for segregationist George Wallace in the 1964 Democratic presidential primary. By 1968, following Hatcher's election, the mood among working-class whites had deteriorated further. In white working-class districts, residents wondered if they would be rendered powerless by Hatcher's election. Would they continue to receive city services? Would their neighborhoods deteriorate as a result of redirected municipal priorities? What made matters worse, as Wright saw it, was the utter indifference on the part of organized labor, particularly his union, the United Steelworkers of America. By ignoring community social problems, organized labor had abandoned its leadership role. Wright concluded that working-class whites desperately needed a positive alternative that would provide them with a sense of power while directing their racial hostilities toward more constructive ends.[91]

Because the conditions that distressed Wright were not peculiar to Gary, he was able to find inspiration and guidance from community leaders elsewhere who were grappling with the same problems. In Chicago, Pittsburgh, Newark, Baltimore, Cleveland, Philadelphia, and other industrial cities, community leaders were addressing precisely the same concern that troubled Wright—disaffection among whites who felt passed over by the civil rights movement—by forming working-class neighborhood organizations. Waving the banner of "ethnic power" as a direct counterpoint to "black power," local activists in these cities organized blue-collar families around issues of immediate concern, ranging from garbage collection to taxation, as a means of combating political alienation.[92] In the nation's capital, Monsignor Geno Baroni, an Italian immigrant miner's son, launched a national movement, establishing the Task Force on Urban Problems to monitor and coordinate the activities of disparate local groups. As for Wright, he attended training sessions with Saul Alinsky, the renowned working-class community organizer from Chicago. When he returned early in 1970, along with colleague Mike Barnes, a former Catholic seminarian, he was ready to build his own organization. Defining his mission as "an attempt to reach and to organize for fundamental and progressive social change a constituency which many have written off: white, working class, union belonging and home-owning, ethnic, often racist and Wallace voting America," Wright set out to win converts.[93]

The cast of characters embracing the concept of establishing a mass working-class organization included radicals from the labor movement as well as more mainstream community leaders. The assertive style advocated by Wright held particular appeal to individuals who came from a tradition of labor militancy and union dissidence. George Patterson, a labor veteran from the early days of organizing the steel mills, had captained a picket line during the Memorial Day massacre at Republic Steel in 1937. Ken Tucker presented more recent credentials; late in the 1960s, he had seized control of the union at Dupont Chemical in East Chicago, leading workers off the job to protest excessive pollution.

George Sullivan earned his reputation by challenging the autocratic Teamsters Union, coaxing steel haulers from the Gary area into forming an independent labor organization.[94] For Patterson, Tucker, Sullivan, and other frustrated unionists, the Calumet Community Congress not only complemented their union activities but also offered the possibility of rank-and-file empowerment that had eluded them within the labor movement. Many leading participants in the congress, however, had no background in radical movements. John Blosl from the Glen Park Izaak Walton League, Vivian Meyers, a Gary resident who helped run the Neighborhood Helping Hand Program, and other community leaders simply recognized the need for an aggressive working-class political organization. Moreover, the congress received financial assistance from local churches, largely due to the support of Bishop Andrew Grutka. Grutka, who had never before veered far from the political mainstream, had become so alarmed by the pessimistic mood that prevailed among his parishioners that he believed drastic action was necessary. Thus, an odd amalgamation of union radicals, community activists, and clergy ended up as the driving force behind Wright's Calumet Community Congress.

While assembling a leadership team, Wright searched for issues around which to organize, eventually selecting pollution as the central rallying point. Along with Barnes and a corps of ten volunteers, Wright scanned newspapers, attended church services, visited saloons, and spoke with people on street corners to identify working-class concerns. He discovered many, including high electricity rates, inadequate schools, and inequitable tax schedules. A surprising number of grievances involved environmental quality. Homeowners from Ross Township complained that their basements flooded when sewers overflowed. The dumping of acids in storm sewers elicited the wrath of Hammond, East Chicago, and Whiting citizens. Western Gary residents were disturbed about the lack of fishing piers along the lakefront. Steel mill emissions also ranked high on the list of concerns. Hence, when congress organizers prepared their ballot of resolutions for the first mass citizen meeting, over a third of the items involved pollution.[95]

The founding session on December 5, 1970, resounded with vitriolic attacks on U.S. Steel and other corporations, setting the tone for the group's subsequent actions. With more than 900 delegates in attendance, the opening meeting at George Rogers High School in Hammond attracted attention, not only in Gary but throughout the nation. Senators Edmund Muskie of Maine and Edward Kennedy of Massachusetts sent telegrams of encouragement. John Esposito, an aide to Ralph Nader, delivered a stinging keynote address in which he openly attacked U.S. Steel, urging citizens to force the company to open its books and provide data on emissions from every plant in Gary.[96] J. David Carr, superintendent of Gary Works, was understandably miffed by Esposito's comments and within a few days launched a bitter tirade against the congress. According to Carr, its leaders had communist tendencies and were "dedicated to destroying the American way of life."[97]

This exchange only served to intensify the feud between the blue-collar citizen group and the steel company. Shortly after its founding session, the congress launched a series of direct-action campaigns designed to embarrass U.S. Steel and call public attention to the company's environmental misdeeds. In an effort to humiliate corporate executives at U.S. Steel for failing to comply with pollution regulations, the congress sponsored a trip to Carr's suburban residence, where the thirty-six-member contingent demanded an audience with the steel official. Carr's wife informed the group that her husband was not at home. Undeterred, the protesters distributed leaflets picturing Carr above an inscription reading, "Wanted: Pollution Outlaw."[98] The citizen group also came to the assistance of the Buffington Pier Community Coalition, helping them in their fight to appropriate U.S. Steel property for use as public fishing piers by sending representatives to Gary Parks Board meetings and writing letters to local officials.[99] Although the congress reserved most of its antagonism for opposing the steel giant, it also dogged Gary's second largest polluter, NIPSCO. In leaflets distributed to the public, the congress blamed NIPSCO for a dangerous gas explosion in Glen Park and the deterioration of Lake Michigan due to its hot water discharges. In 1972 congress protests convinced public regulators to reduce NIPSCO's requested rate hike.[100]

Of course, not all blue-collar families embraced the anticorporate philosophy or the disruptive tactics advocated by the congress; indeed, it was internal opposition that ultimately led to the group's collapse. The militant rhetoric and tactics employed by the congress drew heavy criticism, not only from the business community but also from labor leaders and politicians who claimed to represent a more moderate work-ing-class constituency. John Krupa, chairman of the Lake County Dem-ocratic party, for example, publicly accused the congress of conspiring in a master plan for communist revolution.[101] Officials from the Steel-workers Union were less blatant in their opposition, but they quietly maligned the organization and urged workers to abandon their mem-berships.[102] Following these attacks, some church and community groups withdrew their support for the new organization and mem-bership declined. Among those who remained, a growing contingent sought to temper the group's hostile stance toward industry. Divided working-class sentiment finally ruptured the Calumet Community Con-gress in 1973 when George Sullivan, one of the group's founders, steered 180 members into a competing organization, the Calumet Ac-tion League. According to Sullivan, the congress had gone too far in at-tacking industry; his new group would concentrate on a tamer issue—political corruption. This split rendered the Calumet Community Congress ineffective, and it disbanded shortly thereafter.[103]

While it lasted, however, the Calumet Community Congress revived a spirit of working-class militancy that had been dormant since the early 1950s. Its tone was angry, its behavior was assertive, and its anticorpo-rate philosophy was radical. In many respects, the blue-collar commu-nity activists of the early 1970s were reminiscent of the steelworkers who had asserted their autonomy through wildcat strikes after World War II. Both groups protested industry's environmental practices, chal-lenging the authority of both union and management and thereby elic-iting scorn from both. Although insurgent labor groups inside the facto-ry, such as Workers for Democracy, continued the wildcatters' legacy even more directly, it was the Calumet Community Congress that most effectively rekindled working-class insurgency—and it did so by using environmental concerns as the spark.

Environmentalism emerged as the most potent rallying point for the new militancy in Gary because it enabled congress leaders to make older traditions of ethnic solidarity and labor activism relevant to problems that had grown out of more recent social trends. Participants in the con-gress referred to themselves as "white ethnics," a phrase which suggest-ed that ethnic affiliations remained a basis for social organization. How-ever, the social function of ethnicity had changed considerably since the

1940s. By 1970, the force that united Gary's "white ethnics" was more a historical experience shared by sons and daughters of immigrants than an affiliation with any European nationality. In accumulating savings from factory work, moving out of the inner city, purchasing private homes, and engaging in a culture of consumption and leisure, Gary's second- and third-generation citizens followed a path that embodied distinctive aspirations and frustrations. Thus redefined, ethnicity became the code word by which the congress spoke to a common set of working-class concerns. Similarly, the theme of corporate abuse, a major impetus behind the labor movement of the 1930s and 1940s, acquired a new twist when the Calumet Community Congress showed that corporations could frustrate workers' aspirations in the community just as easily as they could in the factory. By emphasizing the ways in which corporate environmental practices interfered with the suburban ideals and recreational interests that bonded Gary's "white ethnics" in the early 1970s, the congress transferred the locus of insurgency from the work place to the community.

As a result of its distinct social history, working-class environmentalism did not develop along identical lines as the middle-class version. Although some concerns overlapped, the two groups' environmental agendas differed with respect to priorities and emphasis. The issue of lakeshore protection provides a useful example. For middle-class activists, industrial encroachment along the Lake Michigan shoreline marred the landscape and threatened bathing beaches; for working-class activists, corporate monopoly of the lakeshore blocked access to fishing piers. Also, although people from both groups sought to reduce air pollution, middle-class environmentalists emphasized this issue much earlier. By the time blue-collar families raised the issue, many environmentalists from Miller had shifted their attention to the lakeshore. Subtle differences in philosophy also divided the two groups. Middle-class organizations, such as CARP, framed environmental problems in terms of excessive growth, whereas the Calumet Community Congress blamed exploitative corporations. Furthermore, with regard to tactics, middle-class demonstrators might hold a protest picnic in the woods, but they would never have harassed a corporate official outside his home. Hence, when blue-collar families finally became active in the environmental movement, they formed their own separate organizations. This is not to say that there was no possibility of cooperation between the two factions; as we shall see later, the two groups did coordinate their efforts on occasion. Nevertheless, efforts to create a united environmental front encountered many obstacles.

Further complicating the social dynamics of environmentalism was the role played by African Americans, who approached environmental matters from a completely different perspective than either the white middle class or the white working class. Between 1945 and 1980, African Americans came to comprise the majority of Gary's citizenry, a development that expanded their political clout commensurately. Hence, their public actions became increasingly important in determining the outcome of environmental conflicts. Moreover, although African Americans counted themselves among both the working and middle classes, pervasive racism so thoroughly influenced their relationship to their surroundings that they developed a unique perspective on issues of work place hazards, pollution, and shoreline protection.

Rats, Roaches,

and Smoke

African American

Environmentalism

When Richard Hatcher, Gary's first African American mayor, addressed a group of white environmentalists at a 1970 picnic rally for lakeshore preservation, he reminded his audience that blacks did not share their definition of ecology. For blacks, the relevant environmental issues were poor sanitation, overcrowded housing, and vermin. As Hatcher put it, "The mothers of poor babies must consider, in their planning for the night, that in their environment there are rats which may bite their children; that there are roaches which crawl over and spoil any food left unprotected."[1] Some people in the audience must have wondered at this point whether the mayor was about to launch into a stinging critique of the environmental movement for its distorted sense of priorities, a position advanced by many contemporary civil rights leaders. But this did not happen. Instead, Hatcher abruptly shifted his tone. Explicitly rejecting the dichotomy between environmental reform and social justice, the mayor reasoned that a nation wealthy enough to send spaceships to the moon surely had the resources to combat both poverty and pollution. Indeed, as he explained, the two causes were linked by a common enemy—"those technological and financial powers" that created the problems in the first place and then demonstrated little interest in solving them.

Relegated to the lowest levels of the urban-industrial hierarchy and systematically accorded lowest priority in the distribution of environmental amenities, African Americans had always understood their environmental dilemma in terms of broader structural inequalities. To most African Americans in Gary, it was painfully obvious that onerous working conditions, blighted neighborhoods, and limited access to recreational space all stemmed from blatant racial discrimination and that, furthermore, the amelioration of these conditions would require full-scale assaults on the structure and distribution of power. But to fully reclaim the city as theirs, it would not be enough to wrest power from racist labor unions, white property owners, and political machines. As Hatcher came to realize by the 1970s, social and environmental progress required a direct confrontation with corporate capital. By embedding the environmental question in a broader critique of industrial capitalism, Hatcher was able to direct the attention of blacks to some of the very same issues that were most pressing to white environmentalists—namely, air and water pollution.

If Hatcher's critique of industrial capitalism resonated in the black community, it was because the African American experience in Gary was inextricably linked to the historical dynamics of steel production. It was industrial employment that first lured African Americans to Gary in large numbers during the 1920s, a time when U.S. Steel desperately needed new sources of labor to compensate for the dwindling supply of European immigrants. For blacks mired in the poverty and exploitative sharecropping arrangements of the American South, a job in the mills was considered a golden opportunity for economic and social advancement. Hence, between 1920 and 1930, more than 15,000 migrants, most of them from Mississippi, Alabama, Tennessee, Arkansas, and Georgia, arrived in Gary to work in the mammoth lakefront factories.[2] The contraction of the industrial job market during the Great Depression slowed migration considerably during the 1930s, but in the following decade, another 20,000 African Americans came to the Steel City to fill industrial positions created by the wartime boom.[3] By the end of World War II, 6,500 African Americans worked for U.S. Steel, and according to the 1950 census, about three out of every four African American males in Gary found employment in the industrial sector.[4] The continued availability of manufacturing jobs through the 1950s and 1960s made Gary somewhat of a mecca for blacks. In 1956 *Ebony* magazine ranked Gary as the best place in the country for African Americans;[5] by 1969, Gary's blacks had a higher median income than their counterparts in any other U.S. city.[6]

Despite these relative advantages, persistent racism in Gary imposed barriers on mobility, thereby fueling an aggressive movement for social equality during the postwar years. Employed only in the most menial jobs, African Americans tended to be poorer than most whites. While more than half of all white families earned over $3,000 in 1950, only one in five black households could boast equivalent incomes.[7] As this statistic suggests, however, income differentials existed within the black community. Black steelworkers, shop owners, and teachers earned substantially more than janitors, elevator operators, and messengers, for example. But the sting of racism had no regard for class boundaries. Even when blacks managed to achieve financial security, they were denied full access to the white consumer world and community institutions. Overt racial discrimination blocked African Americans from acquiring better jobs, better housing, and better recreational opportunities. Thus, black citizens found a common purpose in fighting racial discrimination, an effort that culminated when the African American community united behind Hatcher's mayoral bid in 1967.

The condition of physical surroundings represented a component in each phase of the local civil rights movement. Organized efforts at racial advancement proceeded through distinct stages, emphasizing jobs in the 1940s, the integration of public facilities in the 1950s, and political power in the 1960s. The fight for better jobs in the steel mills incorporated a demand for more healthful working conditions, and the drive to integrate community facilities raised questions about equal access to urban space. Hence, when African Americans finally attained some measure of political power, environmental concerns became part of their public policy agenda. In this way, environmental attitudes developed alongside the evolving struggle for first-class citizenship.

The first phase of the local civil rights crusade centered on the steel mills, where the quest for higher-paying jobs dovetailed with the pursuit of a safer working environment. Although all steelworkers encountered certain environmental hazards in the work place, U.S. Steel assigned black laborers to the most dangerous jobs. African American workers routinely found themselves performing tasks that involved heavy lifting, the potential for serious injury, and exposure to grease, carcinogenic fumes, and toxic chemicals. The corporation placed most African Americans in the coke plant, by far the dirtiest section of the mill. Here, coke ovens reached temperatures of 2,000 degrees, subjecting all workers in the vicinity to scorching heat. For the millhands who toiled directly on top of the coke batteries, the insulated clothing provided by the company offered minimal relief and, thus, did little to prevent the development of circulatory problems. Dust and soot encrusted workers as they fed coal into the ovens and removed the finished product. In the handling department, the constant crushing of coal created conditions that resembled those found in a coal mine. Elsewhere, workers came into contact with dangerous acids, flammable liquids, and hot tar.[8] The cumulative effect of this rampant exposure to toxic substances was poor health. According to a 1972 medical study published in the *Journal of Occupational Medicine*, workers who toiled near coke batteries suffered unusually high rates of lung and kidney cancer.[9]

Although conclusive scientific evidence linking coke emissions to cancer did not emerge until the 1970s, laborers intuitively knew that the coke plant was unhealthy. In the 1940s and 1950s, union representatives filed many petitions and grievances protesting the searing heat in the coke plant.[10] Other formal grievances cited the unhealthy conditions produced by smoke and dust.[11] As early as 1935, thirty-seven black steelworkers, many of them from the coke plant, sued U.S. Steel on the grounds that they had contracted pneumoconiosis, silicosis, and tuberculosis as a result of smoke inhalation.[12] Throughout the mills, therefore, the coke plant had the reputation as the least desirable place to work. Laborers assigned to temporary duty there pleaded for other positions, eager to get out as quickly as possible.[13] For blacks who worked there permanently, however, leaving was usually impossible.

U.S. Steel used several techniques to prevent African American employees in the coke plant from securing transfers to other sections of the mill. A promotion system established by the company in the 1940s virtually trapped blacks in the coke plant by calculating seniority on a unit-by-unit basis. Because the coke plant constituted an independent unit, workers there could not amass seniority for jobs elsewhere in the mills. Moreover, corporate management routinely withheld information about positions available in better areas of the factory. On those rare occasions when a black worker applied for an opening elsewhere, steel bosses resorted to any number of outrageous fabrications and tricks to deny the request. Some applicants were forced to take unreasonably difficult tests, while others were simply told they did not meet the necessary skill requirements. When Joseph Pipkins put in a request for promotion to a tractor job, he was informed that he was not fit for the position on the grounds that he was mentally deranged, a charge that was refuted by the worker's personal physician.[14]

Because the jobs African Americans held were simultaneously the most unhealthful and the lowest paying, black activists viewed a degraded work environment as a component of discriminatory employment practices. In the minds of black steelworkers, poor working conditions were not just a matter of management's refusal to install fans or provide better protective clothing. Something much more insidious was at work—racism. Systematic job discrimination kept blacks shackled to those jobs that white workers did not want, either because of dangerous conditions, low pay, or both. Thus, attacking the root of the problem meant putting an end to unfair hiring and promotion policies. Above all, civil rights leaders sought to integrate those sections of the mill where pay was better and work was safer. Of course, coke plant workers pressed the company for better masks, shoes, and ventilation systems, but their overriding strategy involved the dispersing of blacks more evenly through the plant, thereby equalizing environmental burdens among all workers.

The coke plant emerged as the center of black labor activism in the years after World War II. The movement coalesced around two aggressive leaders, Moses Brown and Curtis Strong, who planned and coordinated civil rights strategy in the mills. Their main weapon was the wildcat strike. After World War II ended, high demand for steel and a tight labor market placed the company in a vulnerable position. Because U.S. Steel used gases generated in the coke plant to heat the entire mill, workers there enjoyed exceptional leverage. As Strong later recalled, "We had the company by the nuts, and we squeezed them."[15] Brown, who served as grievance committeeman for the coke plant in the 1940s, took advantage of this situation by pressuring the company to place blacks in positions previously held by whites only. When the company refused, he led coke workers off the job until management capitulated. Brown used the strike tactic frequently, up to several times a year. In addition to securing the employment of African American workers as gas tenders, Brown forced management to accept applications from black workers for jobs in the heating department, one of the few white enclaves in the coke plant. Curtis Strong, Brown's successor, carried the offensive into the 1950s. A controversial figure, Strong evoked hostility and suspicion among whites, especially those in union leadership positions. Blacks in the coke plant at Gary Works, however, showed their gratitude by consistently reelecting him as their grievance committeeman over a fourteen-year span. Strong's use of unauthorized strikes succeeded in getting blacks employed as foremen, secretaries, and, perhaps most importantly, craftsmen and maintenance workers, positions that usually involved much less exposure to hazardous conditions.[16]

Despite these incremental advancements, Strong found many of his efforts blocked, not just by corporate management but by union officials. Although white steelworkers enjoyed at least some support from their union in the effort to improve working conditions, such was not the case for black steelworkers. Despite presenting a progressive public image on racial issues, the union was an accomplice to the company in its policy of confining African Americans to the least desirable jobs. Many workers received their jobs through union recommendations, and the union office was a conduit of information about new openings and transfer opportunities. Yet when black workers sought the assistance of union representatives, they were customarily told that no jobs were available. Moreover, white union officers blocked Strong's efforts by failing to process grievances and withholding technical expertise.[17]

Thus, in the early 1950s, Strong and other black activists in the mills decided to wage an internal war against the United Steelworkers of America. Marshaling their electoral resources behind designated candidates for local and national leadership positions, they gradually increased black representation in the upper echelons of the union hierarchy. In this way, they were able to force the union to make civil rights reform a priority. The strategy produced some notable gains; through the efforts of a civil rights committee, black workers for the first time gained entrance to higher-paying, less dangerous jobs in the western sections of the steel mills.[18]

Still, U.S. Steel's discriminatory seniority system impeded the advancement of blacks already employed in hazardous parts of the mill. Hence, in the 1970s, activists in the steel mills sought to reform the promotion system. Because U.S. Steel used the same methods to calculate seniority in all of its plants, African American workers developed a national strategy. Taking their case to the courts, black workers across the country sued both U.S. Steel and the Steelworkers Union for supporting a racist promotion system. The legal strategy succeeded; in 1974 the three parties signed a consent decree establishing new promotion guidelines. From then on, seniority was calculated according to time spent with the company rather than in a particular unit.[19]

Through wildcat strikes, union politics, and legal battles, black activists chipped away at obstacles to equal employment opportunities in the steel mills. As a result, black workers became more evenly distributed throughout the mills than they were in 1945. Yet the consequences of racism were not easily eliminated. Although some workers took advantage of the 1974 consent decree, for example, progress was slow. According to one unofficial estimate, as of 1978, African Americans still comprised 90 percent of the coke plant workforce while only a few blacks found employment in areas with the best working conditions: the tin mill, the electro-galvanizing department, and the central maintenance shops.[20] Despite notable advancements in the postwar decades, black workers performed a disproportionate share of steel production's dirtiest and unhealthiest chores through the 1970s.

Outside the steel mills, African American activists sought better clerical and white-collar job opportunities as alternatives to hazardous industrial work. In the years immediately following World War II, African Americans who could not find work in the mills had to settle for low-paying menial jobs. The nonindustrial employment profile of residents in predominantly black census tracts in 1950 suggests that African *difference in race/gender

Americans were concentrated in the service sector.[21] Black males might find work as janitors, dishwashers, or hospital orderlies, but most businesses refused to hire them as clerks or salespersons. Black women, often in need of employment to help support their families, rarely found jobs except as domestic servants.[22] Although the Gary City Council passed an antidiscrimination employment bill in 1950, the commission charged with enforcing the law lacked subpoena power and proved reluctant to impose fines on violators.[23] Hence, civil rights activists opted for a more direct approach. The Gary Urban League took on the mission of securing white-collar employment for African Americans during the 1950s and 1960s by initiating a series of informal negotiations with local business leaders, including representatives from U.S. Steel. In 1951 the league persuaded steel company management to employ its first African American secretary. Six years later, after persistent prodding by the league, U.S. Steel hired its first black foreman.[24] The Urban League also entered into negotiations with beverage companies and local retailers to hire blacks as drivers and sales clerks.[25] While the Urban League was twisting arms behind closed doors, a protest group called the Fair Share Organization relied on more combative tactics to pressure downtown retailers to hire more black salespersons. The group, brandishing its slogan "Don't spend your money where you can't work," organized successful consumer boycotts of establishments that refused to hire blacks, including several grocery stores, a windshield wiper factory, a bank, and a clothing store.[26] The cumulative effect of negotiations and boycotts was a gradual erosion of overt discrimination in white-collar hiring. Yet as late as 1980, seven out of ten African American workers still confronted the choice of either hazardous factory work, meager-paying service jobs, or unemployment.[27]

Just as African Americans interpreted a hazardous working environment as a symptom of employment discrimination, so did they view their environmental predicament outside the work place as a product of racism. Especially after 1950, the demand for full and equal access to urban environmental resources became a prominent component of the civil rights crusade in Gary. In part, this second phase of the civil rights struggle was an outgrowth of the battle for fair employment inside the mills. With somewhat better job opportunities and higher incomes, African American families set their sights on those consumer and environmental amenities that defined the middle-class life-style in the postwar United States. In the process, however, they came up squarely against an urban spatial order that was rigidly segregated along racial lines. Constructed by whites who sought to use the practice of racial exclusion to assert social superiority, this system effectively blocked access to certain beaches, parks, and neighborhoods. For African Americans, then, social mobility was very much a matter of reclaiming control over the urban environment.

The campaign to eliminate the racial segregation of urban space saw black citizens transfer a tradition of militancy from the work place to the community at large.[28] This is not to deny that Gary's activists drew inspiration and borrowed strategy from the civil rights crusade that was sweeping the American South at the time. Gary citizens were well aware of the drive to integrate public facilities in the South; stories about sit-ins, boycotts, and marches filled the pages of Gary's black newspapers. When Martin Luther King, Jr., scheduled a visit to Gary in 1959, 5,000 people gathered to hear him speak, although flight delays due to bad weather caused King to cancel the engagement at the last minute. The next day, however, King met with a much smaller group of activists at Junior's Snack Shop in Midtown.[29] Faced with many of the same problems that confronted blacks in the South, Gary citizens looked to King for guidance. Yet the direct-action tactics advocated by King were quite familiar to black labor activists, some of whom attempted to transfer such techniques to community battles well before King electrified the nation in the mid-1950s. Although ministers and teachers played an important role in Gary's civil rights crusade, as they did elsewhere, so did steelworkers. Curtis Strong, for example, was active in the National Association for the Advancement of Colored People (NAACP), and for much of the 1960s, Jeanette Strong, his wife, served as president of the organization. The confrontational tactics used by local activists—pickets, marches, and boycotts—had as much to do with the infusion of steelworkers into mainstream civil rights organizations in the 1950s as it did with developments in the American South.[30]

Indeed, labor activists played a prominent role in the first postwar effort to open access to public recreational facilities in Gary. Midtown, the neighborhood where almost the entire black population resided, had a severe shortage of open recreational space. The two parks in the neighborhood were small and poorly maintained. Making the matter worse, other city parks were in essence off-limits to Gary's black citizens.[31] Few parks were guarded more vigilantly than Marquette Park, which contained the city's so-called "public" beach. Through intimidation and violence, whites secured exclusive enjoyment of Gary's sand and surf. City government contributed to segregation at the beach by denying black citizens police protection. Indeed, the police routinely drove African Americans from the beach under the pretense that their presence endangered public safety.[32] In order to find a safe haven along the lake, African Americans had to travel over twenty miles to either Chicago or Michigan City, a situation they found intolerable.[33]

It was within this context that a multiracial group of about 100 citizens, many of them active in the labor movement, agitated for open access to Marquette Park in the summer of 1949. Calling themselves the Young Citizens for Beachhead Democracy, the group held a rally in front of city hall and then drove to Marquette Park to "seize" the beach. As the caravan of automobiles entered the suburban community of Miller, the protesters encountered an angry band of whites armed with bats, clubs, and iron pipes. Pelting the cars with rocks, the white mob tried to turn back the demonstrators, but the caravan continued to the beach. Shortly after the civil rights protesters spread blankets, hung banners, and planted an American flag in the sand, police officers approached the group. The law enforcement officials ordered the protesters to leave the park under the pretense that the beach was closed for the day. Obediently, the group packed its belongings and left. To ensure that word of their protest spread quickly, the demonstrators printed leaflets about their excursion and distributed them in front of the steel mill gates.[34]

Although the seizure of the beach generated significant publicity, much of it was negative; indeed, opposition from mainstream civil rights leaders ultimately undermined the campaign. The Gary NAACP found the demonstrators to be unnecessarily militant, condemning the strategy of taking the beach "by force." According to Edna Morris, president of the local NAACP chapter, the protest was unwarranted because the park was never legally closed to blacks.[35] The Anselm Forum, a discussion group of prominent citizens that met regularly to promote racial harmony, rejected invitations to participate in the event on the grounds that revolutionaries had masterminded the event.[36] In a similar vein, the

Midtown Youth Council charged that the rally was "inspired by the pinkos and radicals solely for the purpose of creating dissention."[37] Faced with conflicting community opinion, even within the black community, city officials felt no compulsion to address the problem.

Within a few years, however, city hall was no longer able to ignore the problem since the campaign to integrate Marquette Park now enjoyed the solid backing of civil rights groups. Several developments contributed to this shift. As of 1949, steelworkers had not yet infiltrated civil rights groups in large numbers. By the mid-1950s, however, they formed a dominant voting block in the NAACP.[38] At the same time, several black ministers became convinced of the need for more aggressive action. Through the Interdenominational Ministerial Alliance, these clergymen used their prestige in the community to mobilize citizens in civil rights protests. Finally, the Gary Urban League, which had previously devoted its energies to securing white-collar employment for blacks, decided that the time had come to wrestle with discrimination in the community. In 1953 all three organizations turned their full attention to the situation at Marquette Park.

On a hot summer day in July of that year, two carloads of young black women from the NAACP journeyed to Marquette Park for an outing. Unbeknownst to them, a gang of white youths vandalized their automobiles while they sat on the beach enjoying the afternoon. When they returned to the parking lot, they found the gang waiting for them. A teenaged boy slapped one of the women in the face, while another threatened to "knock the ladies' teeth down their throat." Just as the thugs prepared to overturn one of the automobiles, a police patrol car pulled into the parking lot. The officers dispersed the crowd, allowing the women safe passage back home. To the dismay of the women, however, the police refused to make arrests. Civil rights leaders seized upon this incident, demanding a commitment from the city government to protect black beachgoers. Peter Mandich, Gary's mayor, assured them that in the future, the city would provide adequate police protection. Civil rights leaders, therefore, decided to test the mayor's sincerity. Two weeks later, black representatives from the Gary Urban League and the Interdenominational Ministerial Alliance visited Marquette Park. There was no trouble. Members of the NAACP beach committee organized outings to the beach throughout the summer, and the mayor continued to keep his word. Although some of the black groups encountered hostility, no serious violence erupted. For the moment, civil rights groups claimed victory.[39]

The success of the 1953 campaign turned out to be ephemeral. As the spotlight faded from Marquette Park, so did the police. Whites once again began harassing blacks at the park, and blacks no longer felt secure visiting the beach.[40] But it was not until 1961 that another ugly incident on the beach jolted the civil rights movement back into action. On Memorial Day, a group of whites attacked a black man and beat him severely while a city police officer stood nearby and watched.[41] Astounded, black civil rights leaders insisted on a response from the mayor. Five hundred African American citizens jammed the city council chambers on June 6 to press the local government to do something. Richard Hatcher, then an attorney for the NAACP, demanded a public statement deploring the incident, an investigation of the policeman's actions, the appointment of an African American to the Police Civil Service Commission, and the integration of police squads assigned to Marquette Park. The mayor refused these demands, merely urging patience.[42]

It was not until the late 1960s, after Hatcher's election as mayor, that African Americans felt safe visiting Gary's beaches. Even then, they used the lakefront cautiously, adopting patterns of beach use that minimized conflict. Since whites monopolized beaches during the daytime, blacks planned to enjoy their lakeside recreation in the evenings and at night. Instead of camping at Marquette Park, African Americans frequented the smaller, less populated Lake Street beach further west. Instead of scattering at different locations along the lakefront, they congregated at Lake Street so that they could amass sufficient numbers to ward off hostile whites.[43] Through the 1970s, Marquette Park and beaches further east continued to breed racial hostilities.[44]

A long history of exclusion from Marquette Park certainly gave African Americans a unique perspective on the issue of lakefront preservation. For the most part, black citizens demonstrated indifference to environmental battles to protect the shoreline from industrial development. In the early 1970s, when the shore preservation movement reached its height, African Americans were only beginning to use the beaches. A few saw this newfound ability as a reason to support the environmentalists.[45] Most African Americans, however, lacked the necessary sense of entitlement to the shoreline to become overly concerned about the prospect of industrial encroachment. Denied the use of public beaches, most African Americans were not willing to devote their energies to protecting them. Indeed, some African Americans opposed attempts to improve Marquette Park's recreational facilities in the 1960s and 1970s, arguing that the money would be unfairly spent on the rich.[46]

Whereas the campaign to integrate Marquette Park provided a dramatic focus for efforts to reclaim the urban environment, attempts to achieve more pleasant residential quarters proved far more complex and ultimately produced less satisfactory results. In the years immediately following World War II, black citizens of Gary found themselves firmly trapped within the confines of a segregated housing market. As of 1950, 97 percent of Gary's African American population lived within the two-square-mile area known as Midtown.[47] Originally, Midtown sprang up on the city's southern fringe, well beyond the sturdy homes that U.S. Steel built for its managers and skilled workers. The company absolved itself of responsibility for the flimsy shacks and tenements that developers erected to house unskilled immigrants and later on southern blacks. By World War II, most of Midtown's white residents had moved elsewhere, while deliberate discrimination prevented blacks from doing the same. Realtors refused to show blacks homes in other neighborhoods; city authorities rejected African American applications for public housing projects located outside the Midtown ghetto.[48]

Midtown underwent rapid physical deterioration in the decades following World War II. One consequence of residential confinement was severe overcrowding. Between 1950 and 1960, Midtown's population swelled from 38,000 to 62,000. Housing construction, however, did not keep pace; the number of new dwelling units rose by a meager 33 percent.[49] Overcrowding, in turn, strained the neighborhood's physical resources. Garbage piled in the streets and alleys; rats proliferated in abandoned cars and vacant lots; wear and tear took its toll on the housing stock. According to the 1960 census, one in five homes lacked adequate plumbing facilities. But overcrowding was not the only factor responsible for this environmental deterioration. Local political leaders adopted a policy of neglect, offering little assistance and permitting serious housing code violations. Banks were equally culpable, frequently denying requests for home improvement loans.[50]

In addition to a crumbling infrastructure, Midtown residents had to contend with escalating levels of industrial air emissions during the postwar years. Situated in the geographic center of Gary, Midtown by no means experienced the highest levels of air pollution in the city. The neighborhood was sufficiently close to the steel mills, however, so that the stenches of coke and cooked metal frequently permeated the air. As resident Jim Holland recalled, Midtown inhabitants engaged in a daily ritual of wiping industrial soot from their window ledges each morning.[51]

Although Midtown residents did what they could to stem the tide of environmental decay through occasional cleanup drives and yard beautification competitions, many simply wished to move elsewhere.[52] Especially as black workers earned higher incomes, a private home away from the congestion of Midtown became more alluring. Through the 1950s and 1960s, many black families managed to accumulate sufficient funds to purchase private homes outside of Midtown. Moreover, more housing was becoming available in the surrounding neighborhoods as whites moved to outlying suburbs. Civil rights leaders realized that in order for black families to take advantage of these opportunities, the city would have to outlaw discriminatory real estate practices. A fair housing law did not come easily, however. It took over three years and the coordinated efforts of more than twenty civil rights organizations to convince the city council to pass a civil rights bill in 1965 that included a fair housing provision.[53]

Although the civil rights bill eliminated the most flagrant forms of housing discrimination, it by no means permitted free access to all of Gary's neighborhoods. In some sections of the city, whites fled in large numbers, thereby opening new housing opportunities for aspiring black homeowners. But in other neighborhoods, white resistance hardened and blacks found it as difficult as ever to make inroads. Despite a fair housing code, African Americans still found themselves in direct competition with white residents for limited environmental amenities. As a general rule, white homeowners were determined to preserve their monopoly over the most desirable residential properties. In a city where the absence of industrial features constituted one of the most precious environmental resources, this meant that blacks who wished to move out of Midtown had to settle for housing in some of Gary's most polluted neighborhoods.

Few players had a greater interest in perpetuating a racially divided housing market than real estate firms. Hence, it was largely through the machinations of avaricious realtors that a new social arrangement of residential space emerged in the 1950s and 1960s. As African Americans grew more impatient for better housing, realtors realized they could gain huge profits by exploiting racial tensions. Through a technique known as blockbusting, they scared whites into selling their homes en masse, thereby opening up housing for blacks. Blockbusters initiated their scam by purchasing a home on an all-white block and encouraging a black family to buy it. Next, they contacted the other families on the block and warned them that blacks were about to "invade" the area, which the blockbusters claimed would ruin the neighborhood and depress property values. Realtors urged neighbors to sell immediately, before disaster struck. In many areas of the city, residents succumbed to the blockbusters' threats and sold their homes quickly and cheaply. Realtors then resold the homes at much higher prices to blacks desperate for housing.[54] Through this process, selected areas changed rapidly from white to black, block by block.

The first neighborhood to experience such a rapid transition was Tolleston, located just west of Midtown (see map 4). As population pressure mounted in Midtown during the 1950s, ghetto boundaries pushed into the neighboring community. Between 1945 and 1960, the percentage of blacks residing in Tolleston increased from under 2 percent to 10 percent. Sensing a trend, whites began to offer resistance, and Tolleston suddenly became the scene of racial hostilities. Some homeowners inserted restrictive clauses in their property deeds, forbidding sale to African Americans. Many of those who planned to move pledged their allegiance to an all-white community by planting signs on their lawn reading, "For Whites Only."[55] But realtors had other plans. Making their rounds among the older residents each evening, agents warned homeowners that blacks were moving into the neighborhood and that plummeting real estate values would render their property worthless. The message was clear: sell immediately.[56] Ultimately, most whites took heed, selling their homes as quickly as possible, regardless of the buyer's color. In south Tolleston, where most blacks settled, the white population plunged from 4,769 in 1950 to 1,843 in 1960. By 1980, only 235 whites remained in the entire neighborhood, as compared to a white population of 8,418 thirty years earlier. Once the transition of Tolleston was under way, blockbusters used similar tactics in western Gary and the areas surrounding downtown. In so doing, they instigated a dramatic transformation in the racial composition of Gary's residential neighborhoods. By 1980, 75 percent of Gary's African Americans lived in areas that were once solidly white (see table 5.1). Once restricted to Midtown, African Americans now enjoyed the freedom to live in different sections of the city (see table 5.2).

That freedom did not extend to all parts of Gary, however; black families found it much easier to move into polluted neighborhoods than into clean ones. Ultimately, the ability of African Americans to purchase private houses outside of Midtown depended on the willingness of white residents to sell their homes.[57] Despite the prodding of blockbusters, whites refused to vacate areas that were relatively free from industrial pollution. In Miller, for instance, residents foiled blockbuster efforts by banning the display of "For Sale" signs on homeowners' lawns. Whites in Glen Park used cruder methods, relying on outright intimidation to keep blacks north of the Little Calumet River. Hence, property changed hands slowly in these two areas. Along Gary's western border, on the other hand, upwardly mobile whites were eager to leave the asphalt, carbon black, and slag-processing factories that spewed soot and dust into their backyards. Whereas western Gary was inhabited almost exclusively by whites in 1950, they counted for less than 6 percent of the area's population in 1980. Emissions from the steel mills had a similar effect along Gary's northern tier, where the white population dwindled from 23,000 to 1,700 in the two decades following 1960.[58]

As blacks moved into these vacant homes, they faced higher levels of air pollution than they had encountered in Midtown. Attracted by a quiet neighborhood and affordable homes, many middle-income blacks moved into the Ambridge section of northwest Gary in the early 1970s. What they had not counted on was the unbearable stench from the nearby sewage treatment plant.[59] Recent arrivals to the Emerson district, located just east of downtown, also received a surprise when they examined the exterior surfaces of their homes on May 7, 1972. On that day, unusually high levels of hydrogen sulfide emissions from U.S. Steel's coke plant had reacted with lead-based paint to produce black and

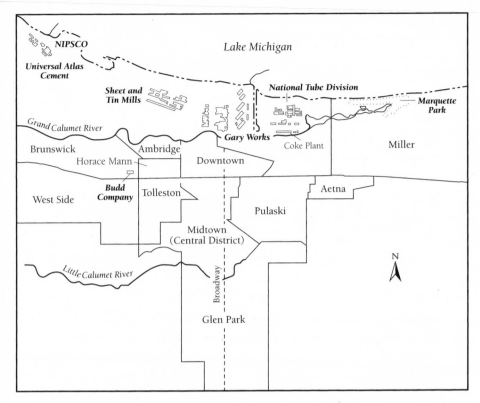

Map 4. Gary Neighborhoods, 1960

brown stains on the house exteriors.[60] In this same neighborhood, some citizens worried about the health effects of such severe pollution. Mary, a twenty-four-year-old mother, worried about her son's health because the ever-present soot in the air made it hard for him to breathe.[61] For these African Americans, along with many others, better housing came at the price of dirty air.

Even the acquisition of better housing often proved to be an ephemeral achievement. Upon gaining access to previously forbidden communities, African Americans discovered that those areas suddenly became subject to deliberate neglect. African American newcomers to Tolleston, for instance, noticed that their arrival coincided with a marked reduction in garbage collection and street cleaning. Anticipating deteriorating conditions, absentee landlords stopped making repairs and private lenders stopped granting home improvement loans in neighborhoods that experienced significant African American in-migration. Of course,

Table 5.1. Percentage of Black Population Residing in Midtown, 1950–1980
(Census Tracts 14, 16, 20, 21, 22, 23)

	Percentage of black population
1950	97
1960	82
1970	49
1980	25

Sources: U.S. Bureau of the Census, *Seventeenth Census of the United States, 1950, Census Tracts*, 65–67, *Eighteenth Census of the United States, 1960, Census Tracts*, 15–17, *Nineteenth Census of the United States, 1970, Population and Housing, Census Tracts*, pp. P-2–P-4, and *Twentieth Census of the United States, 1980, Census Tracts*, pp. P-35, P-36.

their predictions were self-fulfilling. Since blacks were denied the resources to maintain them, their homes, many of which were old and on the verge of collapse to begin with, rapidly succumbed to physical decay. Before long, the blighted conditions characteristic of Midtown followed African Americans not only to Tolleston but to the northern and western sections of the city as well.[62]

The uneven record of social progress in the 1950s and 1960s convinced many African Americans that only a full-scale assault on the local political structure would enable them to fully control their destiny as citizens of Gary. Continued discrimination in public housing, city employment, and municipal services made it apparent that their electoral contribution to the Democratic party, no matter how generous earned them inadequate rewards. Moreover, they still found themselves the losers in the competition for environmental amenities. It was thus with a great sense of hope that African Americans rallied behind the candidacy of Richard Hatcher in his bid for mayor in 1967. With black voters enjoying a numerical majority in the city for the first time, Hatcher barely edged out the incumbent, A. Martin Katz, in the Democratic primary. The massive defection of virtually the entire white electorate to the Republican party in the general election underscored the high stakes involved.

For those expecting a quick fix, however, the first years of the Hatcher administration were undoubtedly disappointing. Despite enacting a

Table 5.2. Census Tracts outside Midtown with Over 50 Percent Black Population, 1950–1980

	1950	1960	1970	1980
		19 (Tolleston)	19	19
			5 (North Side)	5
			6 (West Side)	6
			15 (North Side)	15
			17 (North Side)	17
			18 (North Side)	18
				1 (Miller)
				2 (Miller)
				3 (North Side)
				4 (North Side)
				7 (North Side)
				8 (North Side)
				9 (North Side)
				10 (Northeast)
				11 (Northeast)
				12 (Northeast)
				24 (Glen Park)
				25 (Glen Park)
Totals	0	1	6	18

Sources: U.S. Bureau of the Census, *Seventeenth Census of the United States, 1950, Census Tracts*, 65–67, *Eighteenth Census of the United States, 1960, Census Tracts*, 15–17, *Nineteenth Census of the United States, 1970, Population and Housing, Census Tracts*, pp. P-2–P-4, and *Twentieth Census of the United States, 1980, Census Tracts*, pp. P-35, P-36.

host of new programs and a revamped set of governmental priorities, Hatcher failed to bring about full social or environmental equality. Indeed, by the early 1970s, Hatcher had come to reassess the depth of the problem, a process that sharpened his critique of corporate capital. It was in this context that Hatcher redefined the African American environmental agenda by bringing issues of industrial pollution to the forefront of public attention.

Long before he became mayor, Hatcher recognized that a blighted environment degraded the quality of life for African Americans. Growing up during the depression in nearby Michigan City, Hatcher experienced the environmental hardships that afflicted poor, urban blacks. Slaughterhouse stenches permeated the unpaved streets that ran through his neighborhood. He remembered living in a house where wide cracks in the walls allowed snowfall to blanket his bed during winter storms. When Hatcher moved to Gary as a young attorney in 1959, he discovered similar conditions in the Midtown ghetto. Here residents lived in surroundings that most people "wouldn't allow dogs to live in," Hatcher recalled. Although the physical manifestations of poverty left an indelible imprint on Hatcher's environmental consciousness, he also developed new concerns, among them, air pollution. While serving on the Gary City Council during the mid-1960s, Hatcher came across a study detecting an unusually high level of respiratory disorders in Gary. The report convinced him that factory discharges constituted a public health threat for residents near the steel mills, including most of the city's black population.[63] Hence, Hatcher became one of the staunchest advocates of tough antipollution laws on the city council. For the remainder of his political career, the conditions of slum life and public health would underpin Hatcher's environmental objectives.

During his first few years as mayor, however, Hatcher accorded industrial pollution lower priority than more blatant aspects of racial discrimination. Defining his political mission in terms of the historical struggle for racial advancement, Hatcher ran for mayor making no secret of his primary concern: improving the social and economic status of Gary's blacks. On the campaign stump, the candidate promised to employ more blacks in local government, provide more job opportunities, and improve ghetto housing. And these were precisely the issues he attended to once in office. When the mayor summed up the accomplishments of his first year in office in an article published in *Ebony* magazine, he highlighted the federal funds he had procured for low-income housing construction and job-training programs.[64] Through 1969, Hatcher's environmental program reflected his commitment to improving the plight of poor, inner-city African Americans. Almost immediately upon assuming office, the mayor improved sanitation services and invigorated housing code enforcement in Midtown. In his second year as chief executive, Hatcher introduced a plan for a series of small "vest pocket" parks in Midtown to replace dreary concrete with greenery.[65] Industrial pollution, however, received scant attention. In spite of occasional remarks about the need for vigorous enforcement of pollution regulations, Hatcher's record on reducing industrial waste emissions was unexceptional.

Around 1970, however, a variety of factors catapulted industrial pollution toward the top of the mayor's agenda. By this time, many of his social programs were in place, thereby affording him the luxury of moving on to other problems. Given his record on the city council, it was quite logical to expect the mayor to devote more attention to Gary's pollution menace. Moreover, progress on the civil rights front had altered blacks' relationship with the environment in ways that made industrial pollution a more pressing matter. Not only were more blacks living in the city's most polluted districts, but also some were using Marquette Park beach for the first time. By 1970, a few African Americans even managed to purchase homes in selected areas of Miller.[66] Hence, pollution control and preservation of the lakefront were no longer irrelevant to African Americans. Ultimately, however, Hatcher's sudden preoccupation with industrial despoliation of the environment can only be understood in the context of his evolving political philosophy, particularly his increasing disenchantment with U.S. Steel and his growing conviction that big business was responsible for many of the troubles that plagued not only African Americans but the entire city of Gary.

Recalling his early years as mayor, Hatcher confessed a naïveté in dealing with U.S. Steel. From the start, he had understood that the company represented an obstacle to social progress due to its discriminatory hiring policies and its disregard for community welfare. He sincerely believed, however, that by raising these issues publicly and negotiating with steel management he could swing the company around. At first, this strategy appeared effective. During his first year in office, Hatcher persuaded the company to waive its high school diploma requirement for new employees, thereby making it easier for Gary's most disadvantaged citizens to find jobs. Shortly thereafter, the steel company pledged $10 million for a low-income housing project.[67] Hatcher was unsuccessful in acquiring further gains from U.S. Steel executives, however, and he increasingly found his social programs blocked by the company. The nub of the matter was taxes. As the city's largest taxpayer, U.S. Steel balked at an any social program that required public expenditures. On one occasion, a Gary Works superintendent candidly remarked to Hatcher, "We're willing to work with you on anything as long as it doesn't take taxes."[68] Unfortunately, many housing, education, and anti-poverty programs required public funds, and therefore the mayor and U.S. Steel increasingly found themselves at loggerheads. Moreover, U.S. Steel often worked behind the scenes, using its influence in the state legislature to deny Gary's local government bonding authority for various urban revitalization projects. Faced with an intransigent corporation, Hatcher decided to take the offensive.

Initially, the main issue of contention between the mayor and the steel company was not the environment but corporate taxes. As early as 1967, Hatcher pledged to raise corporate taxes on the grounds that U.S. Steel property was grossly underassessed. Midway through his first year in office, Hatcher demanded an inspection of U.S. Steel's financial record, a move designed to prod the company into negotiations. A series of meetings between city officials and steel executives accomplished nothing, however. Hatcher then issued the company an ultimatum to hand over its property records by October 1, 1968. The company refused, sued the city, and won a restraining order. Shortly thereafter, a frustrated Hatcher hinted that the city would initiate a lawsuit against the company. He decided, however, that the city could ill afford the expense of a lengthy legal battle and thereafter resorted to scathing public remarks about U.S. Steel's preferential tax treatment and more behind-the-scenes negotiations with company officials. In the end, the city obtained a slightly more equitable financial arrangement with U.S. Steel.[69]

While the tax issue simmered, Hatcher turned to industrial pollution, which fit just as neatly into his evolving anticorporate framework. In the fall of 1970, Hatcher showcased his new environmental program by calling on U.S. Steel to slow production during temperature inversions, create a steel reclamation facility, and provide a rapid transport system for its workers.[70] Through a series of critical appointments, Hatcher invigorated the administrative agencies responsible for enforcing the city's pollution regulations. First, the mayor hired Joel Johnson, a Nigerian-born chemist, to head the Air Pollution Control Division. Johnson was no firebrand; at times, he expressed a reluctance to damage the city's relationship with the business community. Nevertheless, the new chief believed that Gary's air pollution control program needed strengthening. Several months after assuming his position in the spring of 1970, Johnson roused U.S. Steel's ire by closing a loophole in the smoke ordinance that had exempted coke ovens from regulation. Herschel Bornstein, who became Hatcher's new health commissioner in 1971, was far more pugnacious. Motivated by having witnessed his father's bout with lung ailments and having observed the scarred lungs of patients while practicing medicine in Gary, Bornstein made air quality his top priority. Thriving on confrontation, Bornstein stirred controversy with his surprise inspections of local factories.[71] Finally, Hatcher altered the character of the business-oriented Air Pollution Advisory Board by stacking it with dedicated environmentalists.[72] These personnel changes had a decisive impact on the tenor of pollution regulation. Previously, the city had devoted much of its energy to policing the practices of small businesses such as steel scrap firms and junkyards, preferring to enter into negotiations with the larger companies.[73] Now the city stalked bigger game, including U.S. Steel.

In extending the critique of corporate exploitation to pollution, Hatcher deliberately kindled a new environmental consciousness among African Americans. Prior to 1970, no black leader in Gary had emphasized air quality. To most African Americans, pollution was a white issue; it had little to do with them. Hatcher attempted to shatter this notion. At public appearances and press conferences, the mayor hammered away at the same theme: industrial emissions damaged the health of Gary's black residents, making pollution a black issue.[74] In national forums, the message was the same. When Gary hosted the 1972 National Black Political Convention, Hatcher warned the prestigious gathering of black activists to avoid any political entanglements involving alliances with giant corporations that exploited workers, cheated on taxes, and poisoned the environment.[75] In Gary, some African Americans heard the message. When *Info*, a newspaper that served Gary's African American community, surveyed its readers in 1972, pollution control made the list of top concerns, although it ranked somewhat lower than drugs and crime.[76] Furthermore, although African Americans did not build any permanent grass-roots environmental organizations during the 1970s, they advanced their new environmental objectives through existing community structures.

In a section of western Gary called Ivanhoe Gardens, residents took on an asphalt manufacturer in the early 1970s. The manufacturer, Bucko Construction, had operated in this area since World War II.

Through the 1940s and 1950s, the neighborhood surrounding the plant was predominantly white. During the late 1960s, the racial composition changed as whites departed and blacks, mostly from Midtown, moved into the small, low-rent homes just across the railroad tracks from the Bucko plant. Although the firm had installed some dust-collecting devices, the new residents complained that emissions from the factory clouded the air and made them ill. For Lillie Numley, who suffered from tuberculosis, the situation was especially dangerous because the smoky air made breathing difficult. In August 1972, Sammie Locke, the local precinct committee representative, circulated a petition among the angry citizens demanding that the Gary Air Pollution Control Division take care of the matter. Within a year, residents of Ivanhoe Gardens breathed a little easier after the city persuaded Bucko Construction to overhaul its pollution control system.[77]

In Midtown, African Americans used the Model Cities Residents Committee to press for tougher pollution regulations. One of many Great Society programs established by Lyndon Johnson's administration in the 1960s, the Model Cities program helped residents in depressed urban areas plan for the social, economic, and physical improvement of their neighborhoods. One of Hatcher's major accomplishments was securing over $13 million from the federal government for a Model Cities program that would serve Midtown and the adjacent neighborhood to the north, which had recently been populated by many impoverished African Americans. Given the mission of enhancing their surroundings, members of the Model Cities Residents Committee organized tree-planting campaigns, abandoned-car removals, and litter collection drives. The committee also defined air pollution as a blighting influence and a threat to public health. Among committee members' stated goals was a provision to reduce air pollution in their neighborhood by 50 percent.[78]

Hatcher's crusade against industrial pollution struck a chord in the African American community because his anticorporate framework fit squarely within the tradition of Gary's civil rights struggle. For thirty years, civil rights activists had targeted local corporations for their discriminatory hiring practices. Hence, there was already the sense in the black community that firms such as U.S. Steel were oppressive. Moreover, blacks had little difficulty transferring these hostilities to issues of community exploitation because the civil rights movement, far more than the labor movement, already combined community and work place in a comprehensive critique of power relations in urban society.[79] Racism pervaded both settings. Indeed, the activists who led the struggle for better jobs also orchestrated campaigns for integrated parks, schools, and neighborhoods. By raising the pollution issue, and for that matter, the tax issue, Hatcher merely added more fuel to an already smoldering fire.

Most importantly, Hatcher's war against corporate polluters signaled a convergence of environmental agendas; for the first time, members representing each of Gary's most salient social groupings—middle-class whites, working-class whites, and African Americans—had placed pollution reform near the top of their list of priorities. Of course, just as many white citizens rejected environmentalism, not all African Americans embraced the cause of clean air and water. For example, editorials in the *Gary Crusader*, one of the city's black newspapers, continued to condemn environmentalists for crippling economic production, thereby placing jobs at risk.[80] However, at least during the early 1970s, such charges were seldom leveled by African Americans in Gary. The sheer weight of Hatcher's influence in the black community would have crushed any incipient environmental opposition movement. Thus, even if some blacks remained indifferent, few were about to challenge the mayor by downgrading the problem of industrial pollution. Furthermore, for those African Americans already inclined toward mainstream environmentalism—either because of high exposure to pollutants or deep animosity toward the steel company—Hatcher's public positioning not only sanctioned grass-roots activism but paved the way for a multiclass and multiracial environmental coalition.

The Rise and Fall

of an Environmental

Coalition

As the Gary City Council met on the evening of December 15, 1970, to consider an amendment to the municipal air pollution ordinance, 350 angry citizens jammed the legislative chambers. The legislation in question was a bill that would for the first time force U.S. Steel to curb air emissions from its coking ovens. The audience, composed of African Americans from inner-city ghettos, affluent white suburbanites from Miller, and blue-collar families from working-class neighborhoods, represented a cross section of Gary's population. Public testimony favored the amendment overwhelmingly. A representative from the Calumet Community Congress scolded the steel company for considering itself outside of the law. Using more subdued rhetoric, Helen Hoock, president of Community Action to Reverse Pollution (CARP), assured legislators that no citizens would lose their jobs on account of pollution control. Mayor Richard Hatcher also put in an appearance, chiding the steel company for its "thinly veiled blackmail threats that the corporation might have to close down the mills if it is compelled to clean up its mess." The only person offering testimony against the bill was Edward Logelin, a U.S. Steel vice president. At one point, Logelin made the mistake of posing the rhetorical question, "Is this action of sufficient importance to warrant the imposition of an insurmountable technological and economic burden on much needed steel production?" In unison, the crowd thundered, "Yes!" Impressed by the breadth of popular support for the bill, the city council passed the measure unanimously.[1] In this battle over coke oven emissions, the people of Gary transcended divisions of race and class to stand together against corporate pollution and power. In so doing, they implicitly rejected the liberal approach to environmental reform that had prevailed for much of the 1950s and 1960s.

Already by 1970, a sizable proportion of Gary's citizenry had expressed disenchantment with the liberal arrangements that had invested private industry with so much power in the community during the postwar years. White middle-class activists from Miller had learned that mild pollution control measures, secured with the cooperation of business leaders, did little to protect their suburban havens from corporate capital's expansionary impulses. At the same time, many working-class whites found themselves strangled by a highly centralized collective bargaining process that failed to confront management on a number of issues, including environmental quality. Among African Americans, the limitations of liberal reform were even more apparent, ultimately inciting challenges to corporate management, organized labor, and the local Democratic party machine. By articulating a critique of U.S. Steel that incorporated its environmental abuses, Hatcher played a critical role in steering African American concerns into line with the concerns of many disaffected whites. It was this convergence of agendas that enabled farsighted civic leaders, including Hatcher, to construct a multiracial and multiclass environmental coalition around the issue of coke oven pollution. Following different historical trajectories, then, diverse members of Gary's community came to link environmental damage with a critique of liberal reform, thereby setting the stage for the most sustained assault on corporate power in the entire postwar period.

Although Gary's environmental activists had good reason to rejoice in their victory over the steel giant in the city council chambers in December 1970, industrial capital demonstrated that it was not prepared to relinquish its environmental prerogatives without a fight. If disgruntled citizens willingly abandoned the liberal compacts that previously undergirded environmental policy, industrialists would show even greater resolve in rejecting the tacit accords by resorting to the crudest displays of intimidation. Assisted by a sudden downturn in the local economy, industrial leaders launched a vicious counteroffensive that reestablished the primacy of race and class by exploiting citizens' economic vulnerabilities. In this way, the environmental contests of the early 1970s demonstrated in blatant fashion the extent to which industrial capital would use its power over people to preserve its control over nature.

The formation of a multiclass and multiracial environmental coalition was remarkable given the severe social tensions that pervaded Gary in the late 1960s and early 1970s. Hatcher's election had polarized the city. Gary's white citizens, most of whom had voted against Hatcher, reacted to the election with a mixture of anger and fear. Many worried that emboldened African Americans would suddenly invade their neighborhoods and suburban enclaves. Unfairly associating Hatcher with more militant black power advocates like H. Rap Brown and Stokely Carmichael, others predicted a breakdown of law and order. During the mayoral race, the incumbent candidate, A. Martin Katz, fueled such notions, warning voters that if Hatcher won, blood would flow in the streets.[2] Hence, when Midtown residents torched three buildings and looted several department stores just months after Hatcher assumed office, some interpreted the incident as a confirmation of their worst fears.[3] Thousands of white residents left Gary altogether over the next several years. In Glen Park, this separatist impulse took the extreme form of a campaign to secede from the city of Gary, a scheme that ultimately failed. Among those who remained, the prevalent feeling was that African Americans had become far too assertive, a conviction that translated into hardened resistance toward Hatcher and his administration. Expressing exasperation with his white opponents in 1969, the mayor commented, "They wouldn't be pacified if I walked down Broadway on my hands."[4]

If fear and anxiety made whites reticent about joining hands with African Americans, the sentiment among blacks was no more conducive to collaboration. In electing Hatcher, African Americans deliberately severed their unproductive alliances with white politicians. When whites attempted to block the mayor's programs, blacks became even more resentful. Interpreting attacks on Hatcher as an affront to the entire African American community, black citizens rallied in defense of the new mayor. As one Hatcher supporter reminded a group of local legislators who attempted to reduce the mayor's appointive powers shortly after the election, "We're going to back Mayor Hatcher from here to hell to eternity."[5] Moreover, the confidence inspired by Hatcher's triumph encouraged African Americans to press their claims more aggressively, even if it meant clashing openly with their white opponents. Protesting the persistence of racial segregation in the city schools, a group of students persuaded 20,000 black youngsters to boycott classes during the third week of May in 1968. When the student leaders learned that a group of white parents from Miller intended to march on city hall in opposition to the boycott, they planned to meet the marchers downtown. Only a last-minute intervention by the mayor convinced the students to call off this potentially explosive confrontation.[6] Amid this atmosphere of mutual suspicion and hostility, blacks and whites were reluctant to collaborate on any political matter, including the environment.

Although the expansion of a national consumer culture in the decades following World War II as well as recent united efforts to defeat Hatcher blurred class differences among whites somewhat, relations between working-class and middle-class families remained strained. With their lakefront homes and white-collar jobs, middle-class residents of Miller lived and worked far apart from the world of union halls, steelmaking furnaces, and the small bungalows that housed industrial laborers and their families in communities such as Aetna and Glen Park. Moreover, the two groups did not entirely trust one another. In particular, middle-class citizens were wary of the Calumet Community Congress, with its leftist philosophy and its militant tactics. Charges of communist influence in the congress's leadership alarmed white-collar suburbanites. Even Miller's environmental activists, who tended to support progressive causes, deliberately distanced themselves from the blue-collar organization.[7]

More than any other individual, Mayor Hatcher was responsible for steering like-minded community leaders into a coordinated popular revolt that targeted industry's environmental abuses. Although Hatcher's priorities remained with Gary's African American community, he also worried about the deteriorating state of race relations and saw in the pollution issue a means of deflecting popular hostilities toward more constructive ends. Following a barrage of reports about violent crime in African American districts, Hatcher lashed out at the press by asking rhetorically, "Why don't the major news media in Gary subject their readers to an incessant exposure of the most damaging criminal activity in all of Lake County, that of U.S. Steel, that giant industry which wrecks the health of the people by belching out smoke containing two pounds of particulate matter per Gary citizen per day?"[8] In this way, Hatcher hoped to emphasize that industrial capital, not any particular race, was responsible for Gary's misfortunes.

Recognizing that pollution was one of the few issues that could bridge the divide between hostile social factions, Hatcher cultivated ties with both working-class and middle-class environmental activists. The mayor was aware that most individuals at the forefront of the environmental movement were among the most progressive-minded members of the white community; he was convinced, for instance, that the leaders of CARP, the Miller environmental group, were sensitive to the problems of African Americans. Helen Hoock, the group's president, had chaired the League of Women Voters' Civil Rights Committee, while several other members were active in the Indiana Civil Liberties Union. A few had even worked on Hatcher's mayoral campaign, gaining for him a smattering of white support. For their part, the Miller activists desperately needed the mayor's support to block the construction of a power plant along the Lake Michigan shore, thereby providing the basis for regular correspondence and a series of meetings between the two parties.[9] Although the Calumet Community Congress came under attack in the black press for being a separatist organization, Hatcher gave his nod of approval to the group after the working-class activists persuaded him that the formation of an all-white organization was merely the first step in a process that would culminate in multiracial cooperation. Thus, in highlighting the pollution issue and opening lines of communication among various environmental groups, Hatcher hoped to advance one of his own causes, divert public attention from racial bitterness, and maintain some political support in the white community.

While Hatcher served as the focal point for multiclass and multiracial cooperation, the task of coordinating the activities of the disparate groups fell to a group of War on Poverty volunteers working under the auspices of the Volunteers in Service to America (VISTA) program. Hatcher proved enormously successful at bringing a variety of federal poverty programs to Gary, among them VISTA, which assigned young men and women from around the country to community projects in urban ghettos. Between 1968 and 1971, the predominantly white VISTA staffers in Gary aided poor black neighborhoods by establishing a recreational center, organizing a food cooperative, administering a breakfast program, and encouraging parents to become more involved with local schools. Because they lived in Midtown and interacted with residents there daily, VISTA workers were among the few whites who earned the trust of African Americans. During their stay in Gary, several VISTA workers developed a concern for the environment, and on their own time, they participated in the Calumet Community Congress and became friendly with some of the Miller activists. Thus, they moved comfortably among Gary's various white and black communities. Two VISTA volunteers in particular, Phil Starr and Robert Baer, decided to incorporate their environmental interests into their work. With Hatcher's assistance, Starr and Baer enlisted the participation of African American youths in a citywide recycling program for household trash.[10]

The issue that ultimately brought blacks and whites together in a united endeavor was coke oven pollution. During the late 1960s, U.S. Steel converted over 5 million tons of coal into coke each year. In the process, 40,000 tons of carbon particles drifted into the atmosphere, along with smaller amounts of hydrocarbons, carbon monoxide, and hydrogen sulfide.[11] Whenever winds blew in from the lake, they carried these discharges across the eastern portion of the city, damaging property and threatening public health. Dense smoke from the plant obscured visibility on the nearby interstate highway, causing traffic accidents, while toxic fumes made breathing hazardous and tarnished house exteriors.[12] Local physicians observed that Gary residents suffered from abnormally high levels of carbon accumulation in their lungs, thus heightening the risk of cancer, emphysema, and bronchitis.[13] Despite the damage they caused, these emissions were entirely legal because, at U.S. Steel's behest, Gary's 1962 pollution ordinance exempted coke oven emissions. At the time, the company argued that the technology needed to control such emissions did not exist, a position it continued to uphold.

Joel Johnson, Hatcher's recently appointed air pollution chief, was skeptical. In his view, there was no reason why coke ovens should not be subjected to the same laws as other industrial processes. During the late 1960s, several members of the Air Pollution Advisory Board raised the question of controlling coke oven emissions, only to be told by steel company representatives that nothing could be done. When Johnson began to attend these meetings in 1970, he too inquired about new technologies for reducing coke oven smoke. Not satisfied with the patented response, Johnson approached the mayor with the idea of removing the coke oven exemption from the air pollution ordinance. Hatcher approved the plan, and in August Johnson introduced legislation to the city council.[14]

U.S. Steel was not about to give in without a fight, however. Through the 1960s, steel officials had cooperated with local pollution regulators in formulating environmental policy and devising compliance schedules. In exchange for its cooperation, the company received lenient treatment. In the view of steel company executives, the coke oven proposal represented a breach of the tacit agreement. This time the corporation would make no attempt to negotiate a mutually acceptable solution. Instead, it adopted a hard line, maintaining that control of coke oven pollution was impossible. In a sharply worded letter to Johnson, J. David Carr, superintendent of Gary Works, warned that passage of the coke oven amendment would "terminate coke making operations within the City of Gary." In testimony before the city council in September, Carr reiterated his threat, reminding legislators that many jobs were at stake.[15]

Unsure of the sincerity of the company's claims, the city council tabled the bill for three months, providing local environmentalists with the time to mount a citizen lobbying campaign. The first group to seize upon the issue was CARP. Upon hearing Johnson's proposal, Miller's environmental activists suspended their battle against the lakeshore power plant to focus their energies on the coke oven problem. Although several hundred acres of woodland buffered Miller from the steel mills, the coke plant, located toward the eastern end of U.S. Steel's property, was the closest source of air pollution. Riding westerly winds, fumes and smoke rose from the ovens and wafted into the affluent lakefront neighborhood, especially during winter and spring.[16] CARP objected to coke plant pollution on a number of grounds: it threatened health, reduced property values, increased the costs of home maintenance, and degraded the landscape to the point that citizens became depressed. U.S. Steel's intransigent behavior convinced the group that the proposed amendment was the only solution to the problem.[17]

The Miller environmentalists realized that in order to persuade the city council to pass the amendment they would have to refute U.S. Steel's arguments. Immediately, they began researching the company's claim that no technology existed to reduce coke emissions. CARP members scoured the technical literature and consulted with chemists, engineers, and union officials. They discovered that U.S. Steel was wrong; methods existed to reduce coke oven smoke.[18] Several companies were experimenting with new devices to capture smoke pouring from coke batteries, including one that dumped coal into the ovens through a completely sealed chute. Furthermore, they found that simple housekeeping improvements—such as sealing cracks on oven doors, replacing oven lids immediately after loading coal, and insulating coal storage sheds—could reduce emissions considerably. Another technique involved eliminating the "green push," a procedure whereby the company speeded the coal-baking process for the sake of higher production. CARP researchers learned that incomplete cooking increased the amount of unfused coke particles released into the atmosphere. By merely keeping coal in the ovens until it was fully baked, the company could cut down drastically on fugitive air emissions.[19] Equipped with an arsenal of engineering reports, technical articles, and expert testimony, CARP representatives submitted their findings to the Hatcher administration, city council representatives, and the local media.

Logical arguments meant little without evidence of strong citizen support for the amendment, however, so the Miller activists sought statements of support from community groups and civic leaders. CARP members had little trouble lining up endorsements from their friends in the League of Women Voters, the Miller Exchange Club, and the Save the Dunes Council. But they encountered much more difficulty locating support outside Miller, support they desperately needed to sway vacillating council representatives from African American and white working-class districts. At first, contacts with working-class groups produced meager results. The major unions showed little interest. Orval Kincaid, subdistrict director of the Steelworkers Union, promised to circulate petitions, but once they were out of CARP's hands, the group never saw them again. CARP received a more positive response from the Buffington Pier Community Coalition, the working-class organization fighting for fishing rights on U.S. Steel property. But it was not until the Calumet Community Congress agreed to back the cause that local legislators became convinced that white working-class citizens were solidly behind the amendment. Congress organizers realized that the issue fit perfectly with their anticorporate environmental theme, so shortly after the first mass meeting, they convened an emergency senate to pledge their support for the cause.[20] Within a week, congress volunteers collected 2,500 signatures to demonstrate the extent of working-class support.[21] The group also staged several publicity stunts, including a trip to the suburban home of steel company executive, J. David Carr, where congress members passed out bags of dust from the coke plant to bystanders so that his neighbors "could reap the same benefits of U.S. Steel's pollution as do the people of the Gary area."[22]

Garnering popular support in the African American community was more problematic since neither the Calumet Community Congress nor CARP had developed working relationships with any black organizations. In this regard, VISTA workers proved themselves invaluable. Attuned to rising alarm about industrial pollution in the African American community, VISTA workers, particularly Starr and Baer, were convinced that they could bring poor, inner-city blacks into the movement. Armed with Hatcher's endorsement, Starr, Baer, and a few colleagues canvassed public housing projects, telephoned civil rights leaders, and wrote to black community clubs, ultimately securing endorsements from the National Association for the Advancement of Colored People (NAACP), the Tolleston Community Council, and Metro Corps, a War on Poverty organization.[23] Jean Thurman, an African American social worker, sent letters to black representatives on the city council, reminding them that for inner-city residents, air quality ranked alongside poverty, delinquency, and urban blight as a serious problem.[24] Perhaps the most positive response among African Americans came from a youth gang known as the Kangaroos. Ever since Hatcher had employed black gang members in his mayoral campaign, offering political activity as a constructive alternative to delinquency, Gary's youth gangs had demonstrated an interest in local politics. Fiercely loyal to Hatcher, gang members occasionally appeared at city council meetings to voice their support for the mayor's programs. Starr and Baer had also become friendly with some members of the Kangaroos who frequented the settlement house where they worked. Worried about the health effects of coke plant emissions, the gang members were easily convinced to join the crusade against the steel company.[25]

Thus, when it came time for the big showdown at city hall, the coalition was well prepared to demonstrate widespread community support. The lineup of speakers on behalf of the amendment was lengthy and diverse. Although several weeks earlier the chances for the bill's passage had seemed uncertain at best, all nine members of the city council voted in favor of coke emission controls. The campaign to arouse public indignation toward the steel company and to unleash citizen pressure on local legislators had succeeded.

The steel company, however, still held more cards up its sleeve, bogging the matter down in the courts, which required the dogged persistence of environmentalists and the Hatcher administration. Under the provisions of the local ordinance, the steel company had the right to appeal the city council decision, an opportunity U.S. Steel seized immediately. The mayor appointed a three-person appeals board, chaired by Milton Roth, who had initiated the movement for a smoke abatement law in the 1950s. Here the battle was played out once more; the steel company held its line that technological limitations prevented compliance with the new regulations, while citizen groups and city attorneys argued otherwise. CARP submitted a brief explaining that U.S. Steel could reduce emissions without applying new technology by sealing cracks in oven doors, baking coal for longer durations, and quenching hot coke with clean water.[26] The board agreed, ruling against the company in August 1971.[27] Still determined to avoid the regulations, U.S. Steel sued the city of Gary, claiming that the Air Pollution Appeal Board lacked legal authority. Once again, U.S. Steel lost its case. In his decision, handed down in May 1972, Superior Court judge James Richards gave the company five years to achieve full compliance with the coke oven amendment.[28] For the moment, the steel giant surrendered. The following month, U.S. Steel promised to retire two old coke batteries, renovate five others, and build a state-of-the-art smokeless coke oven.[29]

By 1973, the city of Gary had secured the support of the federal government in its effort to keep U.S. Steel in compliance with the coke oven regulations. Responding to the nationwide clamor for improved air quality, the U.S. Congress amended the Clean Air Act in 1970 to establish limitations on the concentrations of six atmospheric pollutants, including particulate matter. Charged with executing this law, the U.S. Environmental Protection Agency (EPA) required all states to submit implementation plans for achieving compliance. Generally, the EPA left enforcement to state and local agencies, intervening only when necessary.[30] The severity of steel mill pollution combined with U.S. Steel's nationwide reputation for evading regulations, however, prompted EPA officials to play a more aggressive role in Gary. Hoping to make an example of U.S. Steel, the agency targeted the company for enforcement in the early 1970s. At a public address in 1973, David Kee, EPA's chief enforcement official, declared, "The EPA's number one air pollution control priority is northwest Indiana."[31] The corporation dreaded entanglements with the EPA, with its corps of well-trained lawyers and its authority to levy hefty fines. The Gary Air Pollution Control Division used the threat of EPA involvement to its advantage during negotiations with the steel executives in 1972 and 1973, pressuring the firm to adopt a new pollution abatement schedule that moved up the deadline for coke oven pollution control two years.[32]

The confrontation with U.S. Steel over coke oven emissions forced the issues of manufacturing procedures and technology into the realm of public debate. Prior air pollution regulations had set permissible emission levels and left the precise means of attainment to the corporation. The coke oven affair demonstrated that by 1970 citizens no longer accepted the corporation's authority to decide what was technologically feasible. Although city officials and environmentalists conceded that full compliance with the new law would have to wait until U.S. Steel had time to install sophisticated pollution control devices, they insisted that the company take specific interim steps to reduce emissions: sealing cracks on oven doors, replacing oven lids immediately after charging, and using only the cleanest furnaces at times of lowered production. Other demands required more substantial changes in the production process, including the elimination of the "green push" and a reduction in the quantity of coal baked during each cycle.[33] When Judge James Richards upheld the coke oven law in May 1972, he incorporated these procedures in his decision.[34] By the mid-1970s, U.S. Steel management had acquiesced; the company rebuilt oven doors, improved furnace maintenance, and required workers to observe proper coking times.[35]

The federal government's role notwithstanding, local environmentalists owed their success in the coke oven campaign to the novel social alignment embodied in the 1970 citizen coalition. At a time of severe social turmoil, a common environmental predicament and shared resentment of U.S. Steel transcended the fears and animosities that otherwise separated people. Individuals and groups that often stood on opposite sides of public issues now joined forces. For the first time in a long while, a substantial number of black citizens collaborated with white environmentalists. Hence, the list of groups in support of the measure contained some odd bedfellows; the NAACP and the AFDC (Aid to Families with Dependent Children) Mothers Organization worked alongside the Dune Homemakers Club and the League of Women Voters.[36] Furthermore, although the vast outpouring of community support for coke oven regulation was not soon replicated, the spirit of multiclass and multiracial cooperation spilled over to several other environmental issues in the early 1970s. For example, Miller environmentalists attended several Model Cities Residents Committee sessions to enlist support for lakeshore protection. Responding favorably, Model Cities members twisted arms on the city council to secure a resolution opposing further industrial development along the Lake Michigan shore.[37] Meanwhile, Helen Hoock, president of CARP, returned a favor to the working-class anglers in the Buffington Pier Community Coalition by writing protest letters to U.S. Steel executives, exhorting them to allow public fishing on one of the company's jetties.[38]

The environmental coalition was a product of an unusual convergence of circumstances, some peculiar to Gary, others unique to the period around 1970. The coke oven confrontation occurred in the midst of a national assault on large corporations led by Ralph Nader. During the late 1960s, Nader had galvanized public opinion against big business with his crusade against unsafe consumer products. By the end of the decade, the renowned consumer activist was taking corporations to task for fouling the nation's air and water. Indeed, in a 1970 Chicago address, Nader singled out U.S. Steel's operation in Gary for admonishment. "What right has this company," asked Nader, "to contaminate this city, damage homes, depreciate property, and injure health?"[39] Hence, the broader political climate buttressed aggressive citizen initiatives against seemingly omnipotent industrial giants. Perhaps in a city characterized by greater economic diversity, no single firm could have aroused the level of community wrath that U.S. Steel evoked in Gary. Certainly, U.S. Steel's rigid posture—its refusal to compromise and its insistence on fighting to the bitter end—did little to defuse the tense atmosphere surrounding the controversy.[40] Equally important, a healthy economic climate gave citizens the courage to stand up to the company's threats about worker layoffs.

Such was not the case several years later when a downturn in steel production sent the local economy into a tailspin. A series of national recessions throughout the 1970s struck the steel industry hard. Despite efforts to diversify the city's manufacturing base over the previous twenty-five years, the local economy still depended on the fortunes of U.S. Steel. When hard times hit the steel company, massive layoffs sent waves of economic destruction through the city. The first recession arrived during the summer of 1971. Steel mill employment fell by 30 percent, idling thousands of workers. Mayor Hatcher scrambled to acquire more federal funds to offset widespread joblessness, with some success.[41] But the city was less fortunate two years later when an international energy crisis followed the Nixon administration's decision to eliminate many urban social programs. Nixon's block grant scheme redirected federal aid from antipoverty ventures to a wide variety of projects selected by state governments, and Gary lost several housing and employment programs as a result.[42] When an Arab oil embargo crippled steel production in the fall of 1973, the federal government no longer provided a safety cushion. As Gary's unemployment rate rose to over 10 percent by 1975, local businesses felt the pinch.[43] In 1969, when the economy was still vibrant, civic leaders had optimistically planned the revitalization of the downtown district, designating funds for street improvements, store-front canopies, and additional parking facilities. The cornerstone of the project was a fourteen-story Holiday Inn, suitable for conventions and tourists.[44] In 1975, the hotel shut down. Many downtown merchants shared the same fate, transforming Broadway from a bustling retail center into a row of boarded-up storefronts.[45] By the end of the decade, in the wake of yet another oil crisis, unemployment crept up further, to 14 percent of the workforce.[46]

U.S. Steel used the economic setback to its advantage, dividing supporters of environmental reform. With increasing frequency, the company threatened to close down parts of its operations and lay off workers if pressed too aggressively on pollution control. When the city considered taking legal action against the corporation for failing to meet its 1973 deadline for pollution control at the cement plant, U.S. Steel announced it would stop making cement. A company spokesman placed the responsibility for the loss of 700 jobs on the shoulders of city officials.[47] Two years later, the steel manufacturer threatened to fire 200 workers if federal authorities attempted to enforce a deadline for cleaning coke plant emissions. In a statement to the press, Edgar Speer, chairman of U.S. Steel, accused the EPA of insensitivity to steelworkers, the company, and the city of Gary.[48] When the corporation opened Gary Works to tourists for a special bicentennial celebration, Speer took the opportunity to remind his guests that the costs of pollution control would be incurred by "people who want to work—but can't."[49]

By threatening to eliminate jobs, corporate capital effectively exploited the vulnerabilities of those at the lower end of Gary's social hierarchy for the purpose of maintaining the company's environmental hegemony. Although the company had issued similar threats in the past, a sluggish economy imbued them with far more bite in the mid-1970s. As economic security once again became the overriding concern for many Gary citizens, few were willing to take unnecessary financial risks. Hence, those who felt most vulnerable to job loss—blacks and lower-income whites—withdrew their support for stringent environmental controls. Only affluent professionals from Miller, at least one step removed from the steel economy, could afford to maintain constant pressure on industry without fear of immediate retribution. Local political leaders, including Hatcher, found it increasingly difficult to take a strong stand against industry when public support for environmental reform came from only one neighborhood and one sector of the population.

Industry's success in shattering the environmental coalition was demonstrated most clearly in 1974 when the EPA attempted to shut down U.S. Steel's open-hearth furnaces. In an earlier agreement with local, state, and federal authorities, U.S. Steel had vowed to replace its open-hearth furnaces with cleaner basic-oxygen furnaces by January 1, 1975. As the deadline approached, however, the corporation demanded an extension, threatening to terminate its open-hearth furnace operations entirely and dismiss 2,500 workers if the authorities refused. Suddenly, individuals and organizations that had previously refrained from active involvement in pollution matters clamored for the mayor's attention. Harry Piasecki, president of the Steelworkers Union local, met with Hatcher, begging him to keep the mills open. William Todd, vice president of both the NAACP and the Steelworkers Union at Gary Works, echoed this plea in yet another meeting with the city's chief executive. The Gary Urban League even formed an emergency committee expressly for the purpose of persuading state and local officials to grant U.S. Steel an extension. Alone on the opposite side of the fence, Miller activists argued that the furnaces should be closed as scheduled. Lobbied intensively by labor, civil rights leaders, and environmental groups, Hatcher retreated from his uncompromising environmental stance and attempted to occupy a middle ground. He supported a six-month extension with the stipulation that U.S. Steel pay a hefty fine.[50]

Faced with conflicting pressures, the city council also retreated from its proenvironment posture in the mid-1970s. When local legislators considered a bill to stiffen sulfur dioxide regulations and to mandate the use of low sulfur coal in industrial operations in 1972, the Northwest Indiana Public Service Company (NIPSCO), the primary contributor to sulfur dioxide pollution in Gary, contended that such a law would double consumers' electricity bills. Apparently convinced of the economic argument, the council rejected the bill, passing a much weaker law instead.[51] Shortly thereafter, Thomas Crump, an African American city council representative, urged the Gary Air Pollution Control Division to adopt a more lenient approach toward industry. Crump argued, "NIPSCO is in the process of building a generating plant in Kankakee because the situation prevented them from doing it here. . . . We have a problem with businesses leaving now. U.S. Steel and other companies are now diverting orders to other plants."[52] When the federal government pressed Gary to update its air quality code in 1975, council officials subjected the EPA to a tongue-lashing. Eugene Kirtland, the representative from white, working-class Glen Park, accused the agency of being overzealous and contributing to inflation. Cleo Wesson, the representative from Midtown, concurred with Kirtland, as did a third council member elected at-large. On this particular occasion, five other legislators outvoted the antienvironmentalists.[53] Even when local officials held the line against industrial pollution, however, strict air pollution regulations no longer elicited the unanimous support they received in 1970. Increasingly, the mayor, city council, and local regulatory officials relaxed their war against industrial pollution.

One casualty of the environmental retreat was the city's Air Pollution Control Division. Once known for its aggressive pursuit of environmental outlaws, the agency had become so ineffectual as a result of cutbacks in personnel and resources that the state stripped it of its administrative authority in 1975. In a review of the department's performance the previous year, two state inspectors were disturbed to find that industrial emission readings were not being taken properly and that violators were not being prosecuted.[54] As Indiana's chief air pollution official recalled the situation, "U.S. Steel was creating many problems and the Air Pollution Division wasn't getting the job done."[55] Thus, using its powers of intercession, the state took charge of virtually all day-to-day operations of the division in Gary.

At the same time, EPA administrators were convinced that heavy-handed corporate pressure was hindering the performance of state regulators as well. Indeed, federal officials accused the state of blocking their own enforcement initiatives by working out private deals with pollution offenders. Under federal law, the state agency had every right to do this, leaving more vigilant EPA officials with no recourse.[56]

By the end of the decade, however, the same economic and political pressures that constrained enforcement at the state and local levels also began to weaken federal pollution control efforts. Between 1973 and 1977, the EPA had launched a series of lawsuits against U.S. Steel for violating national air and water quality standards, thereby compensating to some degree for the lax enforcement on the part of state and local officials.[57] But within a few years, the federal government also retreated to a far more lenient position on pollution control. Not just in Gary and Indiana, but throughout the nation, corporate capital used the stagnant economy to weaken the reform impulse and win concessions from government. Pressure from organized labor to protect jobs and high inflation rates convinced the Carter administration to consider the financial costs of regulation when pursuing environmental criminals. The Reagan administration demonstrated even more responsiveness to the costs incurred by businesses subjected to environmental controls. In particular, sympathy for the ailing steel industry prompted the federal government to pass the 1981 Steel Industry Compliance Extension Act, which allowed steel companies to defer pollution control expenditures for three years. By the 1980s, then, the steel industry encountered little governmental pressure to further reduce air pollution.[58]

The rapid retrenchment on pollution reform, a direct consequence of environmentalism's narrowing social base, highlighted the tremendous power of industry to exert its control over society and the political process. In 1970 Gary stood at a crossroads concerning the direction of environmental reform. For years, divergent social experiences and widespread adherence to liberal political arrangements had produced a response to environmental conditions that was not only fragmented but basically accommodating toward industry. Then, in the early 1970s, a broad cross section of activists managed to transcend social barriers in a direct challenge to industrial capital's environmental authority. But Gary's major corporations, most notably U.S. Steel, would only be pushed so far. Just as working-class whites and African Americans were the last to challenge industry's environmental abuses in the community, industrial capital made sure that they were the first to have their commitment tested when economic difficulties forced them to choose between clean air and jobs. When these groups accorded financial security higher priority than environmental quality, it did not reflect a more sanguine view of pollution nor did it signify a more favorable view of industry. Indeed, the rhetoric of civil rights and labor groups in the late 1970s revealed a lingering resentment toward industry for placing Gary's citizens in such an uncomfortable position. Even as Harry Piasecki, president of the Gary Works local, urged Mayor Hatcher to grant U.S. Steel an extension on its open-hearth deadline, he castigated the steel company for using workers as pawns.[59] Thus, although U.S. Steel could generate sufficient animosity to sustain a frontal assault on its environmental practices, it could also, under other circumstances, exploit the dependent status of its workers to defuse environmental activism. It was this dependent relationship that emerged as the most important dynamic in local environmental politics by the late 1970s. Certainly divergent concerns continued to separate the environmental objectives of social groups, but more than ever before, it was an unequal distribution of power that limited efforts to wrest environmental authority from corporate capital.

Environmentalism was not dead in Gary, however, especially among those middle-class citizens far more removed from the steel company. Recognizing the futility of waging a solitary battle against Gary's foul air, Miller activists returned their attention to more immediate surroundings—the lakefront. Indeed, it was during this period of economic decline that they scored their most stunning victory—the inclusion of Miller's undeveloped land in the Indiana Dunes National Lakeshore. Success on this front rested on a very different network of social alliances. Instead of joining forces with inner-city blacks and blue-collar workers, they collaborated with affluent whites who lived in neighboring lakefront communities to the east of Gary. Although large corporations, especially U.S. Steel, continued to play the role of archvillain, this time the controversy would be played out almost exclusively in the arena of national politics. For Miller's environmentalists, the passage of the National Lakeshore Expansion Act in 1976 was cause for celebration for it culminated a decade of persistent struggle to save their shoreline from industrial development. For others in Gary, however, the results did not bode so well.

The Social Geography of Pollution and the Politics of Sand

In the years following World War II, Gary citizens developed a variety of responses to the proliferation of industrial wastes, which as a whole drastically altered the social geography of industrial pollution. While some people could point with satisfaction to noticeable improvements in the quality of their physical surroundings, others found themselves mired in the midst of a rapidly deteriorating environment. In part, the evolving social geography of pollution was a product of demographic change, particularly the differential ability of citizens to relocate to remote suburban communities. But public policy, in the form of environmental laws and regulations, was equally responsible for shifting the burden of pollution from one group to another. Even though industrial capitalists severely dampened the thrust of environmental reform with their counteroffensive in the mid-1970s, the cumulative force of postwar environmental regulations forced manufacturers to make many concessions and adjustments, most notably in the reduction of air and water emissions. However, a fragmented community response to pollution enabled industrial corporations to maintain high levels of waste generation by diverting their refuse to land-based sites in poor and minority neighborhoods where popular resistance was weak. In this way, divisions of race and class continued to undergird industry's basic environmental requirements. Thus, by 1980, perhaps more than ever before, the spatial dimensions of industrial pollution reflected the relative power of social groups and the continued salience of class and race in conditioning the relationship between individuals and their surroundings.

Even as national surveys continued to rank Gary high on the list of the dirtiest cities during the 1980s, many Gary citizens were fond of telling visitors how clear their skies had become in recent years. There was much truth to this claim. Local pollution laws dating back to the 1960s, supplemented by national regulations in the 1970s, had been effective, particularly in curtailing the most visible form of air pollution—particulate emissions. By burning cleaner fuels and installing pollution control equipment to meet local, state, and federal environmental regulations, Gary manufacturers dramatically reduced the amount of thick, dark smoke that poured from their chimneys. Gas boilers at the Budd Company and Taylor Forge, for example, replaced the use of 18,000 tons of coal per year, while dust-collecting devices at the local power plant reduced particulate discharges by 7,000 tons annually.[1] U.S. Steel lagged behind other local industries in meeting air quality standards and frequently initiated lengthy legal proceedings to avoid compliance. Chiding the company for its obstructionist behavior, a federal judge suggested that "instead of spending time in court, blocking every move, it should be spending more time to meet the problem."[2] By 1976, the corporation had earned such notoriety for its staunch resistance to pollution control that John Quarles, deputy administrator of the U.S. Environmental Protection Agency (EPA), cited it as the worst offender of environmental regulations in the entire country.[3] Nevertheless, after considerable kicking and screaming, the steel giant was eventually dragged into compliance, and particulate pollution levels in Gary dropped noticeably. By 1975, the company had already modified procedures at the coke plant, spent well over $100 million on various dust-collecting devices, and retired its last open-hearth furnace, thereby eliminating forever the red haze that residents had come to associate with the Gary skyline. While the giant steel furnaces still spewed over 50,000 tons of particulate matter into the skies each year during the late 1970s, this figure represented half the amount it had been releasing only a decade earlier.[4] As table 7.1 illustrates, particulate concentration in downtown Gary fell commensurately. Although these readings crept upward as government officials relaxed enforcement somewhat in the late 1970s, concentrations of industrial dust never again returned to the high levels of the 1950s and 1960s.

Gary was much slower, however, to curtail less visible forms of air pollution, such as sulfur dioxide. Although U.S. Steel had been emitting sulfur gas for many years, it was not until the Northwest Indiana Public Service Company (NIPSCO) opened its coal generating station in 1956 that this form of pollution presented a serious problem in Gary. Burning large amounts of high-sulfur coal, the local utility company easily doubled the quantity of sulfur dioxide emitted from the city's industrial sources. As the demand for electric power increased over the next two decades, sulfur dioxide levels climbed in direct proportion, reaching a peak around 1973.[5] Over this period, manufacturers faced little pressure to reduce these emissions; with public attention riveted to the smoke menace, city officials ignored colorless fumes. By the time the city council considered a sulfur dioxide pollution law in 1972, the environmental reform movement had lost much of its punch, and hence, the resulting legislation was weak. Still, the new law improved air quality by requiring manufacturers to burn coal with a lower sulfur content. As table 7.2 illustrates, sulfur dioxide levels showed a noticeable drop by the middle of the decade.[6]

Once sulfur dioxide regulations were in place, however, unanticipated complications arose at NIPSCO's power plant, thereby exposing the elusive nature of pollution control. Power plant engineers discovered that the introduction of low-sulfur coal into their boilers interfered with the operation of electrostatic precipitators, the machines that sucked fly ash from the power plant smokestacks. Hence, in switching fuels, NIPSCO had reduced sulfur dioxide emissions but increased the quantity of particulate matter spewing from its smokestacks. At the time, the

Table 7.1. City of Gary Ambient Air Quality: Suspended Particulate, 1964–1980

	Suspended particulate (ug/m^3)
1964	170.6
1965	148.7
1966	135.2
1967	129.7
1968	141.7
1969	119.6
1970	108.1
1971	94.5
1972	99.2
1973	88.9
1974	79.6
1975	76.8
1976	85.9
1977	83.6
1978	83.0
1979	91.5
1980	83.5

Source: City of Gary Ambient Air Quality Data, September 30, 1982, Victor Nordlund Files, USX Corporation, Gary, Indiana.

only other feasible alternative involved the use of wet scrubbing devices in place of the precipitators. But adopting this course would have required the disposal of mountains of toothpastelike sludge generated by the scrubbers. Thus, in each scenario, combating one pollution problem simply created another. It was not until the 1980s that NIPSCO resolved the dilemma by injecting sulfur trioxide into its boilers, a process that improved the performance of dust collectors on low-sulfur coal emissions.[7] This would not be the only occasion, however, when pollution control reforms had unintended consequences.

In the area of water pollution, public policy also contributed to a gradual improvement in environmental quality, although in this case, much of the initiative came from federal lawmakers. Except where drinking water was concerned, city officials paid little attention to water quality. Hence, after the Gary City Council mandated the construction of a water filtration plant in 1951, local authorities left the problem to federal agencies—first the Federal Water Pollution Control Administra-

Table 7.2. City of Gary Ambient Air Quality: Sulfur Dioxide, 1968–1980

	Sulfur dioxide (ug/m^3)
1968	23.6
1969	18.3
1970	21.0
1971	26.2
1972	28.8
1973	28.8
1974	26.2
1975	15.8
1976	19.0
1977	15.7
1978	14.9
1979	13.0
1980	26.2

Source: City of Gary Ambient Air Quality Data, September 30, 1982, Victor Nordlund Files, USX Corporation, Gary, Indiana.

tion, then, after 1970, the EPA.[8] As the city's primary water polluter, U.S. Steel elicited the greatest attention from the federal government. Under the auspices of the Federal Water Pollution Control Administration, U.S. Steel devised a four-year pollution abatement plan in 1966 while simultaneously securing an arrangement to pump its coke plant wastes into the Gary Sanitary District's treatment facilities. Over the next four years, the company invested over $30 million in oil skimmers, settling basins, scale pits, and sedimentation tanks, all of which contributed to sharp reductions in the amounts of oil, grease, and solid matter in the effluent flowing from Gary Works.[9]

Still, EPA administrators found U.S. Steel's efforts lacking when the agency assumed control of the nation's cleanup efforts in 1970. Despite the progress it had made over the previous years, the company continued to release 3,100 pounds of cyanide, 5,100 pounds of ammonia, 82,000 pounds of chlorides, and 180,000 pounds of sulfates into the Grand Calumet River every day through mid-decade.[10] Only after incurring a $4 million fine in 1977 and exhausting all its options for legal recourse did the steel corporation come up with a water pollution control plan that satisfied the EPA.[11] Ironically, when company engineers finally pieced together a complete water pollution control system in the 1980s, government regulators touted it as one of the finest in the nation and used it as a basis for comparison when evaluating pollution control in other steel mills.[12] Federal officials had a much easier time with Gary's second major water polluter, the Georgia-Pacific paper mill, which agreed to divert its effluent to the Gary Sanitary District for treatment in 1969.[13]

As a result of this slow but steady progress in water pollution control, the Grand Calumet River showed some evidence of improvement in the 1970s, although water quality remained poor. Readings for dissolved oxygen content and biological oxygen demand, measures frequently employed to evaluate water quality, indicated that industry's pollution abatement techniques were producing results. Dissolved oxygen is necessary to support a healthy, balanced aquatic environment. Levels under 3 milligrams per liter rarely support life; levels above 6 can support game fish. Biological oxygen demand, which varies inversely with dissolved oxygen content, measures demand placed on oxygen by both municipal and industrial wastes. Table 7.3 shows that according to these indicators, the river experienced the most severe degradation between 1955 and 1969, recuperating gradually thereafter. Pollution controls at U.S. Steel also contributed to a 50 percent reduction in cyanide and ammonia concentrations in the river over the course of the 1970s. The long-term accumulation of toxic sediments along the river bottom, however, continued to poison aquatic life. Sediment analyses conducted in the 1970s revealed a variety of contaminants, including polychlorinated biphenyls (PCBs), polynuclear aromatic hydrocarbons (PAHs), and a variety of toxic metals, while acute toxicity tests conducted in 1972 found river sediments to be highly toxic to both vertebrate and invertebrate test species. As a result, only sludgeworms chose to make their home in the Grand Calumet. Fish were not observed in the river until the 1980s.[14]

In contrast to the Grand Calumet River, Lake Michigan exhibited no signs of water quality improvement in the 1970s. A slow-draining body of water, Lake Michigan took longer to deteriorate than the Grand Calumet River but, once degraded, did not exhibit the same quick response to pollution control programs. Studies of water quality in the lower lake basin conducted after 1963 showed severe degradation be-

Table 7.3. Grand Calumet River Water Quality, 1945–1979

	Dissolved oxygen (mg/l)	Biological oxygen demand
1945–49	4.3	3.9
1950–54	4.8	5.3
1955–59	4.1	10.8
1960–64	4.9	15.5
1965–69	6.2	12.1
1970–74	7.6	5.3
1975–79*	7.7	8.7

Source: Gary Sanitary District, *Annual Report*, 1945–80.
*Readings for some stations were missing for 1976, 1978, and 1979. These figures were estimated based on extrapolations from the previous year's readings.

tween 1963 and 1970 and even worse degeneration by 1976. Eutrophication continued, signaled by the spread of algae further into the lake. Only pollution-tolerant fish, such as alewife, carp, and gizzard shad, flourished in the lake's shore regions. Although the state of Indiana stocked the lake with salmon and trout, these sport fish failed to spawn on their own. Throughout the decade, high concentrations of toxic substances in Lake Michigan fish prompted the Indiana Board of Health to prohibit their commercial sale.[15]

Despite these limited improvements in Gary's air and water quality, the benefits of reform were distributed across the population selectively. Throughout the postwar period, both population movement and shifting industrial location patterns altered the social geography of air and water pollution. In the 1940s, high population density in the city's core subjected most Gary citizens to intense doses of steel mill smoke. Subsequently, both population and industry dispersed. However, although affluent whites generally moved to the south and east, far from the sources of industrial waste, upwardly mobile African Americans tended to move into western Gary, an area increasingly dominated by manufacturing. Due to the presence of NIPSCO's power plant, residents of western Gary suffered the highest levels of sulfur dioxide pollution. Fortunately for them, prevailing winds usually blew the power plant fumes away from Gary, across Lake Michigan or into neighboring East Chicago, a city with a large Latino population. When winds came from the north, however, they immersed western Gary in a bath of sulfur dioxide, raising concentrations to levels that impaired breathing.[16] Even though particulate pollution had improved considerably by this time, malfunctioning equipment and unfavorable wind patterns created hazardous conditions on occasion. As a result of recent demographic shifts, the burdens of heavy particulate pollution fell almost exclusively on low-income African Americans, who by 1980 occupied virtually all the homes closest to Gary Works (see table A.5).

The social geography of water pollution, like that of air pollution, bore the imprint of racial divisions. Despite improvements in the Grand Calumet River, Lake Michigan continued to offer more recreational opportunities and pleasing vistas. As the inhabitants of Gary's only lakefront neighborhood, Miller's affluent whites accrued the benefits of easy access to the lake. Even though African Americans had become accustomed to using the beach at Marquette Park during the 1970s, white residents still monopolized lakefront housing. By contrast, the filthy Grand Calumet River passed through a neighborhood recently settled by working-class African Americans. Homeowners in this northwest Gary neighborhood considered the polluted stream an eyesore, and parents worried about the potential danger to local children who played along the banks and swam in the water. Ann Anderson recalled that her son constantly ignored her admonitions and followed his friends to the river to stalk frogs and catch fish. Although no fish lived in the river at this time, she worried about her son coming into contact with industrial wastes in the water. When a young girl drowned in the river in 1981, parents suspected that the high concentration of toxic wastes had contributed to her death.[17]

Behind this marked social skew stood a series of political decisions about where to direct environmental reform efforts. Not all sources of pollution came under equal public scrutiny, and in part, the degeneration of air quality in western Gary was attributable to minimal citizen resistance. Of all U.S. Steel's facilities, the cement plant in the northwest corner of the city was the most ignored by both environmental activists and local authorities. Yet by the 1970s, this facility spewed more than twice the amount of particulates discharged from all the facilities at Gary Works. An uneven community response to sulfur dioxide pollution had similar consequences for the social geography of air pollution.

Had NIPSCO scattered its generating stations around the city rather than concentrating its facilities in western Gary, the distribution of sulfur dioxide pollution might have been more equitable. But when environmental activists blocked construction of a lakeshore power plant in Miller in the early 1970s, they guaranteed that western Gary would continue to bear the burden of sulfur dioxide pollution. Although most Gary citizens remained oblivious to the dangers posed by power plant emissions, Community Action to Reverse Pollution (CARP) roused community opposition in Miller by warning of a sulfuric acid mist that would wreak havoc on property and human health. At the very moment that NIPSCO announced its plans to build a generating station in Miller, it was putting the finishing touches on yet another 100 megawatt power plant in northwest Gary. Here, the utility company faced no community opposition.[18]

Whatever slight improvements were recorded in water and air quality in Gary during the 1960s and 1970s, they were dramatically offset by the rise in land pollution, which displayed an even greater class and racial bias. The primary legacy of the environmental movement and its resulting regulations was not so much an overall reduction of industrial waste but a transfer of waste from water and air to the land. By the 1970s, precipitators, scrubbers, and baghouses attached to smokestacks at Gary Works, the cement plant, and NIPSCO captured over 100,000 tons of particulate dust each year. At the same time, water pollution facilities amassed surpluses of sediments, oils, greases, and toxic chemicals. What were companies to do with this accumulation of industrial garbage? In the absence of effective solid waste laws, they deposited it into holes in the ground.

Because Gary's marshy soil was conducive to solid waste disposal, some manufacturing refuse had always been dumped on land. In many cases, pits and lagoons located near factory sites simply proved to be the most convenient reservoirs for waste material. For many years, U.S. Steel had deposited pickle liquor, slag, and other wastes into ponds scattered throughout its property. Several smaller firms also used abandoned pits and marshes for discarding solid materials that were too bulky for municipal sewers. But after 1960, the rising demand for dump sites necessitated a far more intensive use of land. Hence, old dumps were enlarged and new ones were opened to accommodate the burgeoning mass of solid wastes.

Gary's larger manufacturers continued to bury wastes on their property, converting even more parcels of land into garbage dumps. At U.S. Steel, engineers designed several new facilities to impound the growing volume of wastes generated after 1965. For the disposal of caustic acids, the company dug a well 4,000 feet deep. To discard unwanted slag, it drove pilings into Lake Michigan to create an enclosed dumping area. Requiring still more waste disposal space, U.S. Steel added a tar sludge dumping area and a special landfill for hazardous wastes, which by the early 1980s amounted to 6,000 barrels annually.[19] NIPSCO's solid waste problem involved finding a dumping site for the fly ash captured by the company's electrostatic precipitators. Like U.S. Steel, the utility benefited from an abundance of open pits on its landholdings. One by one, NIPSCO filled these ponds with the residue, reserving the northwest corner of its property for its most hazardous wastes.[20] The Gary Sanitary District, which treated wastes from a variety of local industries, anticipated that it would run out of room for sludge disposal some time in the 1960s. So, in 1964, it simply purchased a parcel of property one mile west of the treatment plant and pumped its solid wastes there.[21]

The proliferation of solid wastes also produced a rash of independent refuse dumps that accepted garbage from companies lacking sufficient disposal grounds. Numerous small manufacturing concerns simply did not have space on their property to store their garbage. Even several larger firms such as U.S. Steel and NIPSCO eventually generated more waste than they could handle.[22] Hence, shrewd entrepreneurs purchased undeveloped parcels of land and excavated gaping holes in the ground. Or, if they were lucky, they found property that already contained craters. In the process of constructing highways during the 1960s, workers often mined soil and sand for the purpose of building overpasses.[23] The leftover cavities, known as borrow pits, proved ideal for solid waste disposal. Once in possession of a hole, owners invited manufacturers to deposit their wastes for a price. By the 1970s, well over fifteen of these independent dumps operated in Gary, accepting refuse not only from companies within the city but also from industries throughout northwest Indiana.[24]

Largely due to the shifting economic mix in the region, the composition of Gary's buried wastes differed in some respects from the types of material previously discharged into the air and water. In addition to the oils, greases, metals, and ashes trapped by pollution control equipment at U.S. Steel and NIPSCO, the dumps also contained hazardous wastes from newer manufacturers. Following World War II, the U.S. economy moved away from its emphasis on heavy industry toward the production of plastics, chemicals, and other synthetic products. Gary's economic matrix reflected this shift, particularly with regard to the expansion of chemical manufacturing. During the two decades following 1950, the city gained five chemical companies and a plastics manufacturer. By the 1970s, chemical production ranked behind steel as the city's second major industry.[25] Because many of these firms began operations after the passage of air and water pollution laws, they buried their wastes from the start. When the Conservation Chemical Company began manufacturing ferric chloride in Gary in 1967, it decided to store its residue in lagoons, drums, and railroad tank cars sitting on its property. Over the next sixteen years, the chemical firm amassed 555,000 gallons of cyanide-laden sludge in addition to another 286,000 gallons of toxic chemicals.[26] The wastes generated by these newer manufacturers, an assortment of pesticides, solvents, and other synthetic compounds, tended to be highly toxic. Hence, by the 1970s, Gary's dumps had become infested with PCBs, benzene, toluene, methylene chloride, and other recently invented chemicals that were classified as carcinogens by the federal government.[27]

The problem with these exotic wastes was that even after they were buried, they traveled underground and eventually contaminated the surrounding soil and groundwater. Gary's soil, topped with thirty feet of highly permeable sand and intersected by a network of underground streams, facilitated seepage. Once caught in the flow of these aquifers, chemicals could travel as far as 350 feet in a year. If dump operators had lined their pits with clay or plastic, wastes might not have escaped into the soil. But being more concerned with costs than with ecological damage, dump managers rarely utilized any lining whatsoever. Hence, dissolved chemicals leached far and fast from disposal sites.[28] By the time state and federal government officials examined Gary's solid waste facilities in the late 1970s and 1980s, they discovered several instances of ecological devastation in the vicinity of dump sites. At some locations, investigators discovered skeletons of poisoned animals, while at other spots they noted severe damage to local vegetation.[29]

A particularly foul situation developed at the site of the Midwest Solvent Recovery company, called Midco I. Operating between 1975 and 1978, Midco I reclaimed solvents and stored wastes sent by various firms in northwest Indiana. Showing no apparent concern for the ecological consequences, workers tossed barrels of toxic sludge into an unlined trench that flowed with water. As drums leaked their contents, including PCBs, lead, ethylbenzene, strontium, and arsenic, the groundwater became polluted. Water in holes three feet deep glowed a fluorescent green. A 1983 EPA inspection turned up the remains of two rabbits, three mice, two birds, and an opossum, all apparently killed by the poisonous residue.[30]

Although dumps such as Midco I were not uncommon in Gary, they were not scattered indiscriminately throughout the city. Taken in sum, the location of these dumps exhibited a clearly definable geographic pattern. Certain sections of Gary simply afforded insufficient space for landfill construction. Dense urban development stretching south from downtown to Glen Park precluded solid waste dumping in the city's central corridor, for example. The city's eastern and western fringes, on the other hand, still contained large tracts of unused land. Yet, as map 5 clearly illustrates, it was only in the western half of the city that dumps proliferated. In part, economic factors contributed to this geographic skew. Land was relatively cheap in western Gary. Moreover, many manufacturers were already located in this part of the city. Locating disposal sites nearby reduced transportation costs considerably. Still, market dynamics do not tell the whole story. Above all, it was an uneven community response, refracted through political decisions, that determined the geographic contours of solid waste disposal.

The spatial distribution of landfills in Gary was inextricably tied to the politics of sand. The extraction of sand for profit had a long history in Gary, primarily because sand was a valuable commodity that was used extensively as fill material. In western Gary, for instance, mined sand had been used for many years to flatten marshy areas in preparation for factory construction. Over time, the city developed a body of law that made it easier to mine sand in certain parts of the city than in

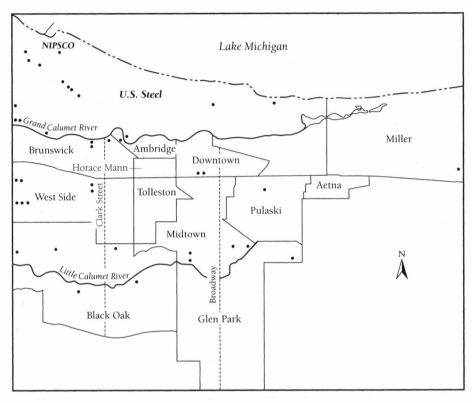

Map 5. Abandoned Waste Sites in Gary, 1986

others. Until the mid-1960s, local regulations merely required that sand miners obtain a permit from the Board of Public Works. Few stipulations governed the awarding of such permits. But as Gary became pockmarked with craters, local legislators decided to impose more control on the permitting process. Thus, in 1964 the city council made sand mining conditional on assurances that owners would eventually convert all holes into recreational facilities. Three years later, responding primarily to pressure from Miller residents who worried about the rape of their sand dunes, the city council amended the municipal code to prohibit sand mining in residential districts.[31] In essence, this provision outlawed the excavation of sand in Miller, where virtually all property was designated for residential use. Western Gary, on the other hand, offered abundant parcels of land zoned for industrial use. In the years after World War II, city officials departed from the rigid classification scheme that had once confined manufacturing to the area north of the Grand

Calumet River. By amending the zoning code, lawmakers increased the availability of manufacturing sites west of Clark Street, thereby creating a hodgepodge of residential, commercial, and industrial land-use designations.[32] Thus, in many areas of western Gary, sand mining remained legal as long as operators secured the appropriate permit.

Still, the effect of sand mining regulations depended on the extent to which they were enforced, and in many instances, crafty dump proprietors managed to hoodwink local officials or ignore the law altogether. Sand miners rarely applied for permits, and when they did, they commonly lied about their intentions. Permit applications announced glorious schemes for converting excavations into recreational centers complete with fishing lakes, boating facilities, and picnic grounds. Such was the case when the Cal-Area Sportsman Club proposed building a recreational lake and apartment complex if permitted to excavate sand from a 120-acre plot in western Gary. Convinced of the firm's sincerity, the city approved the project in 1967. Five years later, a company spokesperson announced a change of plans: the site would not be used for a lake and a housing project after all; rather, the company would operate a landfill.[33] This scenario, in which firms promised to build resort facilities and then reneged, transpired repeatedly. Rumors circulated about landfill owners bribing city council members to look the other way in instances of illegal dumping.[34] Perhaps local officials were merely gullible. Whatever the underlying reason, the letter of the law was not enforced consistently.

While a policy of neglect toward sand mining encouraged the proliferation of landfills in western Gary, such was not the case in Miller, where vigilant citizens kept miners and city officials honest. Even before the city council passed legislation prohibiting sand mining in residential districts, homeowners in Miller kept a watchful eye on interlopers who entered the neighborhood with bulldozers. Hence, when employees of the Alex Metz Construction Company attempted to remove 50 yards of sand from a hill on the eastern edge of the city in the summer of 1964, neighbors immediately notified city attorney Milton Roth, also a Miller resident. Upon discovering that the miners lacked a valid permit, Roth raced to the site with a police officer and arrested two suspects. Incensed, the lawyer representing the construction firm criticized the city for allowing miners to steal a million yards of sand in western Gary while prosecuting two men for removing a bucketful in Miller.[35] The charge contained more than a hint of truth. Over the next decade, local community organizations, first the East Miller Property Association and later the Miller Citizens Corporation, undertook the task of patrolling the neighborhood to ensure that no one defiled their sand. Representatives from these organizations routinely appeared before the Board of Zoning Appeals to oppose any projects that threatened to destroy Miller's rustic character.[36] Indeed, one member of the Miller Citizens Corporation, John Pilzer, secured an appointment to this important agency in the 1970s. In response to constituent pressure, Glen Vantrease, Miller's city council representative, took a vigorous stand against sand mining, making sure that the municipal government denied sand mining permits in his district.[37] Ultimately, it was the menace of sand mining that inspired widespread community support for national park expansion into Miller. For Miller residents, the passage of the National Lakeshore Expansion Act in 1976 was widely interpreted as a victory against sand mining.

Waste dumpers encountered far less community opposition in the city's western neighborhoods. On the rare occasion when western Gary citizens protested their environmental predicament, their efforts proved ephemeral and ineffective. A case in point was the community response to conditions at the Gary city dump. Since the 1940s, private haulers had deposited solid wastes in a large open pit on Colfax Avenue on Gary's far west side. In 1964 the city leased the ninety-acre site and used it as a dump for disposable items, mostly domestic trash.[38] But dump managers also accepted hazardous wastes from nearby manufacturing firms, including several chemical companies. The wastes brought by these customers—heavy metals, industrial solvents, and synthetic chemicals—differed considerably from the material carted in by city garbage trucks. Through the 1960s, the area surrounding the dump was sparsely settled. But in the early 1970s, the city built small subsidized homes for low-income residents adjacent to the dump site, luring several hundred African Americans, mostly from Midtown. It was not long before the recent arrivals began to complain about the nuisance across the street. The object of their anger was not the toxic chemicals brought to the dump but rather sporadic fires and the proliferation of rats. Homeowners expressed revulsion at the pesky rodents that burrowed up to their property and ran in dense packs across their front yards. Fed up with these conditions, local residents held a protest rally in front of the landfill in 1972, halting operations for several hours. Above all, they demanded something be done about the rats and fires. The contents of the dump never emerged as an issue. Eventually, city officials responded by spreading rat poison and closing a portion of the dump. Still, the rest of the landfill operated into the 1980s, contaminating groundwater with PCBs, arsenic, naphthalene, and other assorted toxic substances.[39]

It was not only African Americans who failed to challenge toxic waste dumpers successfully; complaints from poor white residents in the Black Oak neighborhood proved equally ineffective. Wedged between western Gary and Tolleston, Black Oak remained unincorporated until annexed by the city of Gary in 1975. Populated by roughly 10,000 low-income whites, the Black Oak community petitioned to become part of Gary to procure basic city services. The Hatcher administration also favored the arrangement, envisioning the large tracts of vacant land in Black Oak as a potential source of revenue.[40] In accepting Black Oak into the city, however, Gary inherited the problem of Lake Sandy Jo. Originally an abandoned borrow pit alongside the Tri-State Expressway, the water-filled hole was purchased by two men in 1967. Shortly thereafter, the owners circulated flyers throughout northwest Indiana reading, "Accepting all inorganic materials. . . . What are your problem materials?"[41] What incensed nearby residents above all else was not the toxicity of "problem materials" but the smell emanating from the lake, usually likened to rotten eggs. Some homeowners also claimed that leachate from the dump contaminated their well water, but they were unable to identify the pollutants. In 1972 the predominantly white residents of Black Oak joined forces with their African American neighbors just across the city line to lodge formal complaints with the Lake County Board of Health and Mayor Richard Hatcher. Although powerless to act decisively as long as Lake Sandy Jo remained beyond city boundaries, Hatcher demanded action from federal, state, and county officials, describing the dump as "inimical to human health, human dignity, and a flagrant violation of the law."[42] In response, the Indiana Board of Health mandated the cessation of dumping in Lake Sandy Jo. The mandate was ignored, however. Several years later, in 1975, a Superior Court judge ordered the lake drained. This time, the dump owners complied.

Nevertheless, as the smell dissipated, community fervor died down, enabling dumpers to resume their operations for another four years. By this time, groundwater surrounding the site was infested with toxic substances, including tetrachloroethylene, benzene, and toluene.[43]

Ineffective citizen protests and weak law enforcement persuaded dumpers to concentrate their activities in neighborhoods populated by racial minorities and the poor. Landfill protests, such as the ones that targeted the city dump and Lake Sandy Jo, occurred only rarely in Gary's western neighborhoods. More often, dumpers there encountered no opposition. Even after Mayor Hatcher became enlightened about the hazards of solid waste disposal, the city made little headway in solving the landfill problem. In 1974 the mayor announced that there would be no more dumps in Gary, claiming that the proliferation of abandoned pits had caused nothing but trouble. Over the next several years, Hatcher pressured the Gary Plan Commission to reject any questionable sand mining applications.[44] Still, the city found it difficult to close existing dumps and to detect the location of new ones that operated illegally. Part of the problem was that dumpers cleverly concealed their activities. Especially in the desolate industrial district of northwest Gary, dumps were hard to find amid small factories, swamps, scattered homes, and an airport. Indeed, one such site was only discovered as the result of helicopter surveillance. Perhaps dumpers would not have been able to hide so easily had west Gary citizens performed the same sort of watchdog role as their counterparts in Miller. But such was not the case. As Hatcher explained, reflecting on the situation after leaving office, "There was no serious concern in west Gary and no enforcement. The feeling was that you could do almost anything out there. It had to do with who populated the area."[45]

Hatcher's analysis notwithstanding, the uneven community response to toxic waste disposal was not simply a product of greater environmental commitment among Miller's affluent residents but a direct result of power inequities. African Americans in western Gary and poor whites in Black Oak took an intense pride in their neighborhoods, and it was this pride that furnished the inspiration for their campaigns against the city dump and Lake Sandy Jo. But in contrast to Miller environmentalists, they suffered from limited access to information. Until the national media exposed the tragedy at Love Canal in 1979, few Americans recognized the dangers associated with toxic waste disposal. By the early 1970s, however, Miller activists already had an inkling about such hazards. Miller environmentalists were experts at gathering facts; many were long-standing members of the League of Women Voters, a group devoted to research. In 1971 the league selected solid waste disposal as its annual topic for study.[46] The information obtained by Miller activists, however, did not filter into western Gary and Black Oak, where a preoccupation with noxious odors and vermin obscured the more serious threat of toxic contamination. Blocked from access to scientific and academic networks, poor and minority populations lacked the resources to accurately identify their environmental predicament.

Because landfills discharged their contents into the surrounding groundwater, soil, and air, the African American and low-income whites who lived in the affected areas could hardly avoid contact with the poisonous substances. Several hundred households in west Gary and Black Oak continued to rely on wells for their drinking water through the 1970s. Within a two-mile radius of the Gary Municipal Airport, in the northwest corner of the city, fifty-two households depended on the underground aquifer for tap water. At least seven dumps ringed the airport, leaking enough chemicals to contaminate these underground streams with DDT, PCBs, lead, cyanide, and vinyl chloride.[47] Dumps located near Black Oak posed similar hazards to the 350 households that remained unconnected to the city water system. A 1983 EPA investigation revealed traces of toxic substances in the well water of several families residing close to Lake Sandy Jo.[48] But even those who enjoyed the luxury of safe drinking water were not immune from toxic contamination. Unsupervised children used dump sites as playgrounds and waste lagoons as swimming pools. In doing so, they risked absorbing poisonous chemicals through their skin, and on several occasions, youngsters ran home to their parents in pain, reporting strange burns on their bodies.[49] Finally, there was the danger posed by fires. Dump contents were highly flammable, and once they ignited, the blazes were difficult to subdue. At the Midco II landfill, a small fire in a sludge pit generated enough heat to explode several hundred barrels of paint thinner. Flames shot 150 feet into the air, and thick black smoke wafted over northwest Gary.[50] Thus, a solid waste hazard became an air pollution problem for nearby residents.

The skewed social distribution of toxic waste disposal sites represented the most marked example of an environmental regime that discriminated along the lines of race and class. Of all forms of industrial pollution, solid waste disposal had the most concentrated and long-lasting effects. Air emissions eventually dissipated over a large area. Surface water pollution traveled according to specified paths, and the Grand Calumet River flushed much of the waste flow into the vast waters of Lake Michigan. Although buried wastes did not stay put, they moved very slowly; their effects were much more localized. By 1980, the citizens burdened with this long-term danger tended to be either African Americans or poor whites. Significantly, the African Americans subjected to toxic waste contamination from underground burial hailed from a variety of class backgrounds. Although public housing projects drew some low-income blacks to the western part of the city, most African Americans there earned incomes above the city average and were well represented in white-collar occupations.[51] Hence, while class emerged as an accurate predictor of exposure levels among whites, the operative factor for African Americans was race.

In a historical overview of pollution control initiatives in the United States, historian Joel Tarr observed that most reform efforts merely had the effect of transferring wastes from one medium to another. Rarely did they reduce the quantity of wastes entering the ecosystem.[52] Certainly this interpretation fits the situation that developed in Gary during the 1960s and 1970s. But what was especially striking about Gary's history was the extent to which the transfer of wastes among different mediums also reconfigured the social allocation of pollution. Especially as manufacturers shifted wastes from the air and water to the land, the effect of environmental reform was to shift the burden of pollution to low-income groups and racial minorities.

Thus, it was no coincidence that the age of ecology corresponded with the rise of environmental inequality. For some citizens, the environmental movement was empowering. As changes in the urban landscape increasingly became mediated through governmental agencies, those individuals and groups who could negotiate their way through the bureaucratic regulatory process found powerful tools at their disposal. In Gary, there was a clear demarcation between those who were and those who were not successful in this respect. Well connected to scientific and academic circles, white suburbanites from Miller enjoyed a superior ability to assess their environmental predicament and to use the regulatory process to preserve their environmental amenities. Political connections worked in their favor as well. The Miller Citizens Corporation, for example, employed impressive political maneuvers in their effort to include parts of Miller in the Indiana Dunes National Lakeshore. Although the U.S. Congress had passed the necessary legislation, Miller activists feared that the president would refuse to sign the bill, in effect issuing a pocket veto. But they were fortunate to have connections in the White House. The brother of Barbara Hamilton, a member of the Miller community organization, worked with Gerald Ford, and with twenty-four hours remaining on the clock, he persuaded the president to sign the bill.[53] Whether the matter at hand required action from the local zoning board, the EPA, or the president of the United States, middle-class activists were better prepared than any comparable group in Gary to get results. In this way, uneven access to information, technical expertise, and political contacts contributed to selective enforcement of environmental regulations and thereby reinforced environmental inequalities.

Of course, those with white skin and sufficient funds continued to enjoy greater opportunities to create new residential surroundings by moving further from Gary's industrial districts during the 1970s. Although the achievements of civil rights groups and Hatcher's election opened up large segments of Gary to African Americans, racial discrimination remained a rigid barrier to settlement beyond the city's borders. Whereas African Americans comprised more than 70 percent of Gary's population by 1980, black inhabitants accounted for less than 1 percent of the total in Merrillville, Lake Station, Hobart, and Portage, the suburban communities located directly south and east of the city.[54] Poverty imposed similar restrictions on many of Gary's remaining white residents. With layoffs rampant in the steel industry and other forms of manufacturing employment drying up, many blue-collar families simply lacked the financial resources to move to those remote areas of Lake County where air pollution levels were low and toxic waste dumps were few.

Thus, more than ever before, race and class shaped individuals' power to control their environmental destinies and, in particular, to insulate themselves from the worst environmental consequences of manufacturing. Despite the collective efforts of African Americans to secure better jobs, the distribution of environmental burdens had not changed significantly within the steel mills. By 1980, African American workers still toiled at the dirtiest and most dangerous jobs. In the community, on the other hand, the social skew became much more pronounced. Assisted by federal housing and highway programs, affluent white families participated in a mass exodus from the heavily polluted urban core, while poorer whites and African Americans had little choice but to stay put or move into neighborhoods with even higher levels of pollution. But as the saga of toxic waste disposal illustrated, demographic change was only half the story. Rising concern about pollution in the 1950s and 1960s also inspired a spate of pollution control regulations that required manufacturers to adjust their waste disposal practices, a process that profoundly altered the geographic contours of industrial pollution. Despite the sincere efforts of Gary's environmentalists, pollution control proved to be elusive. A fragmented community response to environmental hazards, which was a direct reflection of social inequities, enabled manufacturers to play one group against the other by shifting wastes between different mediums and locations. Because politics reflected the relative power and divergent concerns of various groups within Gary, the cumulative effect of environmental regulation was the movement of industrial pollution toward neighborhoods inhabited by minorities and the poor, where resistance was weakest. Thus, by 1980, the distribution of environmental burdens starkly mirrored divisions of race and class.

Epilogue

Gary and Beyond

Gary appeared a battered city by the 1980s. Shuttered storefronts lined Broadway, interrupted only by the occasional shop selling cheap trinkets, peddling pornography, or offering loans. Across the north side of town and in the neighborhoods of Tolleston and Glen Park, small detached homes that at one time had sheltered prosperous working-class families lay vacant, smothered in fields of overgrown weeds. Even the lakefront suburb of Miller showed signs of dereliction. Due to a lack of maintenance funds, a Japanese footbridge in Marquette Park had collapsed, while the once elegant beachfront bathhouse had begun to crumble.[1] Developments of the 1980s made it clear that the environmental setbacks of the previous decade were not merely products of a cyclical downswing in the economy. Squeezed by declining profits and mounting debt, major American firms such as U.S. Steel restructured their operations to regain a competitive edge in an internationally integrated economy. In the process, they imposed depression conditions on cities such as Gary, thereby severely diminishing opportunities for reversing patterns of environmental decline.

With its high unemployment rates, revenue shortfalls, and decaying physical infrastructure, Gary appeared to share the same affliction as other "Rust Belt" towns of the Northeast and Midwest that had suffered from a vanishing industrial base. But Gary differed from most other dying cities in a fundamental way: heavy industry, and steel manufacturing in particular, performed quite well during the 1980s, demonstrating that the Rust Belt phenomenon was less a product of deindustrialization than a component of a deliberate global strategy on the part of corporate capital that included the geographic decentralization of production activities, speculative financial ventures, increased automation, and a relentless assault on organized labor.[2] Measured by the yardsticks of industrial output and corporate profits, U.S. Steel made an impressive recovery during the 1980s. By the end of the decade, the company's flagship mill in Gary was churning out nearly 7 million tons of steel per year, matching the production levels it had achieved during the 1960s.

However, this economic revival did not translate into prosperity for the inhabitants of Gary. One reason was that much of the corporation's profits went toward the purchase of nonsteel-related businesses such as Marathon Oil. Indeed, the company redubbed itself the USX Corporation several years after it purchased the petroleum firm to reflect its diversified portfolio. Moreover, capital plowed back into steel operations was channeled toward the purchase of labor-saving machinery rather than the creation of new jobs. Due to automation, the giant conglomerate in the 1980s was able to roll as much steel as it had during the halcyon days of the 1950s and 1960s with only one-third the labor force. Largely due to the decline in steel employment, Gary's jobless rate fluctuated between 10 and 20 percent during the 1980s. Even those employees fortunate enough to retain their positions experienced downward mobility. Following a bitter six-month strike in 1987, steelworkers found themselves conceding both wage rates and benefits. In addition, USX adopted a new practice that further eroded the material base of Gary's industrial labor force, contracting out certain jobs to nonunionized firms rather than relying on its own highly paid employees.[3]

In making these structural adjustments, industrialists ensured that the economic conditions that had given them leverage in the environmental battles of the 1970s would become permanent fixtures during the 1980s. Hence, USX continued to exploit social vulnerabilities to ward off challenges to its environmental authority. While hardcore activists in Miller could afford to maintain their environmental vigilance, less-privileged citizens, caught in the crosswinds of conflicting economic and environmental objectives, remained reluctant to press for vigorous enforcement of pollution control regulations. Indeed, it was working peoples' fear of offending business that ultimately accounted for the downfall of Mayor Richard Hatcher. In 1987, after governing the city for almost two decades, Hatcher lost the mayoralty to Thomas Barnes, a candidate who promised to establish more cordial relations with local businesses, including USX. Even though Hatcher had retreated from his virulent anticorporate stance of the early 1970s, many voters still found him too antagonistic toward industry.[4] After observing his successor's behavior in office, Hatcher noted with disappointment that this new relationship with USX involved far more lenient treatment on environmental matters.[5]

As a result, environmental crises continued to plague Gary. In 1989 the *Gary Post-Tribune* reported that during the previous year, smog levels in the area had exceeded federal health standards on twenty-seven occasions. More than once, dangerous fires erupted at the Gary city dump, which was still contaminated with toxic wastes.[6] Revenue shortfalls at the Gary Sanitary District resulted in the direct release of raw sewage and chemical wastes into the already polluted Grand Calumet River.[7] Perhaps no event better captured Gary's environmental plight, especially with regard to the effect on poor and minority residents, than the 1987 hydrochloric acid spill at Gary Products described in chapter 1.

Despite a generally dismal state of environmental affairs, pockets of activism indicated that the legacy of working-class and minority environmentalism was not moribund. During the 1980s, the Grand Calumet River corridor emerged as a hotbed of environmental activism as African Americans from western Gary joined with working-class whites from the neighboring communities of Hammond and East Chicago to protest the transformation of the river into an industrial sewer. Calling themselves the Grand Calumet Task Force, this multiracial coalition adopted the ambitious mission of transforming the river and its wetlands into a scenic recreation facility, complete with bicycle trails, nature observation stations, canoe-launching piers, and picnic grounds. Of course, cleaning the river remained their paramount objective, one that brought their activities into the realm of politics.

Fortunately, the surge of environmental activism among African Americans inspired by Hatcher in the early 1970s provided western Gary with a corps of veterans who were familiar with the intricacies of environmental politics. As director of urban conservation in the Hatcher administration, Nancy Kelly had been assigned the task of improving the physical quality of ghetto neighborhoods. Coordinating her activities with local community groups, Kelly oversaw a program that helped homeowners maintain and improve the appearance of their property, distributing paint to spruce up house exteriors and policing trash removal in alleys and yards. Similarly, Johnny McWilliams had participated in efforts to ameliorate inner-city living conditions by leading the citizen protest against the city dump in 1972. Drawing upon their skills as organizers and lobbyists, Kelly, McWilliams, and others pressured federal regulators to monitor industrial outfalls along the river and to prosecute firms that violated water pollution laws. In the process of trying to revive the Grand Calumet, the task force also became the first grass-roots organization in the area to address the menace of toxic waste disposal. Research revealed that several nearby landfills were slowly leaching their poisonous contents into the river, thereby threatening to offset any gains achieved by reductions in direct industrial discharges. Leaders of the citizen coalition insisted that if the government was serious about improving water quality in the Grand Calumet, it would have to solve the toxic waste problem.

Reacting to citizen pressure, the U.S. Environmental Protection Agency (EPA) devised a comprehensive plan for resuscitating the river, one that included provisions for reducing the threat of toxic wastes. Implementing recent federal laws designed to prevent the improper disposal of hazardous wastes, the EPA effectively terminated operations at seven illegal landfills located in western Gary. Alerted that they would be held accountable for any ecological damages, industries generating toxic wastes began hauling their poisonous cargoes to specially designed facilities in Illinois and Alabama.[8] At the same time, the federal government commenced the costly and laborious task of cleaning up contaminated landfill sites. In 1985 trucks carted away 5,000 cubic yards of soil along with 80,000 abandoned drums from the Midco II landfill. Shortly thereafter, federal authorities initiated an emergency soil removal operation on the grounds of the Conservation Chemical Company.[9] These remedial actions merely scratched the surface of the problem that had been decades in the making, however; it would require a far more sustained and systematic effort to make any meaningful adjustment to an environmental regime that so thoroughly exploited the vulnerabilities of minorities and the poor.

Gary was not the only city where poor and minority citizens confronted a legacy of discriminatory waste disposal practices; indeed, by the 1980s it had become clear that environmental inequality was endemic to urban America. No issue more dramatically exposed the social biases of environmental change in urban America than the decisions about where to locate hazardous waste dumps. Although a handful of social scientists working in the 1970s had discovered that in many U.S. cities, exposure to dirty air correlated directly with socioeconomic status, it was not until the practice of toxic waste dumping created a national furor in the 1980s that the concept of environmental equity entered the mainstream of popular discourse.[10] As reports about Love Canal and other solid waste disposal disasters gained publicity in the early part of the decade, a few observers noted that the afflicted populations tended to be working class and lower income.[11] In Houston, Los Angeles, and Alsen, Louisiana, African American community groups protested decisions to locate toxic waste facilities in their neighborhoods, raising the cry of "environmental racism."[12] The biggest bombshell fell in 1987 when the Commission for Racial Justice released its report, *Toxic Wastes and Race in the United States*. Mapping the social geography of more than 18,000 landfill sites across the nation, the commission discovered evidence of severe racial discrimination, calculating that three out of every five black and Hispanic Americans resided in neighborhoods containing uncontrolled hazardous wastes. Moreover, the civil rights group charged the federal government with complicity in this "insidious form of racism."[13]

By generating widespread publicity, the report forced a response from the federal government. In 1990 the EPA formed an internal committee, the Environmental Equity Workgroup, to investigate the indictments leveled by the commission and to make recommendations for ameliorative action if necessary. When the workgroup concluded its deliberations two years later, it not only admitted the existence of environmental inequalities but also urged that the agency charged with enforcing the nation's environmental laws "increase the priority that it gives to issues of environmental equity."[14] Although unequal access to environmental amenities and resources had constituted an outstanding feature of U.S. cities since the nineteenth century, the situation had worsened by the 1980s such that it was propelled to the fore of national consciousness.

Although neither the Commission for Racial Justice nor the EPA made much attempt to identify the underlying causes of environmental inequality in urban America, Gary's history suggests that the phenomenon was firmly rooted in the dynamics of postwar social arrangements and power relations. Even though all Gary citizens exhibited a strong desire to insulate themselves from the environmental ravages of manufacturing, divisions of class and race conditioned the ability of individuals to procure reliable information, to purchase environmental amenities in the marketplace, and to win battles in the political arena. Each of these proved to be potent variables in determining the course of environmental change.

However, if any place in the United States held forth the promise of a more democratic environmental regime it was Gary, Indiana. Strong labor unions, a civil rights crusade, an environmental movement, and a more pluralistic political structure provided unprecedented opportunities for overturning the prevailing hierarchy of environmental authority. Inside the factories, workers pressed management for better health and safety conditions. In the community, middle-class environmentalists nudged pollution reform onto the political agenda in an effort to remake the city in the image of the suburban ideal. Using the civil rights movement as a vehicle, African Americans pressed for a more democratic allocation of urban environmental amenities. Although divergent perspectives and historical experiences fostered a fragmented social response to environmental problems for much of the postwar period, a broad spectrum of citizens surmounted racial and class barriers to fashion a more radical environmental front once the limitations of liberal reform became apparent.

As events of the 1970s demonstrated vividly, however, entrenched environmental interests were prepared to reinvigorate and exploit divisions of race and class to preserve their prerogatives. Civil rights reforms and a successful drive for black political power notwithstanding, realtors and homeowners associations were able to preserve race as an organizing principle in the distribution of urban space. Furthermore, affluent whites enjoyed unique opportunities to reproduce environmental amenities and racially segregated communities by moving to jurisdictions beyond Gary. Without question, a socially fragmented landscape worked to the advantage of industrial capital, which was even more deliberate in manipulating social behavior for environmental purposes. By reducing workers' bargaining power, holding much of the community hostage to its environmental demands, and shifting wastes to neighborhoods where resistance was weak, Gary's manufacturing concerns satisfied the requirements of industrial production by degrading the working and living environments of lower-income groups and racial minorities.

So although the urban terrain was more fiercely contested in the postwar years than perhaps ever before, divisions of race and class continued to sustain industrial capital's dominion over nature. The corporate restructuring initiatives of the 1980s, aided and abetted by more conservative political regimes at all levels of government, devastated the institutional arrangements of liberal capitalism that once facilitated popular challenges to entrenched environmental hierarchies. Thus, it became unlikely that cities such as Gary would witness any reversal in the patterns of environmental inequality, despite sporadic bursts of grass-roots activism. What the history of urban environmental change adds to our understanding of postwar America is that despite the tenuous commitment to liberal reform, industrial and residential elites would only be pushed so far in extending their privileges to the rest of society. Indeed, the inability of African Americans and many poor whites to improve their environmental conditions testified to liberal capitalism's inability to reconcile the imperatives of economic growth with the goals of public welfare and social equality. Thus, environmental conflicts starkly exposed both the fragility and the limitations of the liberal capitalist consensus, in a way that has rarely been appreciated by historians of the postwar United States. Equally as important, Gary's history directs our attention to the centrality of the physical landscape in struggles for power. After 1970, the environment continued to serve as a battleground for the naked displays of racial and class conflict that contributed not only to a deepening of environmental inequality but also to the growing social inequalities in employment, housing, education, and health care.

Gary's history crystallizes an important truth: the domination of nature involves and necessitates the control of human beings. In 1946, well before the advent of the toxic waste crisis and the rise of an environmental movement, British philosopher C. S. Lewis observed that "what we call Man's power over Nature turns out to be a power exercised by some men over other men with Nature as its instrument."[15] From the perspective of Gary, Indiana, the meaning of these words could not be clearer.

Appendix

Infant Mortality and Air Pollution

The statistics that suggest a direct relationship between infant mortality and air pollution rely on data from the 1950s. Since the spatial distribution of air pollution remained fairly consistent through the 1940s and 1950s, the results of the statistical analysis can be applied to the earlier decade.

Table A.1 shows the results of a regression analysis where infant mortality rates were correlated with particulate levels for eight regions within Gary and the immediate outlying territory. Particulate concentration was measured in milligrams per cubic meter. In the table, the R squared value of .80, which measures the strength of the relationship between variables, means that 80 percent of the variation in infant mortality

Table A.1. Infant Mortality and Particulate Pollution

	R squared	B	Significance
	.80	.07	.00
N = 9			

Source: Raw data compiled by Herschel Bornstein and Leslie Singer from Gary Health Department records, 1950–60, private files of Herschel Bornstein.

levels can be explained by the variation in air pollution levels. Significance values indicate the probability that an R square figure emerged by random chance. Statisticians generally interpret significance levels below .05 as evidence that the correlation is indeed important. The significance level for the equation in table A.1 is .00, well under the .05 threshold. The B value reveals the slope of the regression equation and the direction of the relationship. Thus, according to the data for the 1950s, infant mortality rates varied strongly and directly with air pollution levels.

Multiple regression analysis also allows us to test the effect of air pollution on infant mortality controlling for factors that might better explain why death rates were greater in high pollution areas. I selected race, income, and housing quality as variables that might have been responsible for the high death rates in these districts. The statistics presented in table A.2 show that even when these three variables are added to the regression equation, air pollution maintains its significance. The R squared value increases only slightly, from .80 to .86, indicating that the three additional variables fail to substantially increase the explanatory power of the model. The beta and significance values reveal the relative importance of each variable in the regression equation. Particulate level produces the highest beta value and lowest significance figure, thus establishing itself as the factor most responsible for high infant death rates. None of the remaining three variables produced significance figures below .05.

Table A.2. Infant Mortality and Air Pollution,
Controlling for Income, Race, and Housing Quality

	Beta	Significance
Particulate level (ug/m^3)	1.14	.02
Median income	−.13	.83
Percent white	−.26	.81
Percent housing substandard	−.69	.52
R squared = .86		
N = 9		

Source: Raw data compiled by Herschel Bornstein and Leslie Singer from Gary Health Department records, 1950–60, private files of Herschel Bornstein.

Table A.3. Air Pollution Levels and Socioeconomic Variables

	R squared	B	Significance
Median income	.18	−.02	.03
Median house value	.02	−.00	.54
Percent white collar	.04	−.06	.34
Percent black	.08	.03	.15
Percent white, foreign-born	.01	.00	.68
N = 27			

Sources: U.S. Bureau of the Census, *Seventeenth Census of the United States, 1950, Census Tracts*, 65–67, 191–93, 267–68; Air Quality Reading Files, 1964–66, GAPCD; Suspended Particulate Monitoring Network, Lake County, Indiana, untitled map of geographic distribution of particulate pollution in Gary, Indiana, 1965–66, private files of Elaine Beck.

The Social Distribution of Air Pollution, 1950

Table A.3 shows the results of a regression analysis correlating 1950 particulate levels in census tracts with variations among census tracts in five socioeconomic variables: median income, median house values, percentage of residents employed in white-collar occupations, percentage of blacks, and percentage of foreign-born whites. The only socioeconomic variable that correlated with air pollution was income. While statistically significant, the relationship between income and air pollu-

Table A.4. Proximity to Industry and Socioeconomic Variables

	R squared	B	Significance
Percent black	.29	.09	.01
Median income	.06	−.00	.23
Percent white collar	.05	−.20	.25
Median house value	.02	−.00	.50
N = 26			

Sources: U.S. Bureau of the Census, *Nineteenth Census of the United States, 1970, Population and Housing, Census Tracts*, pp. P-10–P-12, P-18–P-20, P-26–P-28, H-2–H-4; Gary Plan Commission, *Physical Data*, 23.

Table A.5. Air Pollution Levels and Socioeconomic Variables, 1950 and 1980

	Year	R squared	B	Significance
Median income	1950	.18	−.02	.03
	1980	.26	−.98	.00
Median house value	1950	.02	−.00	.54
	1980	.37	−1.20	.00
Percent white collar	1950	.04	−.06	.34
	1980	.29	−90.51	.00
Percent black	1950	.08	.03	.15
	1980	.18	.30	.01
1950, N = 27				
1980, N = 34				

Sources: Gary Air Pollution Control Division, air quality readings, 1965–80, private files of Herschel Bornstein; Air Quality Reading Files, GAPCD; U.S. Bureau of the Census, *Seventeenth Census of the United States, 1950, Census Tracts*, 65–67, 191–93, 267–68, and *Twentieth Census of the United States, 1980, Census Tracts*, pp. P-35, P-36, P-65–P-67, P-79–P-81, H-4–H-6.

tion was weak, as indicated by the low R squared value of .18. Other class-related indicators, such as value of home and white-collar employment, showed no significant correlation. The statistics also fail to indicate any direct connection between particulate levels and either ethnic or racial residential patterns.

Race and Industrial Location

A regression analysis of the relationship between various socioeconomic variables and proximity to industry confirms race as the leading social category associated with industrial location patterns for the late 1960s. The percentage of Gary's industrial acreage in census tracts for 1966 was correlated with racial composition, median income, occupation, and property values for the same tracts in 1970. The vast lakefront property containing the steel mills and power plant were excluded from the analysis because tract boundaries were drawn in such a way that the residents located in the same tracts did not necessarily live near those factories. As it stands, the correlations emphasize the effects of more recent industries in Gary. Table A.4 reports the results. The only variable that registered a significant R squared value was the percentage of blacks within census tracts. The R squared value of .29 fell far below the .05 threshold level determining significance. The regression analysis suggests that by the late 1960s, newer industries were located in neighborhoods inhabited by blacks of various income and occupational levels.

The Social Distribution of Air Pollution, 1950 and 1980

The social skew in the distribution of particulate air pollution, which had become marked by 1980, can be demonstrated statistically. Table A.5 presents the results of a regression analysis that measured the relationship between particulate pollution patterns and both class and race. The percentage of blacks in census tracts was chosen to represent race, while median income, median house value, and occupational status were taken as measures of class. For the sake of comparison, statistics for 1950 correlations are also shown. The analysis reveals significant correlations among all the socioeconomic variables in 1980. By contrast, only income correlated with particulate pollution in 1950. Since higher R squared values indicate stronger correlations, property values emerged as the best predictor of dust levels, followed by income, percentage of white-collar residents, and race. By 1980, then, residents who lived in the most valuable homes, earned the greatest income, and held white-collar jobs breathed the purest air.

Notes

Abbreviations

The following abbreviations are used throughout the notes.

CERCLIS-EPA	Comprehensive Environmental Response, Compensation, Liability, Inventory System Files, U.S. Environmental Protection Agency, Chicago, Illinois
CERCLIS-IDEM	Comprehensive Environmental Response, Compensation, Liability, Inventory System Files, Indiana Department of Environmental Management, Indianapolis, Indiana
CPL	Vivian Harsh Collection, Chicago Public Library, Carter Woodson Branch
CRA	Calumet Regional Archives, Indiana University–Northwest, Gary, Indiana
GAPCD	Gary Air Pollution Control Division, Gary, Indiana
GPL	Gary Public Library, Gary, Indiana
IDEM	Indiana Department of Environmental Management, Indianapolis, Indiana
LA	United Steelworkers of America Collection, Historical Collections and Labor Archives, Pennsylvania State University Library, State College, Pennsylvania
RCRA Files	Resource Conservation and Recovery Act Files, U.S. Environmental Protection Agency, Chicago, Illinois
USW	United Steelworkers of America, Local 1014, Gary, Indiana
USW-CHS	United Steelworkers of America, District 31, Collection, Chicago Historical Society, Chicago, Illinois

Preface

1. For a more elaborate critique along these lines, see Cronon, "Modes of Prophecy and Production."

2. Worster, "Transformations of the Earth," 1092–93.

Chapter 1

1. *Chicago Tribune*, April 15, 1987, sec. 2, p. 1.

2. For a more elaborate treatment of the relationship between control over humans and dominion over nature, see Leiss, *The Domination of Nature*, 167–98, and Worster, *Rivers of Empire*, 19–60.

3. Robert S. Lynd and Helen Merrell Lynd, *Middletown*, 21–24.

4. Judd, *Politics of American Cities*. For case studies of particular cities, see Cum-

bler, *Social History of Economic Decline*; Edsforth, *Class Conflict and Cultural Consensus*; and Swanstrom, *Crisis of Growth Politics*.

5. Foner, *Organized Labor and the Black Worker*, 129–35; Bodnar, Simon, and Weber, *Lives of Their Own*, 55–87; Zunz, *Changing Face of Inequality*, 222–23, 321, 373–75; Gordon, Edwards, and Reich, *Segmented Work, Divided Workers*, 152–53.

6. Mills, *White Collar*; Kenneth Fox, *Metropolitan America*, 50–78. Mills, however, remained skeptical about the ability of the new middle class to realize its political potential.

7. Much of this analysis draws upon Logan and Molotch, *Urban Fortunes*.

8. Kennedy and Porter, "Air Pollution"; Laitos, "Continuities from the Past"; Hurley, "Creating Ecological Wastelands."

9. Rudwick, *Race Riot*, 5.

10. Hoerr, *And the Wolf Finally Came*, 190–91.

11. Melosi, *Coping with Abundance*, 199–274.

12. Commoner, *Closing Circle*, 160–62; Bookchin, *Our Synthetic Environment*; Brown, *Laying Waste*, 45–52, 297–309.

13. For summary accounts of the post–World War II environmental movement, see Hays, *Beauty, Health, and Permanence*; Rosenbaum, *Politics of Environmental Concern*; Petulla, *American Environmentalism*; and Stephen Fox, *American Conservation Movement*, 250–329.

14. Hays, *Beauty, Health, and Permanence*. While Hays expounded on the general social conditions that promoted environmental values, he did not associate environmental activism with any particular class. Rather, he tended to view the benefits of environmental protection in terms of the general public interest.

15. Jones, *Clean Air*, 140–54; Erskine, "The Polls"; Davies, *Politics of Pollution*, 80; James Noel Smith, "The Coming Age of Environmentalism in American Society," in Smith, *Environmental Quality and Social Justice*, 5–6.

16. Commoner, *Closing Circle*, 205.

17. Cited in Roos, *Politics of Eco-Suicide*, 46.

18. Peter Marcuse, "Conservation for Whom?," in James Noel Smith, *Environmental Quality and Social Justice*, 18.

19. Tucker, *Progress and Privilege*. For a similar analysis, see Aaron Wildavsky, "Aesthetic Power or the Triumph of the Sensitive Minority over the Vulgar Mass: A Political Analysis of the New Economics," in Revelle and Landsberg, *America's Changing Environment*, 147–60.

20. Ellis, "At the Forefront of Social Progress"; Kazis and Grossman, *Fear at Work*, 243–50.

21. Woodcock, "Labor and the Politics of Environment," 11–16.

22. Marcuse, "Conservation for Whom?," 18.

23. *Gary Post-Tribune*, March 11, 1972, p. 1.

Chapter 2

1. Graham Romeyn Taylor, *Satellite Cities*, 180–81; Lane, *City of the Century*, 13–14; Moore, *Calumet Region*, 275; Indiana Department of Environmental Management, *Northwest Indiana Environmental Action Plan*, 13.

2. Moore, *Calumet Region*, 258; Greer, *Big Steel*, 59.

3. Moore, *Calumet Region*, 275–76; Greer, *Big Steel*, 57–61; U.S. Steel Corporation, *Gary Steel Works 50th Anniversary* (Gary, 1956), 7–8, box 1, U.S. Steel Corporation Collection, CRA.

4. The Gary Land Company, a U.S. Steel subsidiary, originally owned most of Gary's urban property and took charge of town building.

5. Mohl and Betten, *Steel City*, 10–25.

6. Indiana Department of Natural Resources, *Inventory of Man-Made Land*; Gary Zone Map, 1933, and "Map of Lake County, Indiana, Showing Ownerships," 1950, both in Mid-City Investment Company Records, CRA.

7. Except for the cement plant, which was established in 1903, all subsidiary manufacturing structures were built subsequent to Gary Works. Prior to 1908, the cement plant received its slag from U.S. Steel's South Works in Chicago. Once steel manufacturing began at Gary Works, the cement plant became integrated into U.S. Steel's production network along the Gary lakeshore. Graham Romeyn Taylor, *Satellite Cities*, 172; Moore, *Calumet Region*, 258, 327–30; *Gary Post-Tribune*, May 25, 1960, Press Clipping Collection, Indiana Room, GPL; U.S. Steel Corporation, *Gary Steel Works 50th Anniversary*, 9; interview with James L. Dickerson, former U.S. Steel executive in charge of waste management, Gary, Indiana, November 23, 1986. Unless otherwise noted, all interviews cited throughout the notes were conducted by the author.

8. "Map of the City of Gary and Vicinity," in Dickens, *Economic Factors*; Gary Land Company, *Gary, "The Magic City"* (1941), Indiana Room, GPL; Kerns, *Study of the Social and Economic Conditions*, 6.

9. Varga and Lownie, *Final Technological Report*, pp. V-2–V-4.

10. Community Action to Reverse Pollution, "Why We Need Ordinance #70-60," December 1, 1970, folder 7, box 1, Community Action to Reverse Pollution Records, and "Mission: Coke Minus Emissions," 1971, pp. 10–11, folder 5, box 11, John Schnurlein Collection, both in CRA; Elbert, "U.S. Steel Corporation"; Dickerson interview.

11. Elbert, "U.S. Steel Corporation"; Varga and Lownie, *Final Technological Report*, pp. V-5–V-12; *Gary Post-Tribune*, September 12, 1946, p. 1; *Gary Post-Tribune*, February 15, 1965, Newspaper Clipping Memory Book, GAPCD.

12. The Gary Tube Works was the only U.S. Steel subsidiary that was not located west of Gary Works. The Tube Works stood just north of the coke plant.

13. Varga and Lownie, *Final Technological Report*, pp. V-18–V-20; U.S. Department of the Interior, Federal Water Pollution Control Administration, *Proceedings, Conference, Pollution of Lake Michigan*, 910–12; U.S. Steel Corporation, *United States Steel and the Environment*, 35–45; Dickerson interview; U.S. Environmental Protection Agency, *Master Plan for Improving Water Quality*, 2–39; *Gary Post-Tribune*, July 24, 1944, Press Clipping Collection, Indiana Room, GPL. Although its charges were denied by corporate engineers, a 1949 report published by the Gary Sanitary District charged U.S. Steel with dumping some pickle liquors into the city sewer system. Gary Sanitary District, *Ninth Annual Report: Sewage Treatment Works for 1949* (1949).

14. *Gary Post-Tribune*, May 25, 1960, Press Clipping Collection, Indiana Room,

GPL; Atlas Cement folder, Compliance Files, GAPCD; Lehigh Portland Cement folder, Stream Pollution Control Board Files, IDEM.

15. U.S. Bureau of the Census, *Sixteenth Census of the United States, 1940, Characteristics of the Population, Indiana*, 811, and *Seventeenth Census of the United States, 1950, Characteristics of the Population, Indiana*, pp. 14-214–14-218.

16. Interview with Curtis Strong, United Steelworkers of America, Gary, Indiana, November 20, 1986.

17. Richards, "Steelworker to Minister," 28.

18. Interview with Larry Regan, United Steelworkers of America, Gary, Indiana, December 15, 1986.

19. Strong interview.

20. Interview with Chris Malis, Gary, Indiana, December 2, 1986.

21. Interview with John Howard, Gary, Indiana, April 2, 1986.

22. "Specific Instructions for Job Classification Production and Maintenance Jobs," International Executive Board Proceedings, June 30–August 4, 1945, pp. 114–27, box 2, International Executive Board Minutes, LA; United Steelworkers of America, District 31, "Contract Gains Summary—United States Steel Corporation, 1936–1958," folder 3, box 138, USW-CHS.

23. Greer, "Racism and U.S. Steel"; Paul S. Taylor, *Mexican Labor*, 42–43, and "Mexican Labor in the Calumet Region," in Lane and Escobar, *Forging a Community*, 45; Kerns, *Study of the Social and Economic Conditions*, 31; Mohl and Betten, *Steel City*, 74–75; Greer, *Big Steel*, 86–87; Howard interview; interview with Hubert Dawson, United Steelworkers of America, Gary, Indiana, December 19, 1986.

24. Ruth Hutchinson Crocker, "Gary Mexicans and 'Christian Americans': A Study in Cultural Conflict," in Lane and Escobar, *Forging a Community*, 115.

25. Paul S. Taylor, "Mexican Labor in the Calumet Region," 36.

26. Dawson interview.

27. Gary Plan Commission, *Physical Data*, 19; Gary Health Department, *Annual Report* (1966); Gorman, "Pollution of Lake Michigan," 521; Kenneth R. Spring, "Health and the Steel Industry Environment," in Szekely, *The Steel Industry and the Environment*, 27–42; Radner, *Study and Technical Recommendations*, 12.

28. Gary Redevelopment Commission, *Community Renewal Program*, 39; Gary Plan Commission, *Physical Data*, 48.

29. Inland Steel operated an integrated steel mill just beyond the Gary city limits, west of the cement plant.

30. Because pollution levels were never measured during the 1940s, figures for the immediate postwar period were estimated based on measurements made during the mid-1960s, prior to the implementation of most pollution control projects. Since major sources of pollution remained stable from 1945 through 1965, the geographical distribution of pollution should not have changed significantly over this period. Annual particulate emission readings, 1964–75, Gary Air Pollution Control Division, private files of Herschel Bornstein; Suspended Particulate Monitoring Network, Lake County, Indiana, untitled map of geographic distribution of particulate pollution in Gary, Indiana, 1965–66, private files of Elaine Beck.

31. *Gary Post-Tribune*, April 22, 1973, Newspaper Clipping Memory Book, GAPCD.

32. Spring, "Health and the Steel Industry Environment"; U.S. Department of Health, Education, and Welfare, Public Health Service, *Air Quality Criteria for Particulate Matter*.

33. The history of residential settlement in Gary deviated from the model most frequently employed to describe twentieth-century urban development—the concentric ring theory. Developed by urban sociologists in the 1920s, this model held that free-market dynamics distributed neighborhoods in a series of rings around the central business district. The rings closest to the downtown core housed the working class, while those successively further from the center contained increasingly wealthy populations. According to the theory, as inner-city residents enjoyed upward social mobility, they moved to more peripheral locations. See Park, Burgess, and MacKenzie, *The City*, 1–62. For an example of a historical application of the concentric ring theory, see Warner, *Streetcar Suburbs*. Historians have found it necessary to modify the concentric ring theory to explain urban development in particular cities. See Bodnar, Simon, and Weber, *Lives of Their Own*. See also Rudolph J. Vecoli, "The Formation of Chicago's 'Little Italies,'" in Mohl, *The Making of Urban America*, 157–69.

34. Graham Romeyn Taylor, *Satellite Cities*, 184–93.

35. U.S. Bureau of the Census, *Seventeenth Census of the United States, 1950, Census Tracts*, 65–67, 190–93; interview with Verne Washburn, realtor, Merrillville, Indiana, April 2, 1987. Information about real estate advertising was taken from sample listings in the *Gary Post-Tribune* during the period 1945–50. The following dates were scanned for realty advertisements: September 9, October 4, November 5, December 4, 1945, January 2, May 1, September 1, 1948, January 4, March 4, May 4, July 5, September 4, 1950.

36. Cutright, "Party Organization," 17.

37. For examples of this phenomenon in other industrial cities, see Bodnar, Simon, and Weber, *Lives of Their Own*; Vecoli, "Formation of Chicago's 'Little Italies,'" 157–69; and Slayton, *Back of the Yards*, 111–48.

38. Mohl and Betten, *Steel City*, 161–78.

39. Ibid.; Millennium Committee, *The Polish Americans of Indiana: Their History and Their Jubilee* (Munster, 1966), Frank Roman Collection, CRA; U.S. Bureau of the Census, *Seventeenth Census of the United States, 1950, Census Tracts*, 65–67; *Gary City Directory*, 1947, 1948. Recent scholarship on immigrant settlement warns us not to lump all foreigners into a homogeneous category for the purposes of analysis. Ethnic groups varied according to the motivations they brought to the United States as well as the types of employment they found. These variations produced different settlement patterns. See Bodnar, *The Transplanted*, and Bodnar, Simon, and Weber, *Lives of Their Own*. Although all major European ethnic groups tended to cluster in Gary, this approach helps explain why some groups preferred to concentrate closer to downtown than others. Census data suggests, for instance, that Poles, Serbs, and Croatians tended to find employment in the steel mills more often than Italians, perhaps explaining why Italians settled in Glen Park rather than closer to downtown. U.S. Bureau of the Census, *Seventeenth Census of the United States, 1950, Census Tracts*, 65–67, 190–92, and *Eighteenth Census of the United States, 1960, Population and Housing, Census Tracts*, 15–17, 33–35.

40. See, for instance, Drake and Cayton, *Black Metropolis*, and Osofsky, *Harlem*. Pittsburgh, with a steel economy like Gary's, came closer to replicating Gary's residential developments. Blacks there remained scattered throughout the city as late as 1930, although racially homogeneous neighborhoods were beginning to form. See Bodnar, Simon, and Weber, *Lives of Their Own*, 192–99, 216, 275.

41. Mohl and Betten, *Steel City*, 65–73.

42. U.S. Bureau of the Census, *Sixteenth Census of the United States, 1940, Characteristics of the Population, Indiana*, 797, and *Seventeenth Census of the United States, 1950, Census Tracts*, 65–67.

43. U.S. Bureau of the Census, *Seventeenth Census of the United States, 1950, Census Tracts*, 65–67.

44. The median incomes reported for the four census tracts closest to the steel mills in 1950 were $3,090, $3,263, $3,953, and $3,444. The median income for the entire city was $3,615. Fourteen percent of this community's population was foreign-born, slightly higher than the city average of 11 percent. U.S. Bureau of the Census, *Seventeenth Census of the United States, 1950, Census Tracts*, 65–67, 190–93.

45. Interview with Charles Lazerwitz, realtor and developer, Gary, Indiana, November 17, 1986.

46. Dickens, *Economic Factors*, 5; Vela, "Simple and Uncomplicated," 40; *Gary Post-Tribune*, January 3, 1948, p. 11.

47. Interview with George Kolettis, Gary Air Pollution Control Division, Gary, Indiana, October 9, 1986.

48. "Profile of 'The Old Prophet,' Dr. L. K. Jackson, 'The Servant of the Lord's Servant,'" n.d., box 1, Reverend L. K. Jackson Collection, CRA.

49. Kerns, *Study of the Social and Economic Conditions*, 29; Joseph Chapman, executive secretary, Gary Urban League, to Mr. Prettyman, July 15, 1946, microfilm reel 3, Gary Urban League Papers, CPL.

50. I have estimated these quantities of waste emissions by extrapolating backward from 1965 data according to changes in overall steel production levels. U.S. Department of Health, Education, and Welfare, Public Health Service, *Report on Pollution of the Waters of the Grand Calumet River*, 20.

51. Gorman, "Pollution of Lake Michigan."

52. *Gary Post-Tribune*, July 11, 1953, p. 3.

53. U.S. Department of Health, Education, and Welfare, Public Health Service, *Report on Pollution of the Waters of the Grand Calumet River*, 30–31.

54. Interview with Fred Carr, Portage, Indiana, December 12, 1986.

55. U.S. Department of the Interior, Fish and Wildlife Service, *Physical and Ecological Effects of Waste Heat*, 16.

56. Stanford H. Smith, "Pushed toward Extinction: The Salmon and Trout," in Rousmaniere, *The Enduring Great Lakes*, 34–40; Eugene F. Stoermer, "Bloom and Crash: Algae in the Lakes," in ibid., 18–19; U.S. Department of the Interior, Fish and Wildlife Service, *Physical and Ecological Effects of Waste Heat*, 16.

57. Carr interview.

58. Gary Chamber of Commerce, Governmental Affairs and Tax Research Department, *Public versus Private Ownership of the Local Water Company*.

59. *Gary Post-Tribune*, January 6, 1948, p. 1.

60. Banner, *Social and Economic Conditions*, 22; U.S. Bureau of the Census, *Seventeenth Census of the United States, 1950, Census Tracts*, 65–67. The major hazardous wastes discharged from the coke plant were phenols, cyanide, and ammonia-nitrogen. For health hazards associated with these chemicals, see Sittig, *Handbook of Toxic and Hazardous Chemicals*.

61. Gary Zone Map, 1933, Mid-City Investment Company Records, CRA.

62. As late as 1963, over 8,000 acres of industrially zoned land lay vacant. Gary Plan Commission, *Physical Data*, 43; David Graham Nelson, "Black Reform," 51.

63. Lane, *City of the Century*, 25.

64. Ibid., 22–28.

65. Gary Planning Commission, *Planning Gary's Tomorrow, 1945–1955*.

66. Paul E. Peterson, *City Limits*.

67. Lane, *City of the Century*, 43–47, 202.

68. Interview with William Staehle, former city planner, Gary, Indiana, December 4, 1986.

69. Bloomberg, "Power Structure," 205; Greer, *Big Steel*, 166–67.

70. Although standard historical interpretations identify the New Deal as the beginning of the end for ethnic machine politics in the urban United States, several cities besides Gary witnessed the rise of machine politics in the wake of the Democratic resurgence of the 1930s. See Stave, *New Deal*.

71. William E. Nelson and Meranto, *Electing Black Mayors*, 179–80; *Gary City Directory*, 1948; Bloomberg, "Power Structure," 203–4; interview with Earline Rogers, former state representative, Gary, Indiana, May 22, 1986; interview with Milton Roth, former city councilman, Highland, Indiana, March 7, 1986; Polish American Democratic Club, Twenty-fifth Anniversary Banquet Program, April 22, 1956, folder 30, box 2, Frank Roman Collection, CRA; interview with John Mayerick, former president of USWA Local 1014, Merrillville, Indiana, January 28, 1987; United Steelworkers of America, "By-Laws, Lake County Political Action Committee," December 4, 1946, folder 7, box 105, USW-CHS.

72. Bloomberg, "Power Structure," 204–5; Cutright, "Party Organization," 98, 171; Rogers interview.

73. Mayerick interview.

74. *Gary Post-Tribune*, September 6, 1945, pp. 1, 8.

75. *Gary Post-Tribune*, September 27, 1945, p. 1; "Gary Cuts Loose," 50–52.

76. "Gary Cuts Loose," 50–52; *Gary Post-Tribune*, January 18, 1950, Press Clipping Collection, Indiana Room, GPL; Dickens, *Economic Factors*, 58.

77. *Gary Post-Tribune*, January 3, 1946, p. 1, January 5, 1951, p. 1; Dickens, *Economic Factors*, 60.

78. *Gary Post-Tribune*, May 15, 1950, scrapbook, Philip Rosenbloom Collection, CRA.

79. Tarr, "Historical Perspectives," 97; Rosenkrantz, *Public Health*, 98–109; Tomes, "The Private Side of Public Health."

80. Gorman, "Pollution of Lake Michigan," 520; *Gary Post-Tribune*, August 16, 1940, and "City to Revise Plan for Test of Raw Water," *Gary Post-Tribune*, n.d., [1948], scrapbook, Philip Rosenbloom Collection, CRA.

81. *Gary Post-Tribune*, January 1, 1950, p. 17; *Gary Post-Tribune*, January 14,

1949, Press Clipping Collection, Indiana Room, GPL; *Gary Post-Tribune*, May 15, 1950, scrapbook, Philip Rosenbloom Collection, CRA.

82. Indiana Department of Natural Resources, *Inventory of Man-Made Land*.

83. Stream Pollution Control Board of Indiana, "Resolution 1" (November 17, 1943) and "Resolution 2" (March 15, 1944), in "Reports of Activities, Stream Pollution Control Board, 1943–1945," "Activities of the Indiana Stream Pollution Control Board," memorandum, May 26, 1945, and Minutes, 1945–50, all in Stream Pollution Control Board Files, IDEM; Dickerson interview.

84. *Gary Post-Tribune*, October 3, 1943, Press Clipping Collection, Indiana Room, GPL.

85. Stream Pollution Control Board of Indiana, "Progress Report, Stream Pollution Control Board of Indiana, 1946–1948, Reports of Activities," Stream Pollution Control Board Files, IDEM.

86. *Gary Post-Tribune*, October 1, 1949, p. 1.

87. Greene, "Can We Clean Up Our Rivers?"

88. "Health Aspects of Air Pollution," in Smoke Prevention Society of America, *Forty-Second Annual Meeting, Smoke Prevention Society of America*, 1–18; Hemeon and Hatch, "Atmospheric Pollution," 570–71; Drinker, "Atmospheric Pollution."

89. *Gary Post-Tribune*, July 24, 1944, Press Clipping Collection, Indiana Room, GPL.

90. *Gary Post-Tribune*, January 18, 1950, Press Clipping Collection, Indiana Room, GPL.

91. For a discussion of how this notion of cities influenced political elites in other urban communities, see Daly-Bednarek, *The Changing Image of the City*, 1–40, 107–48.

Chapter 3

1. Telephone interview with Helen Hoock, Gary, Indiana, January 15, 1993; telephone interview with Naomi Stern, Gary, Indiana, January 16, 1993; Helen Hoock to David Comey, Businessmen for the Public Interest, November 2, 1970, folder 2, box 1, Community Action to Reverse Pollution Records, CRA.

2. Between 1948 and 1967, the number of retailers in Gary fell from 1,567 to 1,087. U.S. Bureau of the Census, *United States Census of Business, 1948, Retail Trade, Area Statistics*, p. 13-31, and *United States Census of Business, 1967, Retail Trade, Area Statistics*, p. 16-52.

3. Unless otherwise noted, Gary employment statistics come from the following sources: U.S. Bureau of the Census, *Sixteenth Census of the United States, 1940, Characteristics of the Population, Indiana*, 811, *Seventeenth Census of the United States, 1950, Characteristics of the Population, Indiana*, pp. 14-213–14-218, *Eighteenth Census of the United States, 1960, Characteristics of the Population, Indiana*, pp. 16-462–16-465, and *Nineteenth Census of the United States, 1970, Characteristics of the Population, Indiana*, p. 16-318.

4. By 1967, three-fourths of top and upper-middle management at U.S. Steel lived beyond the city limits in affluent suburban communities. Lower-level supervisors, however, tended to remain in Gary. U.S. Steel Corporation, "Gary, Indiana," 1967, Public Relations Files, USX Corporation, Gary, Indiana.

5. *Gary Post-Tribune*, January 5, 1951, January 1, 1956.

6. *Gary Post-Tribune*, September 24, October 8, 1964, and *Chicago Tribune*, August 11, 1957, all in Press Clipping Collection, Indiana Room, GPL; Gary Chamber of Commerce, "Gary Industrial Directory," 1959, folder 35, box 5, Purdue-Calumet Development Foundation Records, CRA; NIPSCO, "Annual Report," 1956, box 1, NIPSCO Annual Reports Collection, CRA; NIPSCO, "Northern Indiana, 'The Workshop of America': Community Analysis," November 1967, folder 32, box 2, Gary Chamber of Commerce Collection, CRA.

7. "Employment and Regularly Scheduled Work Week of Steelworkers," 1957, folder 2, box 51, employment statistics, July 17, 1961, folder 2, box 51, and employment statistics, May 5, 1969, folder 1, box 206, all in USW-CHS.

8. U.S. Bureau of the Census, *Seventeenth Census of the United States, 1950, Census Tracts*, 190–93, *Eighteenth Census of the United States, 1960, Population and Housing, Census Tracts*, 33–35, and *Eighteenth Census of the United States, 1960, Characteristics of the Population, Indiana*, pp. 16-462–16-465.

9. Thompson, "Woman Worker."

10. Stupar, "One Woman's Experience."

11. For general discussions of the middle class in the postwar United States, see Mills, *White Collar*, and Baritz, *The Good Life*, 166–288. On the connection between the rise of the middle class and postwar suburbanization, see Kenneth Fox, *Metropolitan America*, 50–78. For earlier evidence of the link between suburbanization and changing standards of family life, see Marsh, "From Separateness to Togetherness."

12. Jackson, *Crabgrass Frontier*, 238; Polenberg, *One Nation Divisible*, 130–32.

13. U.S. Bureau of the Census, *Sixteenth Census of the United States, 1940, Housing, Block Statistics*, 5, *Seventeenth Census of the United States, 1950, Census Tracts*, 65–67, and *Eighteenth Census of the United States, 1960, Population and Housing, Census Tracts*, 15–17.

14. On nineteenth-century suburbs, see Warner, *Streetcar Suburbs*; Fishman, *Bourgeois Utopias*, 121–54; Stilgoe, *Borderland*; and Binford, *The First Suburbs*, esp. chap. 6.

15. *Gary Post-Tribune*, July 1, 1956, p. D6, July 15, 1956, pp. C8, C9, July 28, 1956, pp. 16–17.

16. Gary Redevelopment Commission, *Community Renewal Program*, p. 38.

17. Complaint Log, June 15, 1971, GAPCD.

18. Purdue University, Division of Educational Reference, Purdue Opinion Panel, "Greater Calumet Area Housing Survey, Report Number Two: Analysis of the Housing Market by Community of Primary Preference," May 1954, pp. 62–68, folder 14, box 3, Purdue-Calumet Development Foundation Records, CRA; Dickens, *Economic Factors*, 6.

19. U.S. Bureau of the Census, *Eighteenth Census of the United States, 1960, Population and Housing, Census Tracts*, 15–17, 33–35.

20. City Planning Associates, *Gary, Indiana, Community Renewal Program, Report #3: Selected Social Characteristics* (1966), vi, box 9, City of Gary Collection, CRA.

21. During the 1950s, the city gave Gleason Park a face-lift by building a new athletic field, Gilroy Stadium, and adding new tennis courts. Near the end of the de-

cade, Mayor George Chacharis inaugurated a recreational program that opened city schools in the evenings for leisure activities. Lane, *City of the Century*, 260, 263.

22. U.S. Bureau of the Census, *United States Census of Business, 1948, Retail Trade, Area Statistics*, p. 13-32, and *United States Census of Business, 1967, Retail Trade, Area Statistics*, p. 16-52.

23. *Gary Post-Tribune*, January 13, 1950, p. 17.

24. *Gary Post-Tribune*, March 8, 1967, Newspaper Clipping Memory Book, GAPCD.

25. *Gary Post-Tribune*, [August 1953], Anselm Forum Collection, Indiana Room, GPL.

26. Gary Plan Commission, *Planning Gary's Tomorrow, 1945–1955*; "A Mayor for All the People," 1959, scrapbook, Orval Kincaid Collection, CRA; U.S. Department of Health, Education, and Welfare, Public Health Service, *Report on Pollution of the Waters of the Grand Calumet River*, 13; *Gary Post-Tribune*, March 5, 1967, p. A8.

27. U.S. Department of the Interior, Fish and Wildlife Service, *Physical and Ecological Effects of Waste Heat*, 15–20; interview with Fred Carr, Portage, Indiana, December 12, 1986.

28. U.S. Department of the Interior, Federal Water Pollution Control Administration, *Proceedings, Progress Evaluation Meeting*, second session, 23–24, 180; *Gary Post-Tribune*, March 4, 1965, Newspaper Clipping Memory Book, GAPCD.

29. Letter to the editor from Mrs. Horace Gale, *Gary Post-Tribune*, January 19, 1963, p. 4.

30. U.S. Department of the Interior, Federal Water Pollution Control Administration, *Proceedings, Conference, Pollution of Lake Michigan*, 1096–97; *Gary Post-Tribune*, [spring 1967], Newspaper Clipping Memory Book, GAPCD.

31. Skolnick, *Embattled Paradise*, 52–70; May, *Homeward Bound*.

32. For a similar analysis of women's involvement in turn-of-the-century environmental reform campaigns, see Hoy, "'Municipal Housekeeping.'"

33. League of Women Voters Board Meeting Minutes, November 4, 1953, and list of board members, 1961–62, box 4, Gary League of Women Voters Records, CRA; *Gary City Directory*, 1953, 1962.

34. "I Think She's Got It," skit script, [1964], "Recreation" folder, box 2, Gary League of Women Voters Records, CRA.

35. Interview with Elaine Beck (formerly Elaine Kaplan), Gary, Indiana, March 7, 1986.

36. League of Women Voters Board Meeting Minutes, January 4, 1953, "Agenda of the League of Women Voters of Gary, 1953–1954," and Gary League of Women Voters General Meeting Minutes, April 17, 1957, all in box 4, Gary League of Women Voters Records, CRA; telephone interview with Lotte Meyerson, Gary League of Women Voters, Gary, Indiana, January 29, 1993.

37. Meyerson interview.

38. Campaign literature, scrapbook, private files of Milton Roth; interview with Milton Roth, former city councilman, Highland, Indiana, March 7, 1986.

39. Roth interview.

40. Beck interview; Gary League of Women Voters General Meeting Minutes, January 8, 1961, box 4, Gary League of Women Voters Records, CRA; Crenson, *The Un-*

Politics of Air Pollution, 58–73; *Gary Post-Tribune*, December 15, 1962, November 6, 1966, Press Clipping Collection, Indiana Room, GPL.

41. Gary Chamber of Commerce, "Gary: The Nation's Largest 20th Century City," March 1961, folder 34, box 5, Purdue-Calumet Development Foundation Records, CRA.

42. Roth interview.

43. Crenson, *The Un-Politics of Air Pollution*, 59, 72.

44. Greer, *Big Steel*, 188.

45. Crenson, *The Un-Politics of Air Pollution*, 69–73; Greer, *Big Steel*, 188–89; *Gary Post-Tribune*, December 29, 1962, Press Clipping Collection, Indiana Room, GPL; minutes of special meeting between U.S. Steel and city officials, "Discussion of Variance Request by U.S. Steel on the 1965 Agreement," September 1, 1972, U.S. Steel Corporation, "Draft Report: Proposed Air Pollution Control Program for Gary Steel Works," June 1965, and Gary Air Pollution Advisory Board Meeting Minutes, September 2, 1966, all in private files of Elaine Beck.

46. *Chicago Sun-Times*, March 5, 1965, Newspaper Clipping Memory Book, GAPCD.

47. *Gary Post-Tribune*, March 5, 1965, Newspaper Clipping Memory Book, GAPCD; U.S. Department of the Interior, Federal Water Pollution Control Administration, *Proceedings, Conference, Pollution of Lake Michigan*, 1427–29; U.S. Department of Health, Education, and Welfare, Technical Committee on Water Quality, *Water Quality in the Calumet Area*, 41.

48. J. H. Dickerson, "'Overview of Environmental Control,' U.S. Steel—Gary Works," March 14, 1975, private files of James Dickerson; U.S. Department of the Interior, Federal Water Pollution Control Administration, *Proceedings, Progress Evaluation Meeting*, second session, 236–37; U.S. Steel Corporation, "USS Is Winning in Its Fight to Safeguard Air and Water in Chicago-Gary Area: A Special Report of U.S. Steel People in the Chicago-Gary Area," July 1971, "Environmental Quality" folder, box 1, Gary League of Women Voters Collection, CRA.

49. Interview with James L. Dickerson, former U.S. Steel executive in charge of waste management, Gary, Indiana, November 23, 1986.

50. *Gary Post-Tribune*, July 2, 1969, p. A5; interview with F. Leonard Coventry, former superintendent of Gary Sanitary District, Rockville, Indiana, November 11, 1986.

51. NIPSCO, "Annual Report," 1967, box 1, NIPSCO Annual Reports Collection, CRA; interview with Earl Mann, formerly with NIPSCO, Portage, Indiana, November 17, 1986.

52. Compliance Files, GAPCD.

53. U.S. Department of the Interior, Federal Water Pollution Control Administration, *Proceedings, Progress Evaluation Meeting*, second session, 153–57.

54. U.S. Department of Health, Education, and Welfare, Technical Committee on Water Quality, *Water Quality in the Calumet Area*, 46.

55. *Gary Post-Tribune*, March 6, 1967, Newspaper Clipping Memory Book, GAPCD.

56. *Gary Post-Tribune*, January 13, 1963, p. C6; *Gary Post-Tribune*, January 6, 1966, Press Clipping Collection, Indiana Room, GPL; "Gary Works," 1975, Public Relations Files, USX Corporation, Gary, Indiana.

57. NIPSCO, "Northern Indiana," and Gary Chamber of Commerce, "Annual Re-

port," 1964–65, folder 46, box 2, both in Gary Chamber of Commerce Collection, CRA.

58. Gary League of Women Voters Board Meeting Minutes, March 6, 1967, box 4, Gary League of Women Voters Records; *Gary Post-Tribune*, March 3, 1967, p. 1.

59. *Lake County Democrat*, November 1965, p. 8.

60. *Gary Post-Tribune*, December 23, 1965, Press Clipping Collection, Indiana Room, GPL.

61. *Gary Post-Tribune*, March 2, 7, 1967, Newspaper Clipping Memory Book, GAPCD; *Gary Post-Tribune*, March 11, 1967, p. 11.

62. Mann interview.

63. *Gary Post-Tribune*, November 13, 1968, folder 8, box 1, Community Action to Reverse Pollution Records, CRA.

64. Hoock interview, January 15, 1993; Stern interview.

65. Interview with Helen Hoock, Gary, Indiana, April 2, 1986.

66. Membership list, 1972, folder 1, box 1, Community Action to Reverse Pollution Records, CRA; Hoock interview, April 2, 1986.

67. CARP statement at meeting with Richard Hatcher, January 14, 1970, folder 3, box 1, and Helen Hoock to Joe Hopkins, July 10, 1970, folder 2, box 1, both in Community Action to Reverse Pollution Records, CRA; CARP, untitled position paper, [1970], and statement before public hearing, January 21, 1971, both in private files of Elaine Beck; *Gary Post-Tribune*, May 16, 1970, p. A7.

68. Correspondence, 1969–71, folder 2, box 1, Community Action to Reverse Pollution Records, CRA.

69. *Gary Post-Tribune*, November 13, 1968, folder 8, box 1, Community Action to Reverse Pollution Records, CRA.

70. Hoock interview, April 2, 1986; proceedings of public hearing, January 1–February 4, 1971, folder 11, box 1, list of groups cosponsoring CARP picnic, folder 3, box 1, CARP press release, May 11, 1970, folder 3, box 1, CARP statement at meeting with Richard Hatcher, January 14, 1970, folder 3, box 1, and Helen Hoock to Richard Hatcher, November 26, 1969, folder 2, box 1, all in Community Action to Reverse Pollution Records, CRA.

71. Richard Hatcher, speech at CARP picnic, May 17, 1970, folder 3, box 1, Community Action to Reverse Pollution Records, CRA.

72. *Gary Post-Tribune*, July 15, 1971, p. A4.

73. Statement of Carol Wilmore, CARP, to Great Lakes Basin Commission at public hearing, November 29, 1972, folder 2, box 1, Community Action to Reverse Pollution Records, CRA.

74. Franklin and Schaeffer, *Duel for the Dunes*, 124–79; Engel, *Sacred Sands*, 253–89; interview with Charlotte Read, Save the Dunes Council, Chesterton, Indiana, April 4, 1986.

75. "Report Describing Areas Proposed as Additions to the Indiana Dunes National Lakeshore as Included in Bills Introduced in the Congress of the United States, S.2380, H.R. 10209," October 1971, folder 4, box 6, John Schnurlein Collection, CRA.

76. "Why I Want to Leave Miller," unsigned flyer, [1971], scrapbook, 1971–73, Miller Citizens Corporation Collection, Wildermuth Branch, GPL.

77. Interview with Judy Smith, Miller Citizens Corporation, Gary, Indiana, March 14, 1986; interview with Nathan Cooley, manager, Marquette Park pavilion, Gary, Indiana, May 2, 1986; Fred Grady, "The Message of Miller," typescript, September 1973, box 1, Miller Citizens Corporation Records, CRA.

78. *Miller Message*, August 2, 1971, p. 2, Press Clipping Collection, Indiana Room, GPL.

79. Smith interview.

80. *Chicago Tribune*, April 7, 1968, and *Gary Post-Tribune*, November 11, 1968, both in Press Clipping Collection, Indiana Room, GPL.

81. Grady, "Message of Miller."

82. Miller Citizens Corporation, "Fact Sheet," [1972], scrapbook, 1971–73, Miller Citizens Corporation Collection, Wildermuth Branch, GPL.

83. Transcript of public hearing on Indiana Dunes National Lakeshore West Beach Development plan and environmental impact statement, October 16, 1974, folder 10, box 1, John Schnurlein Collection, CRA.

84. Indiana Dunes National Lakeshore Advisory Committee Meeting Minutes, March 14, 1975, folder 11, box 1, John Schnurlein Collection, CRA.

85. Testimony of C. W. Thomas, U.S. Steel Corporation, before Senate Subcommittee on Parks and Recreation, May 26, 1976, folder 2, box 1, Community Action to Reverse Pollution Records, CRA.

86. Statement of L. Keith Smith, February 1, 1975, folder 6, box 6, John Schnurlein Collection, CRA.

87. *Gary Post-Tribune*, May 16, 1970, p. A7; *Gary Post-Tribune*, March 18, 1972, Newspaper Clipping Memory Book, GAPCD.

88. *Gary Post-Tribune*, [1966], Newspaper Clipping Memory Book, GAPCD.

89. Interview with Dennis McGuire, Gary Air Pollution Control Division, Gary, Indiana, October 26, 1986.

90. Statement of Gregory Reising before House Subcommittee on Parks and Beautification, May 9, 1975, folder 6, box 6, John Schnurlein Collection, CRA.

91. For a recent version of this critique, see Davis, *City of Quartz*, 151–220.

92. *Gary Post-Tribune*, March 23, 1972, scrapbook, 1971–73, and "The Miller Message," January 1972, box 1, both in Miller Citizens Corporation Collection, Wildermuth Branch, GPL.

93. Overall Economic Development Committee, *Initial Overall Economic Development Program*, 42.

Chapter 4

1. *Gary Post-Tribune*, February 5, 1973, folder 12, box 12, Lotte Meyerson Collection, CRA.

2. On the homogenization of the postwar working class, see Lichtenstein, "The Making of the Postwar Working Class."

3. Lane, *City of the Century*, 194–96; Nyden, *Steelworkers Rank-and-File*, 17–32.

4. Lichtenstein, *Labor's War at Home*.

5. Lipsitz, *Class and Culture*, 14–36, 231–32.

6. *Gary Post-Tribune*, March 2, 1953, p. 1.

7. *Gary Post-Tribune*, March 17, 1953, folder 3, box 174, USW-CHS.

8. Bloomberg, "Gary's Industrial Workers," 204.

9. Petition of coke plant loaders of number 7 station, September 22, 1945, Grievance A-46-125, First Step, November 19, 1946, and unnumbered grievance concerning coke loaders at number 6 and 7 stations, First Step, [1946], all in Grievance Files, USW.

10. Fourth Step Minutes, Grievance A-51-48, April 23, October 22, 1952, Grievance Files, USW.

11. Interview with Larry Regan, United Steelworkers of America, Gary, Indiana, December 15, 1986; interview with Al Samter, formerly with United Steelworkers of America, Gary, Indiana, March 14, 1986.

12. An important step in this process occurred in 1960 when David McDonald, president of the International United Steelworkers of America, began transferring bargaining authority from the union's Wage Policy Committee, composed of locally elected members, to the new Human Relations Committee, whose members were appointed from above. Herling, *Right to Challenge*, 122–25, 319; Workers for Democracy, "How the Steelworkers Gave Away the Right to Strike, or Where's I. W. Abel?," [1973], private files of William Walden; Betheil, "The ENA in Perspective," 2, 6–16.

13. Statement of David McDonald, International Executive Board Proceedings, September 16, 17, 1953, pp. 130–32, box 5, International Executive Board Minutes, LA.

14. Workers for Democracy, "How the Steelworkers Gave Away the Right to Strike"; Betheil, "The ENA in Perspective," 1–22.

15. Joint Safety Meeting Minutes, U.S. Steel Corporation and United Steelworkers of America, November 19, 1957, January 21, March 3, 1958, November 8, 1965, April 11, 1966, Grievance Files, USW.

16. Grievance 58-115, Second Step, February 18, 1959, Grievance 55-105, Second Step, October 12, 1955, Grievance A-52-10, Third Step, August 1, 1952, and Grievance A-52-59, Third Step, May 18, 1959, all in Grievance Files, USW.

17. Interview with Curtis Strong, United Steelworkers of America, Gary, Indiana, November 20, 1986.

18. Interview with Willie Moore, United Steelworkers of America, Gary, Indiana, December 15, 1986; Joint Safety Meeting Minutes, Gary Works, November 8, 1965, and Safety Meeting Minutes, 44-inch Blooming Mill, Gary Works, June 18, 1974, both in Grievance Files, USW.

19. Strong interview; Joint Safety Meeting Minutes, January 21, 1958, Grievance Files, USW.

20. Noble, *Liberalism at Work*, 68–98; Greenstone, *Labor in American Politics*, xxii; Berman, *Death on the Job*, 148–49.

21. Berman, *Death on the Job*, 152.

22. Noble, *Liberalism at Work*, 137.

23. Ibid., 146, 179–80.

24. For an opposing point of view, see Greenstone, *Labor in American Politics*, xxii–xxiii.

25. Joseph Odorich to Bronko Stankovich, June 26, 1973, folder 1, box 30, USW-CHS; Samter interview.

26. Edward Sadlowski to James W. Smith, July 14, 1975, Health and Safety Files, USW; Berman, *Death on the Job*, 149–50.

27. Letter from Bronko Stankovich to "whom it may concern," November 6, 1972, Health and Safety Files, USW; *Gary Post-Tribune*, June 2, 1968, Press Clipping Collection, Indiana Room, GPL.

28. Samter interview.

29. Francis P. Grimes to Joseph Germano, May 8, 1973, and R. W. Raybrook to J. F. Keppler, December 31, 1975, both in Health and Safety Files, USW; Calumet Environmental and Occupational Health Committee, *Calumet Safety and Health News*, no. 2 (January 1973): 3, private files of Elaine Beck; *Local 1014 Journal* 2 (August 1972): 1, John Mayerick Collection, CRA.

30. Lichtenstein, "The Making of the Postwar Working Class."

31. Lizabeth Cohen, *Making a New Deal*, 99–158; Edsforth, *Class Conflict and Cultural Consensus*.

32. Memorandum from Otis Brubaker, USWA research director, "Basic Steel Gains," September 30, 1968, folder 2, box 18, Civil Rights Department Records, LA; Betheil, "The ENA in Perspective," 2.

33. U.S. Bureau of the Census, *Seventeenth Census of the United States, 1950, Census Tracts*, 65–67, 190–93, and *Eighteenth Census of the United States, 1960, Population and Housing, Census Tracts*, 15–17, 33–35.

34. Lizabeth Cohen, *Making a New Deal*, 144.

35. Mohl and Betten, *Steel City*, 170–77.

36. *Gary City Directory*, 1947, 1967.

37. U.S. Bureau of the Census, *Sixteenth Census of the United States, 1940, Business, Retail Trade, 1939*, 326, and *United States Census of Business, 1963, Retail Trade, Summary Statistics*, p. 4-128.

38. *Gary City Directory*, 1957, pp. 73–75.

39. Millennium Committee, *The Polish Americans of Indiana: Their History and Their Jubilee* (Munster, 1966), Frank Roman Collection, CRA.

40. *Nasa Nada*, 1956, 1961.

41. *Steel Labor* (Midwest edition), February 1951, pp. 7, 10, July 1951, p. 12, October 1951, pp. 5, 6.

42. *Gary Post-Tribune*, September 1, 1948, p. 33.

43. U.S. Bureau of the Census, *Eighteenth Census of the United States, 1960, Population and Housing, Census Tracts*, 15–17, 23–26; interview with Verne Washburn, realtor, Merrillville, Indiana, April 2, 1987.

44. U.S. Bureau of the Census, *Eighteenth Census of the United States, 1960, Population and Housing, Census Tracts*, 33–35, 42–44. Information on housing prices was obtained from real estate listings in the *Gary Post-Tribune* during March, July, and November 1953.

45. Gary Land Company, *Gary, "The Magic City"* (1941), Indiana Room, GPL; Gary Chamber of Commerce, "Gary Industrial Directory," June 15, 1959, folder 35, box 5, Purdue-Calumet Development Foundation Records, CRA; *Gary Post-Tribune*, May 22, 1960, Press Clipping Collection, Indiana Room, GPL.

46. In addition, workers received either a three- or thirteen-week vacation every five years. Memorandum from Brubaker, September 30, 1968.

47. On the role of saloons in working-class life, see Jon M. Kingsdale, "The 'Poor Man's Club': Social Functions of the Urban Working-Class Saloon," in Mohl, *The Making of Urban America*, 122–37.

48. Horvath, "Magrac," 39.

49. Mohl and Betten, *Steel City*, 23; *Gary City Directory*, 1957, pp. 102–3.

50. *Nasa Nada*, January 26, 1955, p. 6.

51. *Steel Labor* (Midwest edition), July 1951, p. 12, October 1951, p. 5; *Steelworker News*, July 12, 1945, p. 6, February 27, 1949, p. 1, box 1, Thomas Colosimo Collection, CRA.

52. *Nasa Nada*, June 15, 1955, p. 6.

53. Bloomberg, "Five Hot Days," 36.

54. Bloomberg, "State of the American Proletariat," 211–16; interview with Fred Widlak, Izaak Walton League, Evanston, Illinois, December 17, 1986; list of charter members, Glen Park Izaak Walton League, Hobart, Indiana; *Gary City Directory*, 1941.

55. *Steelworker News*, December 25, 1947, p. 8.

56. Bloomberg, "State of the American Proletariat," 212.

57. Lake County Political Action Committee, "By-Laws," December 4, 1946, folder 7, box 105, USW-CHS; Bloomberg, "State of the American Proletariat," 213; interview with John Mayerick, former president of USWA Local 1014, Merrillville, Indiana, January 28, 1987; Bloomberg, "Gary's Industrial Workers," 207; Orval Kincaid to Joseph Germano, January 26, 1968, folder 1, box 29, USW-CHS.

58. Mayerick interview; *Steelworker News*, May 4, 1951, p. 1; Orval Kincaid to Joseph Germano, August 28, 1959, folder 4, box 78, USW-CHS.

59. Lane, *City of the Century*, 232; David Graham Nelson, "Black Reform," 78; Samter interview.

60. *Gary Post-Tribune*, March 1965, Newspaper Clipping Memory Book, GAPCD.

61. *Gary Post-Tribune*, May 25, 1965, Newspaper Clipping Memory Book, GAPCD.

62. Interview with Helen Hoock, Gary, Indiana, April 2, 1986; interview with Charlotte Read, Save the Dunes Council, Chesterton, Indiana, April 4, 1986; Petition for Organized Labor for the Industrial Development of Northern Indiana, n.d., folder 34, box 6, John Schnurlein Collection, CRA.

63. Frady, "Gary," 36–37; *Gary Post-Tribune*, May 6, 1964, p. D3. The final tally showed Wallace receiving 14,421 votes to 15,855 for Matthew Welsh, the Johnson delegate.

64. Curtis Strong to Alex Fuller, January 4, 1968, folder 1, box 29, USW-CHS.

65. Strong interview; *Wall Street Journal*, October 24, 1969, Press Clipping Collection, Indiana Room, GPL.

66. Samter interview.

67. Developments in national politics also contributed to labor's political demise. The Vietnam War split the Democratic party and weakened labor's position. As many elements of the Democratic coalition came out against the war in the late 1960s, labor found itself isolated from the mainstream. The AFL-CIO clung to its virulent anticommunist stance. When the Democrats nominated George McGovern on an antiwar platform in the 1972 presidential election, the AFL-CIO took the un-

precedented position of endorsing no one. See Brody, *Workers in Industrial America*, 239–40.

68. Interview with Elaine Beck (formerly Elaine Kaplan), Gary, Indiana, March 7, 1986.

69. Gerald W. Grandey, Lawrence S. Grossman, and Alan P. Donaldson, "The Manischewitz Caper," May 1971, unpublished paper, Northwestern School of Law, pp. 21–22, appendix, p. 8; *Gary Post-Tribune*, December 16, 1970, p. 1; Samter interview; interview with Judy Smith, Miller Citizens Corporation, Gary, Indiana, March 14, 1986; notes on CARP meeting, October 22, 1970, folder 7, box 1, Community Action to Reverse Pollution Records, CRA.

70. Strong interview.

71. *Calumet Safety and Health News*, no. 4 (April 1973): 2–3, private files of Elaine Beck.

72. Noble, *Liberalism at Work*, 52.

73. *Daily Calumet*, February 9, 1973, box 2, David Nelson Collection, CRA.

74. Bogdanich, "Labor Maverick," 15.

75. Staughton Lynd, "Blue Collar Organizing," 28–29; interview with William Walden, formerly with CEOHC, Hammond, Indiana, December 3, 1986.

76. Walden interview; Samter interview.

77. "Remarks by William H. Walden, Jr., at Safety and Health Conference Sponsored by Lake and Porter County AFL-CIO Central Labor Union," May 24, 1972, private files of Elaine Beck; Staughton Lynd, "Blue Collar Organizing," 29–32; Walden interview.

78. Workers for Democracy press release, January 24, 1973, private files of Elaine Beck; *Gary Post-Tribune*, March 2, 1973, Press Clipping Collection, Indiana Room, GPL; "Remarks by Mike Olzanski at a Public Meeting on Industrial Compliance Schedules in Gary, Indiana," May 7, 1973, private files of Elaine Beck; *Gary Post-Tribune*, January 25, 1973, folder 16, box 7, John Schnurlein Collection, CRA; Workers for Democracy, "Recommended Compliance Schedule for Lake County Coke Plants," May 7, 1973, private files of Elaine Beck.

79. "Remarks by Mike Olzanski."

80. Walden interview; *Gary Post-Tribune*, April 22, 1973, Press Clipping Collection, Indiana Room, GPL.

81. Interview with Winzell Stocker, Lake County Fish and Game Association, Hammond, Indiana, December 18, 1986.

82. U.S. Department of the Interior, Federal Water Pollution Control Administration, *Proceedings, Conference, Pollution of Lake Michigan*, 2065–66.

83. *Gary Post-Tribune*, October 15, 1972, p. D3.

84. Buffington Pier Community Coalition, "Buffington Pier Fact Sheet," [1970], folder 34, box 1, Community Action to Reverse Pollution Records, CRA.

85. *Gary Post-Tribune*, September 27, 1972, folder 20, box 5, John Schnurlein Collection, and Gary Parks and Recreation Board, "Proceedings of Public Hearing," January 7–February 4, 1971, folder 11, box 1, Community Action to Reverse Pollution Records, both in CRA.

86. Buffington Pier Community Coalition, "Buffington Pier Fact Sheet"; *Gary Post-Tribune*, September 27, 1972.

87. *Gary Post-Tribune*, March 19, 1971, p. A8.

88. *Gary Post-Tribune*, April 29, 1972, folder 20, box 5, John Schnurlein Collection, CRA.

89. *Gary Post-Tribune*, March 22, 1973, p. B6.

90. Stocker interview.

91. *Washington Post*, March 4, 1973, p. B2; Jim Wright, "Report to Inner City Task Force," October 22, 1968, private files of Beverly Wright; Levine, *Racial Conflict*, 74.

92. "A Rising Cry," 32–33.

93. Ibid., 33; *Washington Post*, December 7, 1970, box 1, Calumet Community Congress Collection, CRA; Lake County Project, Calumet Community Congress, "Project Proposal, Calumet Community Congress," October 15, 1970, private files of Beverly Wright.

94. Alice Lynd and Staughton Lynd, *Rank and File*, 201–32.

95. Interview with Beverly Wright, formerly with Calumet Community Congress, Gary, Indiana, May 27, 1986; Krickus, "Organizing Neighborhoods," 74; Calumet Community Congress, "Resolutions Ballot," 1970, private files of Beverly Wright.

96. "Remarks by John C. Esposito at the Calumet Community Congress," December 5, 1970, private files of Beverly Wright.

97. Krickus, "Organizing Neighborhoods," 78; *Gary Info*, December 11, 1970, p. 1.

98. *Gary Post-Tribune*, July 11, 1971, Press Clipping Collection, Indiana Room, GPL.

99. Calumet Community Congress Executive Committee Meeting Minutes, December 16, 1970, January 6, 1971, private files of Beverly Wright.

100. "What Do You Know about NIPSCO?," n.d., private files of Beverly Wright; *Gary Post-Tribune*, April 2, 1972, Press Clipping Collection, Indiana Room, GPL.

101. *Gary Post-Tribune*, November 24, 1970, box 1, Calumet Community Congress Collection, CRA.

102. Krickus, "Organizing Neighborhoods," 77.

103. *Gary Post-Tribune*, February 11, 1972, January 1973, box 1, Calumet Community Congress Collection, CRA; CAL mailing list, n.d., private files of Beverly Wright.

Chapter 5

1. Richard Hatcher, speech at CARP picnic, May 17, 1970, folder 3, box 1, Community Action to Reverse Pollution Records, CRA.

2. Mohl and Betten, *Steel City*, 49–50.

3. U.S. Bureau of the Census, *Seventeenth Census of the United States, 1950, Census Tracts*, 65–67.

4. Kerns, *Study of the Social and Economic Conditions*, 11; U.S. Bureau of the Census, *Seventeenth Census of the United States, 1950, Census Tracts*, 285–86. The 75 percent figure was arrived at by adding the number of black males employed in craft and operative positions to 80 percent of those employed in laborer positions. In Gary as a whole, only about 20 percent of men classified in the laborer category worked in nonmanufacturing jobs. Data from the 1960 census indicates that the

four to one ratio also applied to blacks, although the precise breakdown is not available for African Americans in 1950.

5. Bloomberg, "They'll Go Democratic Anyway," 13.

6. Greer, "Racism and U.S. Steel," 46.

7. U.S. Bureau of the Census, *Seventeenth Census of the United States, 1950, Characteristics of the Population, Indiana*, p. 14-281.

8. Grievance A-46-125, November 19, 1946, Grievance Files, USW; interview with Curtis Strong, United Steelworkers of America, Gary, Indiana, November 20, 1986; interview with Al Samter, formerly with United Steelworkers of America, Gary, Indiana, March 14, 1986.

9. Redmond et al., "Long Term Mortality Study," 621–29.

10. Memorandum of meeting, October 25, 1951, and grievances, 1945–51, all in Grievance Files, USW.

11. Petition drafted by coke loaders of number 7 station, September 22, 1945, and grievances, 1945–50, all in Grievance Files, USW.

12. Balanoff, "History of the Black Community," 216.

13. Samter interview.

14. Interview with Hubert Dawson, United Steelworkers of America, Gary, Indiana, December 19, 1986; A. Coleman and C. Price to David McDonald, October 1961, folder 3, box 174, USW-CHS; grievances, 1945–75, Grievance 55–4, January 1, 1955, and complaint by Joe Dixon cited in letter from Charles King, Gary Human Relations Commission, to Mr. Dudderar, U.S. Steel, February 16, 1967, all in Grievance Files, USW.

15. Strong interview.

16. Ibid.; Dawson interview; S. M. Jenks and M. N. Brown, "Memorandum of record," January 5, 1949, Grievance Files, USW.

17. Strong interview; Dawson interview. For a discussion of how the Steelworkers Union helped to enforce job discrimination in the steel mills of Birmingham, Alabama, see Norrell, "Caste in Steel."

18. Minutes of meeting with "Negro Delegation" from District 31, February 2, 1968, folder 1, box 29, USW-CHS; Dawson interview; Strong interview.

19. *Gary Post-Tribune*, November 1, 1975, Press Clipping Collection, Indiana Room, GPL; Samter interview.

20. *Steel City Organizer* 1 (June 1978): 1, USW-CHS.

21. U.S. Bureau of the Census, *Seventeenth Census of the United States, 1950, Census Tracts*, 190–93.

22. Ibid.; Mohl and Betten, *Steel City*, 79.

23. Lane, *City of the Century*, 277–78; Gary FEPC, "Fourth Annual Report of Gary, Indiana, 1955–1956," 1956, box 4, Gary League of Women Voters Records, CRA; *Gary American*, January 11, 1957, p. 1.

24. Clifford Minton, "Some of the Things the Gary Urban League Was Instrumental in Doing—Minton's Administration, City-Wide," January 1, 1985, folder 1, box 1, Clifford Minton Papers, CRA.

25. Memorandum from Charles Graves, Jr., vocational services secretary, to Clifford Minton, executive director, Gary Urban League, June 11, 1962, microfilm reel 1, Gary Urban League Papers, CPL.

26. William E. Nelson and Meranto, *Electing Black Mayors*, 188–89; *Gary American*, October 3, 1958, p. 1; interview with Ezell Cooper, United Steelworkers of America, Griffith, Indiana, May 16, 1989.

27. U.S. Bureau of the Census, *Twentieth Census of the United States, 1980, Census Tracts*, pp. P-98, P-104.

28. The infusion of labor activists in mainstream civil rights organizations after World War II was not unique to Gary. See Korstad and Lichtenstein, "Opportunities Found and Lost," 786–811.

29. *Gary American*, January 30, 1959, p. 1.

30. Cooper interview.

31. Clifford Minton, "Leisure Time Activities and Needs of the Midtown Area," speech delivered at Citizens Conference on Local Health, Welfare, and Recreational Needs, Gary, Indiana, September 20, 1950, folder 4, box 1, Clifford Minton Papers, CRA.

32. Reverend L. K. Jackson, "An Open Letter to the Citizens of Gary," 1955, box 1, Reverend L. K. Jackson Collection, CRA.

33. "A Statement Regarding Important Matters Involving Civil Rights and Race Relations in Gary, Indiana," signed by prominent local civil rights leaders, June 5, 1961, folder 5, box 1, Clifford Minton Papers, CRA.

34. *Gary American*, August 1949, Press Clipping Collection, Indiana Room, GPL; Reverend L. K. Jackson, "An Open Letter to the Citizens of Gary"; *Gary Post-Tribune*, August 3, 1949, Anselm Forum Collection, Indiana Room, GPL.

35. *Gary Post-Tribune*, August 27, 1949, Press Clipping Collection, Indiana Room, GPL.

36. Memorandum from Reuben Olsen, 1949, Anselm Forum Collection, Indiana Room, GPL.

37. *Gary Post-Tribune*, August 27, 1949, Press Clipping Collection, Indiana Room, GPL.

38. Cooper interview.

39. Greta Vaughn Brown et al., "Report on Incident at Marquette Park Beach (July 1, 1953) Gary, Indiana," July 7, 1953, memorandum from Clifford Minton to Mayor Peter Mandich, July 14, 16, 1953, memorandum from Clifford Minton to R. Maurice Ross, associate executive director, National Urban League, July 7, 1953, and Clifford Minton, "Gary's (Indiana) Marquette Park and Beach on Lake Michigan: Racial Discrimination and Segregation," July 10, 1984, all in folder 12, box 1, Clifford Minton Papers, CRA; interview with Clifford Minton, Gary Urban League, Gary, Indiana, January 12, 1987; "Brief History of the Gary Branch NAACP, 1916–1967," 1967, box 5, City of Gary Collection, CRA.

40. "A Statement Regarding Important Matters Involving Civil Rights and Race Relations in Gary, Indiana," signed by prominent black community leaders, June 5, 1961, folder 5, box 1, Clifford Minton Papers, CRA.

41. "Summary of Allegation Regarding the Incident at Marquette Park Beach on Memorial Day, May 30, 1961," signed by fourteen community leaders, June 5, 1961, folder 5, box 1, Clifford Minton Papers, CRA.

42. *Gary Post-Tribune*, June 7, 1961, Press Clipping Collection, Indiana Room, GPL.

43. Interview with Nathan Cooley, manager, Marquette Park pavilion, Gary, Indiana, May 2, 1986.

44. John Bubik, president, Miller Citizens Corporation, to Edward Chalko, superintendent, Gary Department of Parks and Recreation, June 19, 1978, folder 1, box 1, Gerald Hebert Collection, CRA.

45. Testimony of Morning Parks, publicity chairman, City Wide Neighborhood Action Council, February 4, 1971, in "Proceedings of Public Hearing at Gary City Hall, Gary Park and Recreation Board," folder 11, box 1, Community Action to Reverse Pollution Records, CRA.

46. Testimony of Annette Long, February 4, 1971, in "Proceedings of Public Hearing"; *Gary Post-Tribune*, October 22, 1968, folder 8, box 1, Community Action to Reverse Pollution Records, CRA.

47. U.S. Bureau of the Census, *Seventeenth Census of the United States, 1950, Census Tracts*, 65–67.

48. City of Gary, "Select Data on Housing," [1965], box 1, Judy Eichorn Collection, CRA.

49. U.S. Bureau of the Census, *Seventeenth Census of the United States, 1950, Census Tracts*, 65–67, 267–69, and *Eighteenth Census of the United States, 1960, Population and Housing, Census Tracts*, 14–17, 42–44.

50. U.S. Department of Health, Education, and Welfare, Bureau of Community Environmental Management, Region V, *An Assessment of Rat Problems*; U.S. Bureau of the Census, *Eighteenth Census of the United States, 1960, Population and Housing, Census Tracts*, 51; *Gary Post-Tribune*, June 27, 1975, box 1, Miller Citizens Corporation Collection, Wildermuth Branch, GPL.

51. Interview with Jim Holland, deputy mayor, Gary, Indiana, November 18, 1986.

52. Gary Urban League, "What Is a Block Unit?," n.d., [1950s], microfilm reel 15, Gary Urban League Papers, CPL.

53. Lane, *City of the Century*, 278–79; William E. Nelson and Meranto, *Electing Black Mayors*, 190–92; Combined Citizens Committee on Open Occupancy, "Letter to Supporters of Fair Housing," March 16, 1963, box 1, Judy Eichorn Collection, CRA.

54. Interview with John McWilliams, former real estate agent, East Chicago, Illinois, December 18, 1986; interview with Louis Comer, conducted by David Nelson, [1969], box 2, David Nelson Collection, CRA.

55. Kerns, *Study of the Social and Economic Conditions*, 63.

56. Gary Urban League, "Special Report on Housing, Race Relations and Neighborhood Conservation," June 1955, microfilm reel 15, Gary Urban League Papers, CPL.

57. A similar phenomenon occurred in Chicago. See Hirsch, *Making the Second Ghetto*, 1–40.

58. U.S. Bureau of the Census, *Eighteenth Census of the United States, 1960, Population and Housing, Census Tracts*, 15–17, and *Twentieth Census of the United States, 1980, Census Tracts*, pp. P-35–P-37.

59. Interview with Ann Anderson, Gary, Indiana, May 20, 1989.

60. Harriet Klinger, chief chemist, Gary Air Pollution Control Division, "Investi-

gation of Paint Discoloration in Near Northeast Gary," May 15, 1972, private files of Herschel Bornstein.

61. *Chicago Tribune*, April 27, 1973, p. 2. Although the article did not specify Mary's race, the neighborhood it described was an area that was becoming increasingly populated by African Americans.

62. Gary Urban League, "Special Report on Housing," 1–4; Comer interview; *Gary Post-Tribune*, January 18, 1968, Press Clipping Collection, Indiana Room, GPL; *Gary Post-Tribune*, June 27, 1975, box 1, Miller Citizens Corporation Collection, Wildermuth Branch, GPL.

63. Interview with Richard Hatcher, Gary, Indiana, May 26, 1989; Poinsett, *Black Power Gary Style*, 27–31.

64. Hatcher, "My First Year in Office," 116–22; Greer, "The 'Liberation' of Gary," 36–38; Levine, *Racial Conflict*, 75–76.

65. *Gary Info*, February 14, 1969, p. 4.

66. Interview with Charles Allen, former city planning commissioner, Chicago, Illinois, December 10, 1986; Cooley interview.

67. Hatcher interview; Hatcher, "My First Year in Office," 117; "Gary Presses a Claim," 40–41.

68. Hatcher interview.

69. Greer, *Big Steel*, 161–81; Holland interview; *Gary Post-Tribune*, February 23, 1973, Newspaper Clipping Memory Book, GAPCD.

70. *Gary Post-Tribune*, September 16, 1970, Newspaper Clipping Memory Book, GAPCD.

71. *Gary Post-Tribune*, January 17, 1971, Newspaper Clipping Memory Book, GAPCD; *Gary Post-Tribune*, April 20, 1971, private files of Herschel Bornstein; interview with Herschel Bornstein, Gary, Indiana, April 8, 1986; Greer, *Big Steel*, 190–91.

72. Gerald W. Grandey, Lawrence S. Grossman, and Alan P. Donaldson, "The Manischewitz Caper," May 1971, unpublished paper, Northwestern School of Law, p. 16.

73. Gary Air Pollution Advisory Board Meeting Minutes, 1964–69, private files of Elaine Beck.

74. Hatcher interview.

75. Hatcher, "We Must Pave the Way," 414.

76. *Gary Info*, December 28, 1972, p. 4.

77. Assorted documents regarding pollution control history of Bucko Construction company, 1957–73, Bucko Construction folder, Compliance Files, and Complaint Log, both in GAPCD.

78. Gary Concentrated Employment Program, "Annual Report," 1971, box 1, Judy Eichorn Collection, and "Model Cities Program Summary," [1970], folder 28, box 1, Community Action to Reverse Pollution Records, both in CRA.

79. For an elaboration of this point, see Katznelson, *City Trenches*, 106.

80. See, for instance, *Gary Crusader*, February 25, 1971, p. 4.

1. *Gary Post-Tribune*, December 15, 1970, p. B3, December 16, 1970, p. 1; telephone interview with Phil Starr, former VISTA worker, Cleveland, Ohio, February 9, 1987.

2. King, *Fire in My Bones*, 101–2.

3. *Gary Info*, August 2, 1968, pp. 1–2.

4. Frady, "Gary," 39–41.

5. Ibid., 39.

6. Lane, *City of the Century*, 294; *Gary Info*, May 24, 1968, p. 1; interview with Steve Morris, student boycott leader, conducted by Joe Haynes, [1969], box 2, David Nelson Collection, CRA.

7. Interview with Helen Hoock, Gary, Indiana, April 2, 1986.

8. *Gary Info*, December 11, 1970, pp. 1, 4.

9. Interview with Richard Hatcher, Gary, Indiana, May 26, 1989; Hoock interview, April 2, 1986.

10. Starr interview; interview with Julie Mortier, former VISTA worker, Gary, Indiana, January 14, 1987.

11. Community Action to Reverse Pollution, "Why We Need Ordinance #70-60," December 1, 1970, p. 1, folder 7, box 1, Community Action to Reverse Pollution Records, CRA.

12. Testimony of Ted Falls, Northwest Indiana Clean Air Co-Ordinating Committee, before Gary Air Pollution Advisory Board, September 3, 1970, private files of Elaine Beck.

13. Jack Troy, Committee on Environmental Health, Indiana Chapter, American Academy of Pediatrics, to Gary, Indiana, City Council, December 15, 1970, folder 7, box 1, Community Action to Reverse Pollution Records, CRA; *Gary Post-Tribune*, April 22, 1973, Press Clipping Collection, Indiana Room, GPL.

14. Gary Air Pollution Advisory Board Meeting Minutes, June 5, 1969, June 4, July 2, 1970, folder 4, box 1, Elaine Kaplan Collection, CRA; *Gary Post-Tribune*, March 8, 1970, p. B1; *Gary Post-Tribune*, September 12, 1970, Newspaper Clipping Memory Book, GAPCD; Hatcher interview.

15. J. David Carr, superintendent, Gary Works, to Joel Johnson, August 31, 1970, private files of Herschel Bornstein; *Gary Post-Tribune*, September 12, 1970, Newspaper Clipping Memory Book, GAPCD; *Gary Post-Tribune*, September 16, 1970, Newspaper Clipping Memory Book, GAPCD.

16. Gary Plan Commission, *Physical Data*, 18.

17. "Statement by Helen Hoock, CARP, before City Council," September 15, 1970, folder 7, box 1, Community Action to Reverse Pollution Records, CRA.

18. Testimony of Helen Hoock before Gary City Council on behalf of CARP, December 15, 1970, folder 7, box 1, Community Action to Reverse Pollution Records, CRA.

19. Community Action to Reverse Pollution, "Why We Need Ordinance #70-60."

20. Krickus, "Organizing Neighborhoods," 78.

21. Calumet Community Congress Executive Committee Meeting Minutes, December 16, 1970, private files of Beverly Wright.

22. *Gary Post-Tribune*, July 11, 1971, Press Clipping Collection, Indiana Room, GPL.

23. CARP, "Coke Oven Project—Results of Org. Contacts," October 1970, folder 10, box 12, Lotte Meyerson Collection, CRA.

24. Jean Thurman to Cleo Wesson, Gary City Council, December 1, 1970, folder 10, box 12, Lotte Meyerson Collection, CRA.

25. Starr interview; Frady, "Gary," 38.

26. Community Action to Reverse Pollution, "'Friend of the Court' Statement to Gary Air Pollution Appeal Board," July 16, 1971, private files of Milton Roth.

27. Decision of Gary Air Pollution Appeal Board, August 26, 1971, private files of Milton Roth.

28. *Gary Post-Tribune*, June 23, 1972, p. A16.

29. *Gary Post-Tribune*, June 29, 1972, Newspaper Clipping Memory Book, GAPCD.

30. U.S. Environmental Protection Agency, *The First Two Years*, 4.

31. *Chicago Tribune*, January 25, 1973, p. 8; Petulla, *American Environmentalism*, 189; interview with David Kee, director, Air and Radiation Divisions, U.S. Environmental Protection Agency, Region V, Chicago, Illinois, May 19, 1989.

32. Minutes of special meeting between U.S. Steel and city officials, "Discussion of Variance Request by U.S. Steel on the 1965 Agreement," September 1, 1972, private files of Elaine Beck; *Gary Post-Tribune*, May 7, 1973, Newspaper Clipping Memory Book, GAPCD; *Gary Post-Tribune*, June 27, 1973, private files of Elaine Beck; interview with Dennis McGuire, Gary Air Pollution Control Division, Gary, Indiana, October 26, 1986.

33. Community Action to Reverse Pollution, "'Friend of the Court' Statement," and "Why We Need Ordinance #70-60."

34. Donald Dreyfus, attorney, Gary Health Department, "Coke Plant Decision Affirmed," press release, May 1972, private files of Herschel Bornstein.

35. Interview with Victor Nordlund, USX Corporation, Gary, Indiana, May 20, 1986; *Gary Post-Tribune*, June 29, 1972, Newspaper Clipping Memory Book, GAPCD.

36. Testimony of Helen Hoock, December 15, 1970.

37. Interview with Charles Allen, former city planning commissioner, Chicago, Illinois, December 10, 1986.

38. Helen Hoock to Archie Adams, Universal Atlas Cement, November 2, 1970, folder 2, box 1, Community Action to Reverse Pollution Records, CRA.

39. *Gary Post-Tribune*, November 18, 1970, Newspaper Clipping Memory Book, GAPCD.

40. U.S. Steel's behavior in this regard was consistent with its rigid posture elsewhere in the country. See Petulla, *American Environmentalism*, 188–89.

41. *Newsweek*, September 13, 1971, p. 59; Hatcher interview.

42. Lane, *City of the Century*, 302.

43. Overall Economic Development Committee, *Initial Overall Economic Development Program*, 44.

44. *Chicago Tribune*, July 19, 1973, Newspaper Clipping Memory Book, GAPCD.

45. Overall Economic Development Committee, *Initial Overall Economic Development Program*, 70.

46. U.S. Bureau of the Census, *Twentieth Census of the United States, 1980, Census Tracts*, p. P-62.

47. *Gary Post-Tribune*, December 2, 1972, p. 1.

48. *Gary Post-Tribune*, December 20, 1975, Newspaper Clipping Memory Book, GAPCD; *Gary Post-Tribune*, December 21, 1975, p. 1.

49. U.S. Steel Corporation, "USS Gary Works, United States Steel Bicentennial," tour brochure, folder 2, box 1, U.S. Steel Corporation Collection, CRA.

50. *Gary Post-Tribune*, December 11, 14, 19, 20, 21, 23, 1974, Newspaper Clipping Memory Book, GAPCD; *New York Times*, January 5, 1975, p. 43; Greer, *Big Steel*, 194–95; interview with Ezell Cooper, United Steelworkers of America, Griffith, Indiana, May 16, 1989.

51. *Gary Post-Tribune*, March 8, 1972, Newspaper Clipping Memory Book, GAPCD.

52. Gary Air Pollution Advisory Board Meeting Minutes, May 5, 1972, private files of Elaine Beck.

53. *Gary Post-Tribune*, June 4, 1975, Newspaper Clipping Memory Book, GAPCD.

54. *Gary Post-Tribune*, July 24, October 2, 1975, Newspaper Clipping Memory Book, GAPCD; State Air Pollution Control Division, "Gary Air Pollution Control Evaluation," August 7, 1974, private files of Elaine Beck.

55. Interview with Harry Williams, director, Division of Air Pollution Control, Indiana State Board of Health, Indianapolis, Indiana, November 12, 1986.

56. Kee interview.

57. *Gary Post-Tribune*, January 25, 1973, p. B1; *Chicago Sun-Times*, December 11, 1975, Newspaper Clipping Memory Book, GAPCD; letter to management from Edgar Speer, chairman, U.S. Steel Corporation, February 23, 1976, private files of Elaine Beck; Greer, *Big Steel*, 201–2.

58. Rosenbaum, *Environmental Politics*, 23; Hays, *Beauty, Health, and Permanence*, 298–300, 313; Petulla, *American Environmentalism*, 185–86; *New York Times*, September 6, 1987, p. F6; interview with Edward Wojciechowski, U.S. Environmental Protection Agency, Region V, Chicago, Illinois, May 19, 1989.

59. *New York Times*, January 5, 1975, p. 43.

Chapter 7

1. Gary Air Pollution Control Division, "Summary of Accomplishments," [1970], folder 3, box 1, Community Action to Reverse Pollution Records, CRA.

2. *Gary Post-Tribune*, June 11, 1972, Newspaper Clipping Memory Book, GAPCD.

3. Cannon and Armentrout, *Environmental Steel Update*, 203. For specific examples of U.S. Steel's recalcitrant actions in other cities, see Petulla, *American Environmentalism*, 189.

4. These figures for U.S. Steel include emissions from its cement plant. Gary Air Pollution Control Division, "Twenty-five Ton Potential Emission," in author's possession; U.S. Department of Health, Education, and Welfare, Public Health Service, *Air Pollutant Emission Inventory*, 19; Cannon and Armentrout, *Environmental Steel Update*, 201; James H. Dickerson, "'Overview of Environmental Control': U.S. Steel, Gary Works," address, March 14, 1975, private files of James Dickerson.

5. U.S. Department of Health, Education, and Welfare, Public Health Service, *Air Pollutant Emission Inventory*, 24; Gary Air Pollution Control Division, "Twenty-five Ton Potential Emission"; Gary Department of Health, "Public Health in New Gary: Public Health Activities in Gary during 1972," [1973], p. 68, Indiana Room, GPL.

6. NIPSCO, "Annual Report," 1974, NIPSCO Annual Reports Collection, CRA.

7. Gary Air Pollution Advisory Board Meeting Minutes, Gary, Indiana, March 24, 1971, private files of Elaine Beck; interview with Roland P. Elvambuena, chief engineer, Gary Air Pollution Department, Gary, Indiana, October 9, 1986; interview with Earl Mann, formerly with NIPSCO, Portage, Indiana, November 17, 1986.

8. *Gary Post-Tribune*, [February 1951], scrapbook, Philip Rosenbloom Collection, CRA; Gary Chamber of Commerce, Governmental Affairs and Tax Research Department, *Public versus Private Ownership of the Local Water Company*.

9. U.S. Department of the Interior, Federal Water Pollution Control Administration, *Progress Evaluation Meeting*, 2:354; U.S. Department of Health, Education, and Welfare, Technical Committee on Water Quality, *Water Quality in the Calumet Area*, 26–27; Dickerson, " 'Overview of Environmental Control' "; "Gary Works Environmental Control, Water Quality," memorandum, 1982, Victor Nordlund Files, USX Corporation, Gary, Indiana.

10. *United States Steel Corporation v. Russell E. Train et al.* and *United States Steel Corporation v. United States Environmental Protection Agency*, 556 F.2d 822 (7th Cir 1977), p. 831.

11. *Chicago Sun-Times*, September 28, 1977, p. 26; testimony of David Ullrich, EPA attorney, Gary Works hearing, Hammond, Indiana, September 27, 1977, Dale Bryson Files, U.S. Environmental Protection Agency, Region V, Chicago, Illinois.

12. Interview with Pete Redmond, U.S. Environmental Protection Agency, Region V, Chicago, Illinois, May 25, 1989.

13. Interview with F. Leonard Coventry, former superintendent of Gary Sanitary District, Rockville, Indiana, November 11, 1986.

14. U.S. Environmental Protection Agency, *Master Plan for Improving Water Quality*, pp. 1-1–1-11, 2-39; Indiana Department of Environmental Management, *Northwest Indiana Environmental Action Plan*, 46, 49, 53–71.

15. U.S. Department of the Interior, Fish and Wildlife Service, *Physical and Ecological Effects of Waste Heat*, 15–20; U.S. Environmental Protection Agency, "Lake Michigan Study Summary," June 1979, private files of Elaine Beck; interview with Nathan Cooley, manager, Marquette Park pavilion, Gary, Indiana, May 2, 1986; Indiana Department of Environmental Management, *Northwest Indiana Environmental Action Plan*, 20–21, 35.

16. Gary Air Pollution Advisory Board Meeting Minutes, April 7, 1972, Elaine Kaplan Collection, CRA.

17. Interview with Ann Anderson, Gary, Indiana, May 20, 1989; U.S. Bureau of the Census, *Twentieth Census of the United States, 1980, Census Tracts*, pp. P-35, P-51.

18. Interview with Charles Kern, NIPSCO, Highland, Indiana, January 23, 1987; interview with William Staehle, former city planner, Gary, Indiana, December 4, 1986.

19. U.S. Steel Corporation, "Gary Works Information Report: Tar Decanter Sludge Disposal Area HWD-2," and "Gary Works Exposure Information Report: Hazardous

Waste Landfill HWD-5," both in folder 3, USS Gary Works and Tubing Specialties Files, RCRA Files; U.S. Department of the Interior, Federal Water Pollution Control Administration, *Progress Evaluation Meeting*, 3:491–94.

20. RCRA Inspection Report, April 29, 1981, DH Mitchell Generating Station, Gary, Indiana, Files, RCRA Files.

21. Coventry interview; interview with Mildred Melton, Gary Sanitary District, Gary, Indiana, April 29, 1986.

22. Gary Plan Commission Meeting Minutes, November 27, 1979, January 29, 1980, City Clerk's Office, City Hall, Gary, Indiana; interview with William Bogner, president, Independent Waste Systems, Gary, Indiana, May 16, 1989; "Preliminary Assessment," [1980], and accompanying documents, Gary Land Development Landfill Files, CERCLIS-EPA.

23. Interview with George Oliver, Indiana Department of Environmental Management, Indianapolis, Indiana, November 13, 1986.

24. This figure was derived from the list of CERCLIS sites. Because the list only includes sites discovered by the EPA, fifteen is a conservative estimate.

25. Northwest Indiana Regional Planning Commission, "The Industrial Heritage of Northwest Indiana," 1974, box 1, Northwest Indiana Regional Planning Commission Collection, CRA; Radner, *Study and Technical Recommendations*, 10–11; Overall Economic Development Committee, *Initial Overall Economic Development Program*, 42.

26. "Site Inspection Report," May 15, 1984, and "Documentation Records for Hazard Ranking System," June 28, 1982, both in Conservation Chemical Company Files, CERCLIS-EPA.

27. This information is based on a survey of CERCLIS and RCRA preliminary investigation reports of hazardous waste sites in Gary, Indiana, conducted under the auspices of the EPA and the Indiana Board of Health. The reports are located in the files of the Indiana Department of Environmental Management in Indianapolis, Indiana, as well as in the files of the U.S. Environmental Protection Agency, Region V, Chicago, Illinois.

28. Oliver interview; Gary Plan Commission, *Physical Data*, 13. For a discussion of similar problems throughout the nation, see Montague, "Limitations of Landfilling," 3–18.

29. This information comes from RCRA and CERCLIS investigation reports.

30. "Site Inspection Report," August 30, 1982, "Midco #1, Gary, Indiana," July 1981, and "Preliminary Assessment," March 10, 1983, all in Midco I Files, and "Midwest Solvent Recovery (MID-CO #1), Midwest Industrial Waste Disposal (MID-CO #2), Lake County, Indiana," n.d., Midco II Files, all in CERCLIS-EPA.

31. *Gary Post-Tribune*, July 22, 1964, November 4, 1967, March 7, 1973, Press Clipping Collection, Indiana Room, GPL.

32. "Results of the 1957 Comprehensive Zoning Plan," *Gary Post-Tribune*, February 1, 1958, pp. 17–27.

33. *Gary Post-Tribune*, April 1, 1968, March 31, 1971, November 15, 1972, March 7, May 2, 1973, Press Clipping Collection, Indiana Room, GPL.

34. *Gary Post-Tribune*, July 8, 1964, Press Clipping Collection, Indiana Room, GPL.

35. *Gary Post-Tribune*, July 23, 1964, Press Clipping Collection, Indiana Room, GPL.

36. *Gary Post-Tribune*, December 28, 1962, p. 16; interview with Judy Smith, Miller Citizens Corporation, Gary, Indiana, March 14, 1986; Board of Zoning Appeals Minutes, 1970–71, folder 9, box 1, John Pilzer Collection, CRA.

37. Staehle interview.

38. Reshkin and Strahun, *Environmental Perspectives*, 131.

39. "Site Inspection Report," 1984, and accompanying documents, Gary City Dump Files, CERCLIS-IDEM; interview with John McWilliams, former real estate agent, East Chicago, Indiana, December 18, 1986; *Gary Post-Tribune*, February 3, 1971, folder 17, box 3, Herschel Bornstein Collection, CRA; *Gary Post-Tribune*, June 12, 1972, Newspaper Clipping Memory Book, GAPCD; *Chicago Tribune*, November 26, 1972, sec. S10, p. 5; *Gary Post-Tribune*, August 27, 1974, Press Clipping Collection, Indiana Room, GPL.

40. Interview with Charles Allen, former city planning commissioner, Chicago, Illinois, December 10, 1986.

41. *Gary Post-Tribune*, January 20, 1972, Press Clipping Collection, Indiana Room, GPL; "Preliminary Assessment," May 3, 1983, Lake Sandy Jo Files, CERCLIS-EPA.

42. *Gary Post-Tribune*, January 5, 1972, Press Clipping Collection, Indiana Room, GPL.

43. "Preliminary Assessment," May 3, 1983, Lake Sandy Jo Files, CERCLIS-EPA; *Gary Post-Tribune*, January 5, 20, 1972, Press Clipping Collection, Indiana Room, GPL.

44. *Gary Post-Tribune*, August 28, 1974, Press Clipping Collection, Indiana Room, GPL; interview with Richard Hatcher, Gary, Indiana, May 26, 1989; Gary Plan Commission Meeting Minutes, May 27, 1980, City Clerk's Office, City Hall, Gary, Indiana.

45. Hatcher interview.

46. Mildred Gruenenfelder, chair, Gary League of Women Voters Environmental Quality Committee, to committee members, August 12, 1971, "Environmental Quality" Folder, box 1, Gary League of Women Voters Records, CRA.

47. "Hazard Ranking System Report," June 13, 1984, and memorandum from Mark Lunsford, Ecology and Environment, Inc., to Jerry Oskavarch, June 7, 1984, both in Midco II Files, "Site Inspection Report," May 15, 1984, and "Documentation Records for Hazard Ranking System," June 28, 1982, both in Conservation Chemical Company Files, and "Preliminary Assessment," December 12, 1982, Roland Dump Files, all in CERCLIS-EPA.

48. The toxic substances detected in wells were tetrachloroethylene, benzene, and toluene. "Preliminary Assessment," May 3, 1983, Lake Sandy Jo Files, CERCLIS-EPA; *Gary Post-Tribune*, January 5, 20, 1972, Press Clipping Collection, Indiana Room, GPL.

49. McWilliams interview; "Preliminary Assessment," February 2, 1983, Ninth Avenue Dump Files, "Preliminary Assessment," February 10, 1983, Midco I Files, and "Potential Waste Site Preliminary Inspection," August 1, 1986, Black Oak Landfill Files, all in CERCLIS-EPA; *Gary Post-Tribune*, August 5, 1970, p. 1.

50. *Chicago Tribune*, August 16, 1977, sec. 1, p. 3.

51. U.S. Bureau of the Census, *Twentieth Census of the United States, 1980, Census Tracts*, pp. P-65–P-67, P-79–P-81.

52. Tarr, "The Search for the Ultimate Sink."

53. Smith interview.

54. U.S. Bureau of the Census, *Twentieth Census of the United States, 1980, Census Tracts*, p. P-34.

Epilogue

1. For descriptions of Gary in the 1980s, see Glastris, "Steel's Hollow Comeback," and *New York Times*, September 4, 1989, p. 1.

2. The study of corporate restructuring, deindustrialization, and Rust Belt cities is extensive. See, for example, Bensman and Lynch, *Rusted Dreams*; Zukin, *Landscapes of Power*, 59–102; Jakle and Wilson, *Derelict Landscapes*; Reich, *The Work of Nations*; Bluestone and Harrison, *The Deindustrialization of America*; Harrison and Bluestone, *The Great U-Turn*; Kochan, Katz, and McKersie, *Transformation of American Industrial Relations*; and Moody, *An Injury to All*, 95–126.

3. *Chicago Tribune*, March 6, 1988, sec. 7, p. 3, April 17, 1988, sec. 7, pp. 1, 8; *New York Times*, September 4, 1989, p. 1; Moody, *An Injury to All*, 1–2; Singer, Lynch, and Holowaty, "Dinosaurs on the Lake?"

4. *New York Times*, May 7, 1987, p. A16, September 4, 1989, p. 1.

5. Interview with Richard Hatcher, Gary, Indiana, May 26, 1989.

6. "Site Inspection Report," 1984, and accompanying documents, Gary City Dump Files, CERCLIS-IDEM.

7. *New York Times*, September 28, 1989, p. 18.

8. Interview with Bill Bogner, president, Independent Waste Systems, Gary, Indiana, May 16, 1989.

9. Indiana Department of Environmental Management, *Northwest Indiana Environmental Action Plan*, appendix A, 15–19.

10. Berry, *Social Burdens*; Brodine, "Special Burden"; McCaull, "Discriminatory Air Pollution."

11. Greenberg and Anderson, *Hazardous Waste Sites*; Bullard and Wright, "Politics of Pollution."

12. Robert D. Bullard, "Anatomy of Environmental Racism and the Environmental Justice Movement," in Bullard, *Confronting Environmental Racism*, 24–29.

13. United Church of Christ, Commission for Racial Justice, *Toxic Wastes and Race*, xiii–xiv.

14. U.S. Environmental Protection Agency, *Environmental Equity*, 1–5.

15. Quoted in Leiss, *The Domination of Nature*, 195.

Bibliography

Manuscript Collections

Chicago, Illinois
Chicago Historical Society
  United Steelworkers of America, District 31, Collection
Chicago Public Library, Carter Woodson Branch
  Vivian Harsh Collection
U.S. Environmental Protection Agency, Region V
  Dale Bryson Files
  Comprehensive Environmental Response, Compensation, Liability, Inventory
    System Files
  Resource Conservation and Recovery Act Files

Gary, Indiana
Calumet Regional Archives, Indiana University–Northwest
  Fosty Bella Collection, no. 177
  Herschel Bornstein Collection, no. 251
  Calumet Community Congress Collection, no. 95
  George Chacharis Collection, no. 18
  City of Gary Collection, no. 10
  Thomas Colosimo Collection, no. 325
  Community Action to Reverse Pollution Records, no. 99
  Judy Eichorn Collection, no. 66
  Samuel Evett Collection, no. 137
  Gary Chamber of Commerce Collection, no. 1
  Gary League of Women Voters Records, no. 4
  Gary Redevelopment Commission Records, no. 154
  Richard Hatcher Collection, no. 86
  Gerald Hebert Collection, no. 171
  John Howard Collection, no. 141
  Indiana Dunes National Lakeshore Collection, no. 22
  Reverend L. K. Jackson Collection, no. 71
  Elaine Kaplan Collection, no. 264
  Orval Kincaid Collection, no. 91
  William Kranz Collection, no. 122
  John Mayerick Collection, no. 168
  Lotte Meyerson Collection, no. 303
  Mid-City Investment Company Records, no. 162
  Miller Citizens Corporation Records, no. 130
  Clifford Minton Papers, no. 160
  David Nelson Collection, no. 67

NIPSCO Annual Reports Collection, no. 235
Northwest Indiana Regional Planning Commission Collection, no. 6
John Pilzer Collection, no. 278
Purdue-Calumet Development Foundation Records, no. 43
Frank Roman Collection, no. 77
Philip Rosenbloom Collection, no. 24
Save the Dunes Council Records, no. 149
John Schnurlein Collection, no. 140
Jean Shiras Collection, no. 269
Jeanette Strong Collection, no. 79
William "Buddy" Todd Collection, no. 188
United Steelworkers of America Collection, no. 13
U.S. Steel Corporation Collection, no. 41
Peter Yesh Collection, no. 241
City Clerk's Office, City Hall
Gary Plan Commission Minutes
Gary Air Pollution Control Division
Air Quality Reading Files
Complaint Log
Compliance Files
Newspaper Clipping Memory Book
Gary Public Library
Anselm Forum Collection, Indiana Room
Miller Citizens Corporation Collection, Wildermuth Branch
Press Clipping Collection, Indiana Room
United Steelworkers of America, Local 1014
Grievance Files
Health and Safety Files
USX Corporation
Victor Nordlund Files
Public Relations Files

Indianapolis, Indiana
Indiana Department of Environmental Management
Comprehensive Environmental Response, Compensation, Liability, Inventory
System Files
Indiana Air Pollution Control Board, Annual Reports
Resource Conservation and Recovery Act Files
Stream Pollution Control Board Files

State College, Pennsylvania
Labor Archives, Pennsylvania State University Library
United Steelworkers of America Collection
Civil Rights Department Records
International Executive Board Minutes

Oral History Collection
Safety and Health Department Records

Private Files
Elaine Beck, Gary, Indiana
Herschel Bornstein, Gary, Indiana
James Dickerson, Gary, Indiana
John Mayerick, Merrillville, Indiana
Milton Roth, Munster, Indiana
William Walden, Hammond, Indiana
Beverly Wright, Gary, Indiana

Federal, State, and Local Reports and Proceedings

City of Gary. *Annual Report*. 1970–80.
Gary Chamber of Commerce. Governmental Affairs and Tax Research Department. *Public versus Private Ownership of the Local Water Company*. 1960.
Gary City Directory. 1939–80.
Gary Health Department. *Annual Report*. 1966–75.
Gary Plan Commission. *Comprehensive Plan, The City of Gary, Indiana: The Master Physical Development Plan for the City of Gary, Indiana*. Evanston: Tec-Search, 1964.
———. *Physical Data: Natural Characteristics and Existing Modifications*. Master Report, no. 1. 1963.
Gary Planning Commission. *Planning Gary's Tomorrow, 1945–1955*. 1945.
Gary Redevelopment Commission. *Gary, Indiana, Community Renewal Program*. Mishawaka: City Planning Associates, 1968.
———. *A Social Survey of Selected Gary Areas*. Gary Community Renewal Program, report no. 6. Mishawaka: City Planning Associates, 1967.
Gary Sanitary District. *Annual Report*. 1945–81.
Indiana Department of Environmental Management. *Northwest Indiana Environmental Action Plan*. Indianapolis, 1988.
Indiana Department of Natural Resources. *An Inventory of Man-Made Land along the Indiana Shoreline of Lake Michigan*. Indianapolis, 1979.
Overall Economic Development Committee, in Cooperation with the City of Gary's Office of Economic Development. *Initial Overall Economic Development Program, City of Gary, Indiana*. 1976.
U.S. Bureau of the Census. *Sixteenth Census of the United States, 1940. Business, Retail Trade, 1939*. Washington, D.C.: Government Printing Office, 1943.
———. *Sixteenth Census of the United States, 1940. Characteristics of the Population, Indiana*. Washington, D.C.: Government Printing Office, 1943.
———. *Sixteenth Census of the United States, 1940. Housing, Block Statistics*. Washington, D.C.: Government Printing Office, 1942.
———. *United States Census of Business, 1948. Retail Trade, Area Statistics*. Washington, D.C.: Government Printing Office, 1951.

————. *Seventeenth Census of the United States, 1950. Census Tracts.* Final Report P-D10. Washington, D.C.: Government Printing Office, 1952.

————. *Seventeenth Census of the United States, 1950. Characteristics of the Population, Indiana.* Washington, D.C.: Government Printing Office, 1952.

————. *Seventeenth Census of the United States, 1950. Housing, Block Statistics.* Washington, D.C.: Government Printing Office, 1951.

————. *Eighteenth Census of the United States, 1960. Characteristics of the Population, Indiana.* Washington, D.C.: Government Printing Office, 1963.

————. *Eighteenth Census of the United States, 1960. Population and Housing, Census Tracts.* Final Report PHC (1)-54. Washington, D.C.: Government Printing Office, 1961.

————. *United States Census of Business, 1963. Retail Trade, Summary Statistics.* Washington, D.C.: Government Printing Office, 1966.

————. *United States Census of Business, 1967. Retail Trade, Area Statistics.* Washington, D.C.: Government Printing Office, 1970.

————. *Historical Statistics of the United States, Colonial Times to 1970.* Bicentennial edition. Washington, D.C.: Government Printing Office, 1975.

————. *Nineteenth Census of the United States, 1970. Characteristics of the Population, Indiana.* Washington, D.C.: Government Printing Office, 1973.

————. *Nineteenth Census of the United States, 1970. Population and Housing, Census Tracts.* Final Report PHC (1)-79. Washington, D.C.: Government Printing Office, 1972.

————. *Twentieth Census of the United States, 1980. Census Tracts.* Final Report PHC 80-2-169. Washington, D.C.: Government Printing Office, 1983.

U.S. Department of Health, Education, and Welfare. Bureau of Community Environmental Management, Region V. *An Assessment of Rat Problems and Associated Environmental Conditions in the City of Gary, Indiana.* Washington, D.C.: Government Printing Office, 1971.

U.S. Department of Health, Education, and Welfare. Public Health Service. *Air Pollutant Emission Inventory of Northwest Indiana: A Preliminary Survey.* Washington, D.C.: Government Printing Office, 1966.

————. *Air Quality Criteria for Particulate Matter: Summary and Conclusions.* Washington, D.C.: Government Printing Office, 1969.

————. *Report on Pollution of the Waters of the Grand Calumet River, Little Calumet River, Calumet River, Lake Michigan, Wolf Lake, and Their Tributaries.* Washington, D.C.: Government Printing Office, 1965.

U.S. Department of Health, Education, and Welfare. Technical Committee on Water Quality. *Water Quality in the Calumet Area: Conference on Pollution of Lower Lake Michigan, Calumet River, Grand Calumet River, Little Calumet River, and Wolf Lake, Illinois and Indiana.* Washington, D.C.: Government Printing Office, 1970.

U.S. Department of the Interior. Federal Water Pollution Control Administration. *Proceedings, Conference, Pollution of Lake Michigan and Its Tributary Basin.* 7 vols. Washington, D.C.: Government Printing Office, 1968.

————. *Progress Evaluation Meeting in the Matter of Pollution of the Interstate Waters of the Grand Calumet River, Little Calumet River, Calumet River, Wolf Lake, Lake*

Michigan, and Their Tributaries. 3 vols. Washington, D.C.: Government Printing Office, 1967.

————. *Proceedings, Progress Evaluation Meeting in the Matter of Pollution of the Interstate Waters of the Grand Calumet River, Little Calumet River, Calumet River, Wolf Lake, Lake Michigan, and Their Tributaries*. Second session. Washington, D.C.: Government Printing Office, 1967.

U.S. Department of the Interior. Fish and Wildlife Service. *Physical and Ecological Effects of Waste Heat on Lake Michigan*. Washington, D.C.: Government Printing Office, 1970.

U.S. Environmental Protection Agency. *Environmental Equity: Reducing Risk for All Communities*. Washington, D.C.: Government Printing Office, 1992.

————. *The First Two Years: A Review of EPA's Enforcement Program*. Washington, D.C.: Government Printing Office, 1973.

————. *Master Plan for Improving Water Quality in the Grand Calumet River/Indiana Harbor Canal*. Washington, D.C.: Government Printing Office, 1985.

————. *National Accomplishments in Pollution Control, 1970–1980: Some Case Histories*. Washington, D.C.: Government Printing Office, 1980.

Periodicals

The following periodicals were reviewed systematically for the years noted:

Gary Info, 1965–75
Gary Post-Tribune, 1945–80
Nasa Nada, 1945–61
Steel Labor (Midwest edition), 1940–60

Books, Articles, and Dissertations

Ackerman, Bruce A., and William T. Hassler. *Clean Coal/Dirty Air, or How the Clean Air Act Became a Multibillion-Dollar Bail-Out for High Sulfur Coal Producers and What Should Be Done about It*. New Haven: Yale University Press, 1981.

Andrews, Richard N. L. "Class Politics or Democratic Reform: Environmentalism and American Political Institutions." *Natural Resources Journal* 20 (April 1980): 221–42.

Balanoff, Elizabeth. "A History of the Black Community of Gary, Indiana, 1906–1940." Ph.D. diss., University of Chicago, 1974.

Banner, Warren M. *The Social and Economic Conditions in Three Minority Groups, Gary, Indiana*. New York: National Urban League, 1955.

Baritz, Loren. *The Good Life: The Meaning of Success for the American Middle Class*. New York: Harper and Row, 1990.

Bell, Daniel. *The Coming of Post-Industrial Society: A Venture in Social Forecasting*. 1973. Reprint, with a new foreword, New York: Basic Books, 1976.

————. *The Cultural Contradictions of Capitalism*. New York: Basic Books, 1978.

Bensman, David, and Roberta Lynch. *Rusted Dreams: Hard Times in a Steel Community*. New York: McGraw Hill, 1987.

Berman, Daniel M. *Death on the Job: Occupational Health and Safety Struggles in the United States.* New York: Monthly Review Press, 1978.

Bernstein, Barton J. "The Truman Administration and the Steel Strike of 1946." *Journal of American History* 52 (March 1966): 791–803.

Berry, Brian J. L. *The Social Burdens of Environmental Pollution: A Comparative Metropolitan Data Source.* Cambridge, Mass.: Ballinger Publishing, 1977.

Betheil, Richard. "The ENA in Perspective: The Transformation of Collective Bargaining in the Basic Steel Industry." *Review of Radical Political Economics* 10 (Summer 1978): 1–24.

Binford, Henry C. *The First Suburbs: Residential Communities on the Boston Periphery, 1815–1860.* Chicago: University of Chicago Press, 1985.

Bloomberg, Warner, Jr. "Five Hot Days in Gary." *Reporter*, August 11, 1955, pp. 36–38.

———. "Gary's Industrial Workers as Full Citizens: They Mean to Use Their New-Won Status and Power." *Commentary* 18 (September 1954): 202–10.

———. "The Power Structure of an Industrial Community." Ph.D. diss., University of Chicago, 1961.

———. "The State of the American Proletariat, 1955: Working Day and Living Time in Gary, Indiana." *Commentary* 19 (March 1955): 207–16.

———. "They'll Go Democratic Anyway." *New Republic*, October 15, 1956, pp. 13–15.

Bluestone, Barry, and Bennett Harrison. *The Deindustrialization of America: Plant Closings, Community Abandonment, and the Dismantling of Basic Industry.* New York: Basic Books, 1982.

Blum, John Morton. *V Was for Victory: Politics and American Culture during World War II.* San Diego: Harcourt Brace Jovanovich, 1976.

Blumin, Stuart. *The Emergence of the Middle Class: Social Experience in the American City, 1760–1900.* Cambridge: Cambridge University Press, 1989.

Bodnar, John. *The Transplanted: A History of Immigrants in Urban America.* Bloomington: Indiana University Press, 1985.

Bodnar, John, Roger Simon, and Michael Weber. *Lives of Their Own: Blacks, Italians, and Poles in Pittsburgh, 1900–1960.* Urbana: University of Illinois Press, 1982.

Bogdanich, George. "Labor Maverick on the March." *Progressive* 40 (August 1976): 13–18.

———. "Never a Kind Word for Abel." *Nation*, May 7, 1973, pp. 591–94.

———. "Steel: No Strike and Other Deals." *Nation*, September 7, 1974, pp. 171–74.

Bok, Derek C., and John T. Dunlop. *Labor and the American Community.* New York: Simon and Schuster, 1970.

Bookchin, Murray. *Our Synthetic Environment.* Rev. ed. New York: Harper Colophon, 1974.

Brodine, Virginia. "A Special Burden." *Environment* 18 (March 1976): 71–78.

Brody, David. *Steelworkers in America: The Nonunion Era.* Cambridge: Harvard University Press, 1960.

———. *Workers in Industrial America: Essays on the Twentieth Century Struggle.* New York: Oxford University Press, 1980.

Brown, Michael. *Laying Waste: The Poisoning of America by Toxic Chemicals*. Rev. ed. New York: Washington Square Press, 1981.

Bullard, Robert D. *Dumping in Dixie: Race, Class, and Environmental Quality*. Boulder, Colo.: Westview Press, 1990.

———. *Invisible Houston: The Black Experience in Boom and Bust*. College Station: Texas A & M University Press, 1987.

———, ed. *Confronting Environmental Racism: Voices from the Grassroots*. Boston: South End Press, 1993.

Bullard, Robert D., and Beverly Wright. "The Politics of Pollution: Implications for the Black Community." *Phylon* 47 (March 1986): 71–78.

Caldwell, Lynton K., Lynton R. Hayes, and Isabel M. MacWhirter. *Citizens and the Environment: Case Studies in Popular Action*. Bloomington: Indiana University Press, 1976.

Cannon, James S., and Frederick S. Armentrout. *Environmental Steel Update: Pollution in the Iron and Steel Industry*. New York: Council on Economic Priorities, 1977.

Center for Investigative Reporting and Bill Moyers. *Global Dumping Ground: The International Traffic in Hazardous Waste*. Washington, D.C.: Seven Locks Press, 1990.

Chandler, Alfred, Jr. *The Visible Hand: The Managerial Revolution in American Business*. Cambridge: Harvard University Press, 1977.

"The Cities: The Price of Optimism." *Time*, August 1, 1969, pp. 41–44.

Clayton, George D., and Florence E. Clayton, eds. *Patty's Industrial Hygiene and Toxicology*. Vol. 3, *Industrial Environmental Health: The Worker and the Community*, edited by L. V. Cralley and L. J. Cralley. New York: Wiley, 1972.

Coburn, Stuart E. "Disposal of Acid-Iron Wastes from a Steel Mill." *Industrial and Engineering Chemistry* 20 (March 1928): 248–49.

Cohen, Lizabeth. *Making a New Deal: Industrial Workers in Chicago, 1919–1939*. Cambridge: Cambridge University Press, 1990.

Cohen, Ronald D. *Children of the Mill: Schooling and Society in Gary, Indiana, 1906–1960*. Midwestern History and Culture. Bloomington: Indiana University Press, 1990.

———. "The Dilemma of School Integration in the North: Gary, Indiana, 1945–1960." *Indiana Magazine of History* 82 (June 1986): 161–84.

Colten, Craig E. "Industrial Wastes in Southeast Chicago: Production and Disposal, 1870–1970." *Environmental Review* 10 (Summer 1986): 93–105.

Commoner, Barry. *The Closing Circle: Nature, Man, and Technology*. 2d ed. New York: Bantam Books, 1972.

———. "The Environment." *New Yorker* 63 (July 1987): 46–71.

Crenson, Matthew A. *The Un-Politics of Air Pollution: A Study of Non-Decision-Making in the Cities*. Baltimore: Johns Hopkins University Press, 1971.

Crile, George. "The Tax Assessor Has Many Friends." *Harpers* 245 (November 1972): 102–11.

Cronon, William. *Changes in the Land: Indians, Colonists, and the Ecology of New England*. New York: Hill and Wang, 1983.

———. "Modes of Prophecy and Production: Placing Nature in History." *Journal of American History* 76 (March 1990): 1122–31.

Cumbler, John T. *A Social History of Economic Decline: Business, Politics, and Work in Trenton*. New Brunswick, N.J.: Rutgers University Press, 1989.

Cutright, Phillips. "Party Organization and Voting Behavior." Ph.D. diss., University of Chicago, 1960.

Cutter, Susan Caris. "Community Concern for Pollution: Social and Environmental Influences." *Environment and Behavior* 13 (January 1981): 105–24.

Daly-Bednarek, Janet R. *The Changing Image of the City: Planning for Downtown Omaha, 1945–1973*. Lincoln: University of Nebraska Press, 1992.

Davies, J. Clarence, III. *The Politics of Pollution*. Studies in Contemporary American Politics. New York: Pegasus Books, 1970.

Davis, Mike. *City of Quartz: Excavating the Future in Los Angeles*. New York: Verso, 1992.

Devall, Bill, and George Sessions. *Deep Ecology: Living as if Nature Mattered*. Salt Lake City: Peregrine Books, 1985.

Dickens, Albert. *Economic Factors for Planning Gary*. Washington, D.C.: Evert Kincaid and Associates, 1955.

Dickerson, Dennis C. *Out of the Crucible: Black Steelworkers in Western Pennsylvania, 1875–1980*. Albany: State University of New York Press, 1986.

Dominick, Raymond. "The Roots of the Green Movement in the United States and West Germany." *Environmental Review* 12 (Fall 1988): 1–30.

Drake, St. Clair, and Horace Cayton. *Black Metropolis: A Study of Negro Life in a Northern City*. New York: Harcourt, Brace, 1945.

Drinker, Philip. "Atmospheric Pollution." *Industrial Engineering Chemistry* 31 (November 1939): 1316–20.

Dulles, Foster Rhea. *A History of Recreation: America Learns to Play*. New York: Appleton-Century-Crofts, 1965.

Edsforth, Ronald. *Class Conflict and Cultural Consensus: The Making of a Mass Consumer Society in Flint, Michigan*. New Brunswick, N.J.: Rutgers University Press, 1987.

Elbert, Paul T. "U.S. Steel Corporation in Indiana." *Indiana Business and Industry* 7 (February 1963): 8–11.

Ellis, Jeffrey C. "At the Forefront of Social Progress: The UAW and the Environmental Movement." Paper presented at the meeting of the American Society for Environmental History, Pittsburgh, Pa., March 1993.

Engel, Ronald J. *Sacred Sands: The Struggle for Community in the Indiana Dunes*. Middletown, Conn.: Wesleyan University Press, 1983.

Epstein, Samuel S., Lester O. Brown, and Carl Pope. *Hazardous Waste in America*. San Francisco: Sierra Club Books, 1982.

Erskine, Hazel. "The Polls: Pollution and Its Costs." *Public Opinion Quarterly* 36 (Spring 1972): 120–35.

Fishman, Robert. *Bourgeois Utopias: The Rise and Fall of Suburbia*. New York: Basic Books, 1987.

Foner, Philip S. *Organized Labor and the Black Worker, 1619–1981*. 2d ed. New York: International Publishers, 1981.

Fox, Kenneth. *Metropolitan America: Urban Life and Urban Policy in the United States, 1940–1980*. Jackson: University of Mississippi Press, 1986.

Fox, Richard Wrightman, and T. J. Jackson Lears, eds. *The Culture of Consumption: Critical Essays in American History, 1880–1980*. New York: Pantheon Books, 1983.

Fox, Stephen. *The American Conservation Movement: John Muir and His Legacy*. Madison: University of Wisconsin Press, 1985.

Frady, Marshall. "Gary, Indiana." *Harpers* 239 (August 1969): 35–45.

Franklin, Kay, and Norma Schaeffer. *Duel for the Dunes: Land Use Conflict on the Shores of Lake Michigan*. Urbana: University of Illinois Press, 1983.

Fraser, Steve, and Gary Gerstle, eds. *The Rise and Fall of the New Deal Order, 1930–1980*. Princeton: Princeton University Press, 1989.

Friedman, Lawrence M., and Jack Ladinsky. "Social Change and Industrial Accidents." *Columbia Law Review* 67 (January 1967): 50–82.

Galambos, Louis, ed. *The New American State: Bureaucracies and Policies since World War II*. Johns Hopkins Symposia in Comparative History. Baltimore: Johns Hopkins University Press, 1987.

Galenson, Walter. "The Unionization of the American Steel Industry." *International Review of Social History* 1 (part 1, 1956): 8–40.

"Gary: A Game of Pin the Blame." *Newsweek*, January 26, 1970, pp. 38–39.

"Gary Cuts Loose," *Business Week*, February 14, 1948, pp. 50–52.

"Gary Presses a Claim." *Business Week*, August 23, 1969, pp. 40–41.

Gilbert, James. *Another Chance: Postwar America, 1945–1969*. Philadelphia: Temple University Press, 1981.

Gladwin, Thomas N. "Patterns of Environmental Conflict over Industrial Facilities in the United States, 1970–1978." *Natural Resources Journal* 20 (April 1980): 243–74.

Glastris, Paul. "Steel's Hollow Comeback." *U.S. News and World Report*, May 8, 1989, pp. 49–52.

Gollmar, Herbert A. "Coke and Gas Industry." *Industrial and Engineering Chemistry* 39 (May 1947): 596–601.

Gordon, David M., Richard Edwards, and Michael Reich. *Segmented Work, Divided Workers: The Historical Transformation of Labor in the United States*. Cambridge: Cambridge University Press, 1982.

Gorman, Arthur E. "Pollution of Lake Michigan." *Civil Engineering* 3 (September 1933): 519–22.

Greenberg, Michael R., and Richard F. Anderson. *Hazardous Waste Sites: The Credibility Gap*. New Brunswick, N.J.: Center for Urban Policy Research, 1984.

Greene, John D. "Can We Clean up Our Rivers?" *Steelways* 3 (May 1947): 6–9.

Greenstone, David J. *Labor in American Politics*. 2d ed., with a new introduction. Chicago: University of Chicago Press, 1977.

Greer, Edward. "And Filthy Flows the Calumet." *Progressive* 40 (June 1976): 27–31.

———. *Big Steel, Black Politics, and Corporate Power in Gary, Indiana*. New York: Monthly Review Press, 1979.

———. "The 'Liberation' of Gary, Indiana." *Trans-Action* 8 (January 1971): 30–39, 63.

———. "Racism and U.S. Steel." *Radical America* 10 (September–October 1976): 45–68.

Grinder, Robert Dale. "The Anti-Smoke Crusades: Early Attempts to Reform the Urban Environment, 1893–1918." Ph.D. diss., University of Missouri, 1973.

Halle, David. *America's Working Man: Work, Home, and Politics among Blue-Collar Property Owners*. Chicago: University of Chicago Press, 1984.

Harrison, Bennett, and Barry Bluestone. *The Great U-Turn: Corporate Restructuring and the Polarizing of America*. New York: Basic Books, 1988.

Hatcher, Richard G. "My First Year in Office." *Ebony* 24 (January 1969): 116–22.

———. "We Must Pave the Way." *Vital Speeches*, April 15, 1972, pp. 413–16.

Hawley, Amos H. *Human Ecology: A Theoretical Essay*. Chicago: University of Chicago Press, 1986.

Hays, Samuel P. *Beauty, Health, and Permanence: Environmental Politics in the United States, 1955–1985*. Studies in Environment and History. Cambridge: Cambridge University Press, 1987.

———. "From Conservation to Environment: Environmental Politics in the United States since World War Two." *Environmental Review* 6 (Fall 1982): 14–41.

Hemeon, W. C. L., and T. F. Hatch. "Atmospheric Pollution." *Industrial and Engineering Chemistry* 39 (May 1947): 568–71.

Herling, John. *Right to Challenge: People and Power in the Steelworkers Union*. New York: Harper and Row, 1972.

Hirsch, Arnold. *Making the Second Ghetto: Race and Housing in Chicago, 1940–1960*. Interdisciplinary Perspectives on Modern History. Cambridge: Cambridge University Press, 1983.

Hoak, Richard. "Waste Pickle Liquor." *Industrial and Engineering Chemistry* 39 (May 1947): 614–18.

Hodge, Willard W. "Wastes Problems of the Iron and Steel Industries." *Industrial and Engineering Chemistry* 31 (November 1939): 1364–79.

Hoerr, John P. *And the Wolf Finally Came: The Decline of the American Steel Industry*. Pittsburgh: University of Pittsburgh Press, 1988.

Hoffman, Victor, and John Strietelmeier. "Gary's Rank-and-File Reaction." *Reporter*, September 10, 1964, pp. 28–29.

Horvath, George. "Magrac." *Steel Shavings* 16 (1990): 39.

Hoy, Suellen M. "'Municipal Housekeeping': The Role of Women in Improving Urban Sanitation Practices, 1880–1917." In *Pollution and Reform in American Cities, 1870–1930*, edited by Martin V. Melosi, 173–98. Austin: University of Texas Press, 1980.

Hurley, Andrew. "Creating Ecological Wastelands: Oil Pollution in New York City, 1870–1900." *Journal of Urban History* 20 (May 1994): 340–64.

Hurst, James Willard. *Law and Economic Growth: The Legal History of the Lumber Industry in Wisconsin, 1836–1915*. Cambridge: Harvard University Press, 1964.

Jackson, Kenneth T. *Crabgrass Frontier: The Suburbanization of the United States*. New York: Oxford University Press, 1985.

Jakle, John A., and David Wilson. *Derelict Landscapes: The Wasting of America's Built Environment*. Savage, Md.: Rowman and Littlefield, 1992.

Janowitz, Morris. *The Last Half-Century: Societal Change and Politics in America*. Chicago: University of Chicago Press, 1978.

Jones, Charles O. *Clean Air: The Policies and Politics of Pollution Control*. Pittsburgh: University of Pittsburgh Press, 1975.

Judd, Dennis. *The Politics of American Cities: Private Power and Public Policy*. Glenview, Ill.: Scott Foresman, 1988.

Judd, Dennis, and Paul Kantor. *Enduring Tensions in Urban Politics*. New York: Macmillan, 1992.

Katznelson, Ira. *City Trenches: Urban Politics and the Patterning of Race in the United States*. New York: Pantheon, 1981.

Kazis, Richard, and Richard L. Grossman. *Fear at Work: Job Blackmail, Labor, and the Environment*. New York: Pilgrim Press, 1982.

Kennedy, Harold W., and Andrew O. Porter. "Air Pollution: Its Control and Abatement." *Vanderbilt Law Review* 8 (June 1955): 854–77.

Kerns, Harvey J. *A Study of the Social and Economic Conditions of the Negro Population of Gary, Indiana*. New York: National Urban League, 1944.

King, Charles, Jr. *Fire in My Bones*. Grand Rapids: Eerdmans, 1983.

Kochan, Thomas A., Harry C. Katz, and Robert B. McKersie. *The Transformation of American Industrial Relations*. New York: Basic Books, 1986.

Kornblum, William. *Blue Collar Community*. Studies of Urban Society. Chicago: University of Chicago Press, 1974.

———. "The Challenge of the Rank and File." *Nation*, January 26, 1974, pp. 114–16.

Korstad, Robert, and Nelson Lichtenstein. "Opportunities Found and Lost: Labor Radicals and the Early Civil Rights Movement." *Journal of American History* 75 (June 1988): 786–811.

Krickus, Richard J. "Organizing Neighborhoods: Gary and Newark." In *The World of the Blue-Collar Worker*, edited by Irving Howe, 72–80. New York: Quadrangle Books, 1972.

Laitos, Jan G. "Continuities from the Past Affecting Resource Use and Conservation Patterns." *Oklahoma Law Review* 28 (Winter 1975): 60–96.

Lane, James B. *City of the Century: A History of Gary, Indiana*. Bloomington: Indiana University Press, 1978.

Lane, James B., and Edward J. Escobar, eds. *Forging a Community: The Latino Experience in Northwest Indiana, 1919–1975*. Calumet Regional Studies Series. Chicago: Cattails Press, 1987.

Lave, Lester B., and Eugene P. Seskin. *Air Pollution and Human Health*. Baltimore: Johns Hopkins University Press, 1977.

Leiss, William. *The Domination of Nature*. New York: George Braziller, 1972.

Leuchtenberg, William E. *A Troubled Feast: American Society since 1945*. Rev. ed. Boston: Little, Brown, 1979.

Levine, Charles H. *Racial Conflict and the American Mayor*. Lexington, Mass.: Lexington Books, 1974.

Lichtenstein, Nelson. *Labor's War at Home: The CIO in World War II*. Cambridge: Cambridge University Press, 1982.

———. "The Making of the Postwar Working Class: Cultural Pluralism and Social Structure in World War II." *The Historian* 51 (November 1988): 42–63.

Lipsitz, George. *Class and Culture in Cold War America: "A Rainbow at Midnight."* New York: Praeger Publishers, 1981.

Logan, John R., and Harvey L. Molotch. *Urban Fortunes: The Political Economy of Place*. Berkeley: University of California Press, 1987.

Lubove, Roy. *Twentieth Century Pittsburgh, Government, Business, and Environmental Change*. New York: John Wiley and Sons, 1969.

———, ed. *Pittsburgh*. Documentary History of American Cities, edited by Tamara K. Hareven and Stephan Thernstrom. New York: New Viewpoints, 1976.

Lynd, Alice, and Staughton Lynd. *Rank and File: Personal Histories by Working-Class Organizers*. Boston: Beacon, 1973.

Lynd, Robert S., and Helen Merrell Lynd. *Middletown: A Study in American Culture*. New York: Harcourt, Brace, 1929.

Lynd, Staughton. "Blue Collar Organizing: A Report on CEOHC." *Working Papers for a New Society* 1 (Spring 1973): 28–32.

McAdam, Doug. *Political Process and the Development of Black Insurgency, 1930–1970*. Chicago: University of Chicago Press, 1982.

McCaull, Julian. "Discriminatory Air Pollution." *Environment* 18 (March 1976): 26–32.

McCraw, Thomas K., ed. *Regulation in Perspective: Historical Essays*. Cambridge: Harvard University Press, 1981.

MacDonald, David J. *Union Man*. New York: E. P. Dutton, 1969.

McEvoy, Arthur F. *The Fisherman's Problem: Ecology and Law in the California Fisheries*. Studies in Environment and History. Cambridge: Cambridge University Press, 1986.

Marable, Manning. *Race, Reform, and Rebellion: The Second Reconstruction in Black America, 1945–1982*. Jackson: University of Mississippi Press, 1984.

Marsh, Margaret. "From Separateness to Togetherness: The Social Construction of Domestic Space in American Suburbs, 1840–1915." *Journal of American History* 76 (September 1989): 506–27.

Matusow, Allen J. *The Unraveling of America: A History of Liberalism in the 1960s*. New American Nation Series. New York: Harper and Row, 1984.

May, Elaine Tyler. *Homeward Bound: American Families in the Cold War Era*. New York: Basic Books, 1988.

Meier, August, and Rudwick, Elliot. *From Plantation to Ghetto*. 3d ed. American Century Series. New York: Hill and Wang, 1976.

Melosi, Martin V. *Coping with Abundance: Energy and Environment in Industrial America*. Philadelphia: Temple University Press, 1985.

———. *Garbage in the Cities: Refuse, Reform, and the Environment, 1880–1980*. Environmental History Series, no. 4. College Station: Texas A & M University Press, 1981.

———. *Pollution and Reform in American Cities, 1870–1930*. Austin: University of Texas Press, 1980.

Mills, C. Wright. *White Collar: The American Middle Classes*. New York: Oxford University Press, 1951.

Mohl, Raymond A., ed. *The Making of Urban America*. Wilmington, Del.: Scholarly Resources Press, 1988.

Mohl, Raymond A., and Neil Betten. *Steel City: Urban and Ethnic Patterns in Gary, Indiana, 1906–1950*. New York: Holmes and Meier, 1986.

Montague, Peter. "The Limitations of Landfilling." In *Beyond Dumping: New Strategies for Controlling Toxic Contamination*, edited by Bruce Piasecki, 3–18. Westport, Conn.: Quorum Books, 1984.

Moody, Kim. *An Injury to All: The Decline of American Unionism*. London: Verso, 1988.

Moore, Powell A. *The Calumet Region: Indiana's Last Frontier*. Indianapolis: Indiana Historical Bureau, 1959.

Nadel, Mark U. *The Politics of Consumer Protection*. Bobbs-Merrill Policy Analysis Series. Indianapolis: Bobbs-Merrill, 1971.

Nader, Ralph. *Unsafe at Any Speed: The Designed-In Dangers of the American Automobile*. New York: Grossman, 1965.

Nelson, David Graham. "Black Reform and Federal Resources." Ph.D. diss., University of Chicago, 1972.

Nelson, William E., Jr. *Black Politics in Gary: Problems and Prospects*. Washington, D.C.: Joint Center for Political Studies, 1972.

Nelson, William E., Jr., and Philip J. Meranto. *Electing Black Mayors: Political Action in the Black Community*. Columbus: Ohio State University Press, 1977.

Newman, Dorothy K., et al. *Protest, Politics, and Prosperity: Black Americans and White Institutions, 1940–1975*. New York: Pantheon, 1978.

Noble, Charles. *Liberalism at Work: The Rise and Fall of OSHA*. Philadelphia: Temple University Press, 1986.

Norrell, Robert J. "Caste in Steel: Jim Crow Careers in Birmingham, Alabama." *Journal of American History* 73 (December 1986): 669–94.

Nyden, Philip W. *Steelworkers Rank-and-File: The Political Economy of a Union Reform Movement*. New York: Praeger, 1984.

O'Gara, James. "Big Steel, Little Steel: The Recent Steel Settlement Has Not Settled Everything." *Commonweal*, November 25, 1949, pp. 206–7.

Osofsky, Gilbert. *Harlem—The Making of a Ghetto: Negro New York, 1890–1930*. New York: Harper and Row, 1966.

Paehlke, Robert C. *Environmentalism and the Future of Progressive Politics*. New Haven: Yale University Press, 1989.

Park, Robert E., Ernest W. Burgess, and Robert D. MacKenzie. *The City*. Chicago: University of Chicago Press, 1925.

Parran, Thomas. "The Public Health Service and Industrial Pollution." *Industrial and Engineering Chemistry* 39 (May 1947): 560–61.

Peterson, Paul E. *City Limits*. Chicago: University of Chicago Press, 1981.

Peterson, Wallace C. *Our Overloaded Economy: Inflation, Unemployment, and the Crisis in American Capitalism*. Armonk, N.Y.: M. E. Sharpe, 1982.

Petulla, Joseph M. *American Environmental History*. 2d ed. Columbus: Merrill, 1988.

———. *American Environmentalism: Values, Tactics, Priorities*. Environmental History Series, no. 1. College Station: Texas A & M University Press, 1980.

———. *Environmental Protection in the United States: Industry, Agencies, Environmentalists*. San Francisco: San Francisco Study Center, 1987.

Plotkin, Sidney. *Keep Out: The Struggle for Land Use Control*. Berkeley: University of California Press, 1987.

Poinsett, Alex. *Black Power Gary Style: The Making of Mayor Richard Gordon Hatcher*. Chicago: Johnson Publishing, 1970.

———. "Uniformity." *Ebony* 27 (June 1972): 45–54.

Polenberg, Richard. *One Nation Divisible: Class, Race, and Ethnicity in the United States since 1938*. New York: Viking Press, 1980.

———. *War and Society: The United States, 1941–1945*. Critical Periods of History. New York: J. B. Lippincott, 1972.

Preis, Art. *Labor's Giant Step: Twenty Years of the CIO*. 2d ed. New York: Pathfinder Press, 1972.

Rabin, Robert L. "Federal Regulation in Historical Perspective." *Stanford Law Review* 38 (May 1986): 1189–1226.

Radner, Samuel. *Study and Technical Recommendations for Air Pollution Control*. Chicago: Armour Research Foundation of Illinois Institute for Technology, 1958.

Rae, John. *The Road and Car in American Life*. Cambridge: MIT Press, 1971.

Redmond, Carol, et al. "Long Term Mortality Study of Steelworkers: VI, Mortality from Malignant Neoplasms among Coke Oven Workers." *Journal of Occupational Medicine* 14 (August 1972): 621–29.

Reich, Robert B. *The Work of Nations: Preparing Ourselves for Twenty-first Century Capitalism*. New York: Vintage Books, 1992.

Renshaw, Patrick. *American Labor and Consensus Capitalism, 1935–1990*. Jackson: University Press of Mississippi, 1991.

Reshkin, Mark, and Lee C. Strahun, eds. *Environmental Perspectives: Northwest Indiana*. Highland: Northwest Indiana Comprehensive Health Planning Council, 1973.

Reutter, Mark. *Sparrows Point: Making Steel—The Rise and Ruin of American Industrial Might*. New York: Summit Books, 1988.

Revelle, Roger, and Hans H. Landsberg, eds. *America's Changing Environment*. Boston: Houghton Mifflin, 1970.

Richards, Luther. "Steelworker to Minister." *Steel Shavings* 7 (1981): 28.

"A Rising Cry: 'Ethnic Power.'" *Newsweek*, December 21, 1970, pp. 32–33.

Roos, Leslie, ed. *The Politics of Eco-Suicide*. New York: Holt, Rinehart, and Winston, 1971.

Rosen, Christine Meisner. *The Limits of Power: Great Fires and the Process of City Growth in America*. Cambridge: Cambridge University Press, 1986.

Rosenbaum, Walter A. *Environmental Politics and Policy*. Washington, D.C.: Congressional Quarterly Press, 1985.

———. *The Politics of Environmental Concern*. 2d ed. New York: Praeger Publishers, 1977.

Rosenberg, Charles E. *The Cholera Years: The United States in 1832, 1849, and 1866*. Chicago: University of Chicago Press, 1962.

Rosenkrantz, Barbara Gutman. *Public Health and the State: Changing Views in Massachusetts, 1842–1936*. Cambridge: Harvard University Press, 1972.

Roskamp, Karl W. *The American Economy, 1929–1970: Resources, Production, Income Distribution, and Use of Product—An Introduction*. Detroit: Wayne State University Press, 1977.

Rousmaniere, John, ed. *The Enduring Great Lakes: A Natural History Book*. New York: W. W. Norton, 1979.

Rudwick, Elliott. *Race Riot at East St. Louis, July 2, 1917*. Carbondale: Southern Illinois University Press, 1964.

Schmidman, John. *Unions in Post-Industrial Society*. University Park: Pennsylvania State University Press, 1979.

Schnaiberg, Allan. *The Environment: From Surplus to Scarcity*. New York: Oxford University Press, 1980.

Singer, Leslie, Gary Lynch, and Michael Holowaty. "Dinosaurs on the Lake?: Steel in the Next Decade." *Indiana Business Review* 68 (Spring 1993): 1–11.

Sitkoff, Harvard. *The Struggle for Black Equality, 1954–1980*. American Century Series. New York: Hill and Wang, 1981.

Sittig, Marshall. *Handbook of Toxic and Hazardous Chemicals and Carcinogens*. 2d ed. Park Ridge, N.J.: Noyes Publications, 1985.

Skolnick, Arlene. *Embattled Paradise: The American Family in an Age of Uncertainty*. New York: Basic Books, 1991.

Slayton, Robert A. *Back of the Yards: The Making of a Local Democracy*. Chicago: University of Chicago Press, 1986.

Smith, Glen. "Swamps Disappear in Gary, Indiana." *American City* 68 (August 1953): 101.

Smith, James Noel, ed. *Environmental Quality and Social Justice in Urban America: An Exploration of Conflict and Concern among Those Who Seek Environmental Quality and Those Who Seek Social Justice*. Washington, D.C.: Conservation Foundation, 1974.

Smoke Prevention Society of America. *Papers Presented at the Forty-First Annual Meeting, Smoke Prevention Society of America*. [St. Joseph, Mich.], 1947.

————. *Forty-Second Annual Meeting, Smoke Prevention Society of America*. Birmingham, Ala., 1949.

Stave, Bruce M. *The New Deal and the Last Hurrah: Pittsburgh Machine Politics*. Pittsburgh: University of Pittsburgh Press, 1970.

Stilgoe, John. *Borderland: Origins of the American Suburb, 1820–1939*. New Haven: Yale University Press, 1988.

Stupar, Pamela. "One Woman's Experience." *Steel Shavings* 4 (1978): 45.

Swanstrom, Todd. *The Crisis of Growth Politics: Cleveland, Kucinich, and the Challenge of Urban Populism*. Philadelphia: Temple University Press, 1985.

Szekely, Julian, ed. *The Steel Industry and the Environment*. New York: Marcel Dekker, 1973.

Tarr, Joel A. "Historical Perspectives on Hazardous Wastes in the United States." *Waste Management and Research* 3 (1985): 95–102.

————. "The Search for the Ultimate Sink: Urban Air, Land, and Water Pollution in Historical Perspective." *Records of the Columbia Historical Society of Washington, D.C.* 51 (1984): 1–29.

Tarr, Joel A., and Bill C. Lamperes. "Changing Fuel Use Behavior and Energy Transitions: The Pittsburgh Smoke Control Movement, 1940–1950—A Case Study in Historical Analogy." *Journal of Social History* 14 (Summer 1981): 561–88.

Taylor, Graham Romeyn. *Satellite Cities: A Study of Industrial Suburbs*. National Municipal League Series. New York: D. Appleton, 1915.

Taylor, Paul S. *Mexican Labor in the United States, Chicago, and the Calumet Region*. Berkeley: University of California Press, 1932.

Teaford, Jon C. *The Rough Road to Renaissance: Urban Revitalization in America, 1940–1985*. Baltimore: Johns Hopkins University Press, 1990.

Thompson, Dorothy E. "Woman Worker." *Steel Shavings* 7 (1981): 30.

Tiffany, Paul A. *The Decline of American Steel: How Management, Labor, and Government Went Wrong*. New York: Oxford University Press, 1988.

Tomes, Nancy. "The Private Side of Public Health: Sanitary Science, Domestic Hygiene, and the Germ Theory, 1870–1900." *Bulletin of the History of Medicine* 64 (Winter 1990): 509–39.

Tucker, William C. *Progress and Privilege: America in the Age of Environmentalism*. Garden City, N.Y.: Anchor Press, 1982.

United Church of Christ. Commission for Racial Justice. *Toxic Wastes and Race in the United States: A National Report on the Racial and Socio-Economic Characteristics of Communities with Hazardous Waste Sites*. 1987.

United Steelworkers of America. *Job Description and Classification Manual, For Hourly Rated Production, Maintenance, and Non-Confidential Clerical Jobs*. Pittsburgh, 1971.

U.S. Steel Corporation. *United States Steel and the Environment*. [New York], 1980.

Varga, J., Jr., and H. W. Lownie, Jr. *Final Technological Report on a Systems Analysis Study of the Integrated Iron and Steel Industry*. Columbus: Battelle Memorial Institute, 1969.

Vela, Richard. "Simple and Uncomplicated." *Steel Shavings* 14 (1988): 40.

Veroff, Joseph, Elizabeth Douvan, and Richard A. Kulka. *The Inner American: A Self-Portrait from 1957 to 1976*. New York: Basic Books, 1981.

Vietor, Richard H. K. *Environmental Politics and the Coal Coalition*. Environmental History Series, no. 2. College Station: Texas A & M University Press, 1980.

Vig, Norman J., and Michael E. Kraft, eds. *Environmental Policy in the 1980s: Reagan's New Agenda*. Washington, D.C.: CQ Press, 1984.

Vogel, David. *Fluctuating Fortunes: The Political Power of Business in America*. New York: Basic Books, 1989.

———. *Lobbying the Corporation: Citizen Challenges to Business Authority*. New York: Basic Books, 1978.

———. *National Styles of Regulation: Environmental Policy in Great Britain and the United States*. Ithaca: Cornell University Press, 1986.

Warner, Sam Bass, Jr. *Streetcar Suburbs: The Process of Growth in Boston, 1870–1900*. Cambridge: Harvard University Press, 1962.

"What Happened to One Model High School: Close-up of Desegregation." *U.S. News and World Report*, April 27, 1970, pp. 37–40.

Williamson, Jeffrey G., and Peter H. Lindert. *American Inequality: A Macroeconomic History*. Institute for Research on Poverty Monograph Series. New York: Academic Press, 1980.

Wilson, William Julius. *The Truly Disadvantaged: The Inner City, the Underclass, and Public Policy*. Chicago: University of Chicago Press, 1987.

Wolfe, Alan. *America's Impasse: The Rise and Fall of the Politics of Growth*. Boston: South End Press, 1981.

Woodcock, Leonard. "Labor and the Politics of Environment." *Sierra Club Bulletin* 56 (December 1971): 11–16.

Worster, Donald. *Rivers of Empire: Water, Aridity, and the Growth of the American West*. New York: Pantheon Books, 1985.

———. "Transformations of the Earth: Towards an Agroecological Perspective in History." *Journal of American History* 76 (March 1990): 1087–1106.

Yankelovich, Daniel. *New Rules: Searching for Self-Fulfillment in a World Turned Upside Down*. New York: Random House, 1981.

Zieger, Robert H. *American Workers, American Unions, 1920–1985*. The American Moment. Baltimore: Johns Hopkins University Press, 1986.

Zukin, Sharon. *Landscapes of Power: From Detroit to Disney World*. Berkeley: University of California Press, 1991.

Zunz, Olivier. *The Changing Face of Inequality: Urbanization, Industrial Development, and Immigrants in Detroit, 1880–1920*. Chicago: University of Chicago Press, 1982.

Index

Abel, I. W., 83
Aetna, Indiana, 51, 90
African Americans: in occupational hierarchy, 4, 24–25, 112–13; northern migration of, 4, 112; residential patterns of, 5, 30, 65, 71, 123–28, 131, 133–34, 160–61, 187; environmental objectives of, 8, 10–11, 111–35; social life of, 33–34; political activity of, 40, 66, 128, 139; income of, 113; beach use, 120–23, 131, 161; and coke oven coalition, 136–37, 144–45; disenchantment of with liberal reform, 137; and community recycling program, 141; and youth gangs, 145; opposition of to environmental protection, 149–51; and toxic waste dumps, 168–69, 170–72, 179. *See also* Racial discrimination; Pollution, effects of on social groups
Air pollution. *See* Pollution, air
Air Pollution Advisory Board, 94, 97, 133, 142
Air Pollution Appeal Board, 145
Alewife: as pest, 35; die-offs, 55–56, 62
Alex Metz Construction Company, 167
Alinsky, Saul, 105
American Bridge Plant, 18. *See also* United States Steel Corporation
Anderson Company, 36
Anselm Forum, 120
Automation: in steel industry, 49, 176

Baer, Robert, 141, 144–45
Barnes, Mike, 105, 106
Barnes, Thomas, 177
Baroni, Geno, 105
Basic-oxygen furnaces: replace open-hearth furnaces, 63, 150
Bazin, Steve, 94
Bear Brand Hosiery, 36

Bethlehem Steel Corporation, 70
Black Oak, Indiana, 169–70, 171
Black power movement, 104, 105
Blast furnaces: wastes generated by, 20; and African American labor, 24
Blockbusting, 125–26
Blosl, John, 106
Board of Zoning Appeals, 168
Borns, Clarence, 71, 72
Bornstein, Herschel, 133
Borrow pits: and solid waste disposal, 163, 170
Bowling: as working-class recreational activity, 92
Brown, Moses, 115–16
Brunswick Community Club, 44
Brunswick neighborhood, 44
Bucko Construction Company, 133
Budd Company, 41, 44, 155
Buffington Pier, 102–3, 147
Buffington Pier Community Coalition, 103, 107, 144, 147
Business class: in the U.S., 3–4; in Gary, 48; exodus of from Gary, 48, 196 (n. 4)

Cal-Area Sportsman Club, 167
Calumet Action League, 108
Calumet Community Congress, 103–9, 136, 139, 140, 144
Calumet Environmental and Occupational Health Committee, 99–100
Candiano, Dick, 92
Capitalism. *See* Industrial capitalism
Carr, Drusilla, 37
Carr, Fred, 35
Carr, J. David, 107, 142, 144
Cement making: and pollution, 22, 161
Chacharis, George, 198 (n. 21)
Chain stores: and decline of ethnic culture, 88–89

Environmental protection. *See* Pollution control; Shoreline preservation

Environmental racism, 179

Equilibrium: as inadequate standard for measuring environmental change, xiv

Esposito, John, 107

Ethnic parishes, 31 Map 2

Ethnicity: and politics, 4; and labor recruitment, 24–25; and settlement patterns, 28, 29–30, 193 (n. 39); declining influence on working-class social life, 88–89; as force for social cohesion among working class, 108–9

Ethnic power, 105

Eutrophication: in Lake Michigan, 150

Experimental Negotiating Agreement, 83, 101

Fair Share Organization, 118

Federal Highway Act, 51

Federal Housing Authority, 51

Federal Water Pollution Control Act: amendments to (1972), 9, 11

Federal Water Pollution Control Administration, 62, 64, 157–58

Feminine Mystique, The, 56

Fish: in the Little Calumet River, 16; in the Grand Calumet River, 16, 34, 159; in Lake Michigan, 35, 160; die-offs, 55–56, 62

Fishing: as working-class recreational activity, 93, 101–3

Fishing piers: demands for public access to, 93, 102–3, 106, 107

Ford, Gerald, 173

Friedan, Betty, 56, 57

Gary, Indiana: as setting for historical investigation, 13–14; early environmental characteristics of, 16; industrial development of, 16–18, 41, 48–49, 64, 91; population of, 17; early history of, 17–18, 28, 38–39; resi-dential patterns of, 28–31, 51–54, 65, 90–91, 123–26, 160, 193 (n. 33); central business district of, 32; politics in, 38–40, 89, 128; economic decline of, 148–49, 175–77; pollution levels in, 155–60; unemployment rate in, 176; environmental conditions of during 1980s, 177; and promise of environmental democracy, 180–81

Gary Air Pollution Control Division, 53, 69, 132, 134, 146, 150, 151

Gary Chamber of Commerce, 39, 40, 60, 61, 103

Gary city dump, 168–69, 177

Gary Crusader, 135

Gary Health Department, 55

Gary-Hobart Company, 42

Gary Industrial Foundation, 40–41

Gary Junior Chamber of Commerce, 60, 74

Gary National Bank, 32

Gary Parks Board, 67, 69, 103, 107

Gary Parks Department, 37, 67

Gary Plan Commission, 69, 170

Gary Post-Tribune, 60, 102, 177

Gary Products factory, 1–2

Gary Public Health Department, 42

Gary Real Estate Board, 44

Gary Sanitary District, 158, 159, 163, 177

Gary Sheet and Tin Mill, 18, 21, 80, 81. *See also* United States Steel Corporation

Gary Urban League, 118, 121, 150

Gary Works: building of, 17; expansion of, 18; production flow of, 19–21; and labor force, 24; and waste disposal and pollution, 44, 161; and clerical workers, 49; and union drive, 79; and OSHA, 86; becomes target of Calumet Environmental and Occupational Health Committee, 99; and support for Curtis Strong among African Americans, 116; opened to tourists, 149; and pollution control,

158, 162. *See also* United States Steel Corporation

Genesis Convention Center, 1

Georgia-Pacific Corporation, 63, 159

Gilroy Stadium, 32, 33, 197 (n. 21)

Gleason Park, 197 (n. 21)

Glen Park, Indiana, 30, 31, 41, 57, 58, 151; pollution in, 26, 55; growth of, 29, 51; environmental characteristics of, 52, 53; social characteristics of, 65; and working-class suburbanization, 90; gas explosion in, 107; racial segregation in, 126; efforts of to secede from Gary, 138; absence of solid waste dumps in, 165; dereliction of, 175

Golf: as working-class recreational activity, 92–93

Grand Calumet River, 16, 17, 37, 44, 102; waste disposal and water quality, 20, 21, 34–36, 63, 64, 159–60, 172, 177; limited public access to, 22; in African American neighborhood, 161; plan to rehabilitate, 178–79

Grand Calumet Task Force, 177–78

Green push, 143, 147

Groundwater contamination: from solid waste disposal sites, 164, 171

Grutka, Andrew, 106

Hamilton, Barbara, 173

Hammond, Indiana, 102, 107, 177

Hatcher, Richard: role of in three-way deal, 69–70; and election of 1967, 96, 113, 128; environmental views, 111–12, 129–30; role of in Marquette Park integration, 122; first years as mayor, 128–29, 130–31; childhood, 129–30; relationship with U.S. Steel, 131–33; crusade against industrial pollution, 132–35; role of in coke oven coalition, 137, 140–41; popular perceptions of, 138–39, 177; and coke oven pollution control, 142, 143; efforts to attract federal funds,

148; role of in open-hearth controversy, 150, 152; and solid waste disposal, 169, 170; and election of 1987, 177

Hays, Samuel P., 9, 190 (n. 14)

Highway construction: as stimulus to suburbanization, 8, 51, 174; and creation of borrow pits, 163

Hoock, Helen, 46, 67–69, 70, 136–37, 140, 147

Horace Mann neighborhood, 29, 53, 57, 65, 72

Horvath, George, 92

Hotel Gary, 32, 40

Housing: conditions of in Gary, 28, 123, 127–28; and federal government policies, 51, 53. *See also* Suburbanization

Howard, John, 23

Howell, Granville, 60–61

Immigrants: European, 3, 4, 6, 24–25, 29, 88–89; Mexican, 24–25, 36

Indiana Board of Health, 160, 169

Indiana Civil Liberties Union, 140

Indiana Department of Conservation, 42

Indiana Dunes National Lakeshore, 70, 71, 73, 153, 173

Indiana Harbor, 103

Indiana Harbor Canal, 34, 35,

Indiana Stream Pollution Control Board, 42, 43

Indiana University, 32

Industrial capitalism: and class formation, 3–5; Hatcher's critique of, 112, 134–35

Industrial land use, 18, 36–37, 44, 70, 73, 91. *See also* United States Steel Corporation

Infant mortality: and air pollution, 27, 183–85

Info, 133

Inland Steel Corporation, 104

Interdenominational Ministerial Alliance, 121

Ivanhoe Gardens, 133
Izaak Walton League, 93, 102

Jedenoff, George, 67
Job blackmail, 11, 142, 149, 150
Johnson, Joel, 132–33, 142
Johnson, Lyndon B., 96, 134
Joint safety committees, 84
Jones, Georgia, 1
Journal of Occupational Medicine, 114

Kangaroos (youth gang), 145
Kaplan, Elaine, 57–58
Katz, A. Martin, 66, 96, 128, 138
Kee, David, 146
Kelly, Nancy, 178
Kincaid, Orval, 96, 144
King, Martin Luther, Jr., 119
Kirtland, Eugene, 151
Knotts, Tom, 38
Kranz, Carey, 95, 96
Krupa, John, 108

Labor relations: during World War II, 79–80; and grievance procedures, 80–82, after World War II, 82–83; and 1987 steel strike, 176
Labor unions: environmental objectives of, 7, 10–11; as means of social mobility, 78; organizing drives in Gary, 79; opposition to Indiana Dunes National Lakeshore expansion, 95; declining political influence of, 204–5 (n. 67). *See also* United Automobile Workers; United Mine Workers; United Steelworkers of America
Lake County Fish and Game Association, 93, 102, 103
Lake Michigan, 25, 58, 161; advantages of for steel production, 16; shoreline, 17, 37, 64–71; limited public access to, 22, 91; waste disposal and water quality, 34–35, 42–43, 55–56, 62, 107, 159–60, 172; and steel mill wash water, 86; fishing piers on, 93,

102–3; and lake-stocking program, 102
Lake Sandy Jo, 169–70, 171
Lake Street beach, 122
Landfills, 18, 65–66, 162–72, 178–79
Latinos: and sulfur dioxide emissions, 160; exposure of to toxic wastes, 179. *See also* Immigrants, Mexican
League of Women Voters, 46, 57–60, 62, 65, 68, 74, 140, 171
Lee, Duke, 23
Lewis, C. S., 182
Liberal capitalism: crystallization of, 7–8; environmental implications of, 8; and industrial corporations, 13; and quality-of-life concerns, 51; and pollution control laws, 56; disenchantment with, 137; limitations of, 181–82
Little Calumet River, 16
Locke, Sammie, 134
Logelin, Edward, 137
Long Lake, 71
Love Canal, 170, 179
Low-sulfur coal: use in NIPSCO boilers, 156–57
Lynd, Helen, 3–4
Lynd, Robert, 3–4

McDonald, David, 83, 202 (n. 12)
McWilliams, Johnny, 178
Malis, Chris, 23
Mandich, Peter, 59, 121–22
Manufacturing: environmental impacts of, 6–7, 55, 64, 124, 141–42, 162–63, 181; growth of in the U.S., 7; technologies and, 7. *See also* United States Steel Corporation, environmental impacts of in Gary
Marathon Oil Corporation, 176
Marcuse, Peter, 10
Marquette Park: beach use affected by pollution, 55–56; and U.S. Steel landfill, 65–66; and racial integration, 120–23, 131; dereliction of, 175
Merrillville, Indiana, 52

Olzanski, Mike, 101
Open-hearth ovens, 92; waste generation of, 20; pollution of, 23; and Mexican labor, 24; replaced by basic-oxygen furnaces, 63; and protective clothing for workers, 84; EPA efforts to close, 150; retired at Gary Works, 156
Organized labor. *See* Labor unions; United Automobile Workers; United Mine Workers; United Steelworkers of America

Particulate matter, 7, 25–27, 64, 68, 156, 161, 183–84, 185–86, 187
Patch neighborhood, 28
Patronage politics, 39–40, 57
Patterson, George, 105
Paulk, Don, 77–78, 100
Pennsylvania: mill towns in, 6
Piasecki, Harry, 86–87, 97, 99, 150, 152–53
Pilzer, John, 168
Pipkins, Joseph, 115
Pittsburgh, Pennsylvania, 16, 60, 194 (n. 40)
Polish American Democratic Club, 39
Polish National Alliance, 89
Politics. *See* Gary, Indiana, politics in
Pollution: effects of on social groups, 1–2, 6, 15, 22–38, 126–27, 154–55, 160–61, 172, 173–74, 179–80, 181–82, 185–87; hydrochloric acid fumes, 1–2, 177; effects of on human health, 2, 26–27, 36, 55, 64, 77, 127, 130, 134, 141, 171, 183–85; after World War II, 7; and meteorological conditions, 25–26; air, 25–28, 31–33, 64, 68, 123, 134, 141–42, 143, 160–61, 171, 177; sulfur dioxide emissions, 26, 68, 156–57; water, 34–36, 41–43, 55–56, 58–59, 64, 102, 177; popular perceptions of, 43–44, 55; effects of on residential locations, 52–53, 124, 126; fragmented community response to, 155,

161–62, 167–71, 172–74, 180–81. *See also* Manufacturing, environmental impacts of; Occupational health and safety; Solid waste; United States Steel Corporation, environmental impacts of in Gary
Pollution control: absence of in Gary, 38–43; smoke abatement ordinance, 59–62; and airborne wastes, 63, 133–34, 155–57; and waterborne wastes, 63, 157–59; undermined by economic growth, 64; and coke oven emissions, 136–37, 141–47; and sulfur dioxide emissions, 156–57, 158; unintended consequences of, 156–57, 162, 174
Power relations: in the U.S., 2–3, 12–13; in Gary, 112, 134–35, 137–38
Progress and Privilege, 10

Quarles, John, 155
Quillen, Ray, 77–78, 100

Race: in urban America, 4; and organization of urban space, 5, 30; and exposure to industrial pollution, 6, 25, 37, 160–61, 173–74, 179; divisions of muted in environmental campaigns, 12–13, 137; divisions of exploited to preserve environmental control, 138, 181–82; and exposure to toxic wastes, 172, 179. *See also* African Americans; Racial discrimination
Racial discrimination, 4, 33, 113, 128; housing and, 5, 30, 54, 123–25, 173; recreation venues and, 37, 119–20; hiring practices and, 114–18; legislation outlawing, 118, 124; in education, 139. *See also* African Americans
Racial polarization, 138–39
Rats: in African American neighborhoods, 111, 123, 168–69
Reising, Gregory, 75
Republic Steel Corporation, 105
Reuther, Walter, 11

United Automobile Workers, 11
United Mine Workers, 98
United States Steel Corporation, 91;
    decision to locate in Gary, 16; land
    use, 17–18, 37, 65–67, 102–3; envi-
    ronmental impacts of in Gary, 17–38,
    42–43; solid waste disposal, 18, 162–
    63; labor force and recruitment, 22,
    24, 41, 49, 112–13, 114, 118, 176;
    company housing, 28, 123; commu-
    nity relations, 38–39; steel produc-
    tion of, 48, 176; support for smoke
    abatement, 60–62; compliance with
    environmental regulations, 62, 63,
    155–56, 158–59; plant expansion of,
    64, 70, 73; role in three-way deal,
    66–67; opposition to environmental
    protection measures, 74, 138, 142,
    145, 148; recognizes union, 79; criti-
    cism against, 107; promotion system,
    115, 117; and Richard Hatcher, 131–
    32; and taxes, 131–32; threats to dis-
    miss workers, 142, 149, 150; viola-
    tion of environmental laws, 155, 158;
    corporate restructuring, 175–77;
    becomes USX Corporation, 176. See
    also Coke ovens; Gary Sheet and Tin
    Mill; Gary Works; Open-hearth ovens
United Steelworkers of America, 23, 40;
    failure to address environmental haz-
    ards, 77, 78, 95–97; efforts to address
    environmental hazards, 78, 81–82,
    84–85, 94–95, 114; early accom-
    plishments of, 79; rank and file
    activism of, 79–80, 82–83; and
    Occupational Safety and Health Act,
    85–87; social programs, 89; political
    influence, 94, 96–97; civil rights
    reform, 94, 116–17; rank and file
    insurgency of, 97–98, 101; indiffer-
    ence of to social problems, 104–5;
    opposition to Calumet Community
    Congress, 108; opposition to open-
    hearth shut down, 150; violation of
    federal environmental laws, 151. See
    also Steelworkers

Urban space: as contested terrain, 3,
    5–7, 181
U.S. Army Corps of Engineers, 42, 65,
    66, 69
U.S. Department of the Interior, 66
U.S. Environmental Protection Agency:
    and coke oven pollution, 101;
    enforcement of environmental laws,
    146; attacked in Gary, 149, 151; cites
    U.S. Steel as worst offender of pollu-
    tion laws, 155; and water pollution
    control, 158; inspection of toxic
    waste disposal sites, 165, 171; and
    rehabilitation of Grand Calumet
    River, 178; investigation of environ-
    mental equity, 179–80
USX Corporation. See United States
    Steel Corporation

Veterans Administration, 51
Volunteers in Service to America
    (VISTA), 141, 144

Walden, Bill, 99–100
Wallace, George, 96, 104
Washburn, Verne, 44
Waste disposal. See Pollution; Landfills;
    Solid waste
Waste dumping. See Landfills; Solid
    waste
Water fluoridation, 58
Water pollution. See Pollution, water
Wesson, Cleo, 151
"Where's Joe?," 83
White-collar employment, 48–50;
    among African Americans, 117–18
White flight, 65, 71, 72, 124–26
Wiggerly, Hobart, 41
Wildcat strikes, 80–81, 83, 115–16
Wilmore, Carol, 70
Wolf Lake, 93
Women: and employment, 22, 49–50,
    56; and political activities, 56–59
Woodcock, Leonard, 11
Workers For Democracy, 100–101,
    103–4

Working class: exposure to pollutants, 6; residential patterns of, 65, 90–91, 173; environmentalism, 77–110; homogeneity of, 78, 87; militance of, 79, 80, 99–109; and mass culture, 87–89; and decline of ethnic culture, 88–89; leisure activities, 92–93; political alienation of, 104–5; participation of in coke oven coalition, 136–37, 144; disenchantment of with liberal reform, 137; opposition to environmental protection, 149–51; and toxic waste disposal, 179

Wright, Jim, 104–6

Young Citizens for Beachhead Democracy, 120–21
Young Men's Christian Association (YMCA), 32, 33
Young, Whitney, 10

Zoning, 5, 36–37, 39, 44, 91, 166–67